SO-BNI-245

D1527026

An Introduction to the Sagas of Icelanders

New Perspectives on Medieval Literature: Authors and Traditions

UNIVERSITY PRESS OF FLORIDA

Florida A&M University, Tallahassee
Florida Atlantic University, Boca Raton
Florida Gulf Coast University, Ft. Myers
Florida International University, Miami
Florida State University, Tallahassee
New College of Florida, Sarasota
University of Central Florida, Orlando
University of Florida, Gainesville
University of North Florida, Jacksonville
University of South Florida, Tampa
University of West Florida, Pensacola

AN INTRODUCTION TO

THE SAGAS
OF ICELANDERS

Carl Phelpstead

Foreword by R. Barton Palmer and Tison Pugh

UNIVERSITY PRESS OF FLORIDA
Gainesville / Tallahassee / Tampa / Boca Raton
Pensacola / Orlando / Miami / Jacksonville / Ft. Myers / Sarasota

25 24 23 22 21 20   6 5 4 3 2 1

Library of Congress Cataloging-in-Publication Data
Names: Phelpstead, Carl, author.
Title: An introduction to the sagas of Icelanders / Carl Phelpstead.
Other titles: New perspectives on medieval literature.
Description: Gainesville : University Press of Florida, 2020. | Series: New
    perspectives on medieval literature: authors and traditions | Includes
    bibliographical references and index.
Identifiers: LCCN 2020001910 (print) | LCCN 2020001911 (ebook) | ISBN
    9780813066516 (hardback) | ISBN 9780813057569 (ebook)
Subjects: LCSH: Sagas—History and criticism. | Iceland—History.
Classification: LCC PT7182.P48 2020 (print) | LCC PT7182 (ebook) | DDC
    839/.63—dc23
LC record available at https://lccn.loc.gov/2020001910
LC ebook record available at https://lccn.loc.gov/2020001911

The University Press of Florida is the scholarly publishing agency for the
State University System of Florida, comprising Florida A&M University, Florida
Atlantic University, Florida Gulf Coast University, Florida International University,
Florida State University, New College of Florida, University of Central Florida,
University of Florida, University of North Florida, University of South Florida,
and University of West Florida.

University Press of Florida
2046 NE Waldo Road
Suite 2100
Gainesville, FL 32609
http://upress.ufl.edu

CONTENTS

The Icelandic sagas—tales of feud and family, of vengeance and violence, and of surprising humor and humanity—have entranced readers
for hundreds of years. Such works as *Egils saga, Gísla saga, Laxdœla saga,*
and *Njáls saga* introduce readers to a world virtually unimaginable to
contemporary society, but the issues they touch upon—honor, integrity, relationships, identity—are enduring concerns of great literature
that probes the deepest questions of the human condition. In this book,
An Introduction to the Sagas of Icelanders, Professor Carl Phelpstead offers a wide-ranging overview of these works, detailing with astute insights their complexities and their enduring allure. He offers a fresh perspective by relating the sagas to issues central to contemporary literary
studies.

Few scholars are better qualified to introduce readers to the Icelandic sagas than Professor Phelpstead. A professor in the School of English, Communication, and Philosophy at Cardiff University and former
president of the Viking Society for Northern Research, he is the author
of such works as *Holy Vikings: Saints' Lives in the Old Icelandic Kings' Sagas* and *Tolkien and Wales: Language, Literature and Identity* and the editor of translations of *A History of Norway and the Passion and Miracles of
the Blessed Óláfr.* He has also published numerous articles on Old Norse
and medieval English literature, as well as on how modern British authors reimagine and re-create the past in their writings.

With each volume in *New Perspectives on Medieval Literature: Authors and Traditions,* we hope that readers will discover the joys and wonders of medieval literature, a body of work that ages yet will never die. The body count in Icelandic sagas is, on the other hand, often rather high, though this contributes to the fascinating mix of familiar and alien that is such a strong part of their powerful appeal.

R. Barton Palmer and Tison Pugh
Series editors

PREFACE

On May 26, 2017, two people were killed and another injured in Portland, Oregon, allegedly by a man who had earlier that month posted
"Hail Vinland!!! Hail Victory!!!" on Facebook. The short-lived Vínland
settlement in North America is, as we will see later in this book, the central subject of two of the sagas of Icelanders (also known in English as
Family Sagas): *Eiríks saga rauða* (*The Saga of Eirik the Red*) and *Grœnlendinga saga* (*The Saga of the Greenlanders*). The Vínland settlement was
a long way from Oregon, but racists across North America have long
seen it as somehow prefiguring and justifying white dominance of the
entire continent. Such claims lose all credibility the moment that they
are confronted with the surviving historical sources, including the saga
narratives: the Vínland settlement was a short-lived and never extensive
failure that, far from demonstrating the inherent superiority of "white"
people, could rather be said to confirm that the indigenous population
was much better able to thrive in the region. Soon after the Portland attack, the journalist and historian David Perry wrote a piece for the *Wash-
ington Post* under the heading "White supremacists love Vikings. But
they've got history all wrong." Toward the end of his article, he writes,
"History has never just been 'the past.' As a historian, I study the way
that groups have always tried to assert control over their story, seeking
to mold legend, myth and reality into a useful narrative about identity
and destiny."[1] That molding of material into narratives about identity
(and destiny) by people seeking to control their own story continues
today, but it also occurred in medieval Iceland. In this book, I seek to

show how our understanding both of the medieval sagas of Icelanders and of our own responses to them can be deepened by sensitivity to the ways in which the texts work as narratives of identity.

An Introduction to the Sagas of Icelanders focuses especially on issues of national, religious, and legal identity, gender and sexuality, and the relations between human beings, nature, and the supernatural. Some of these topics have received considerable attention from previous scholars, while others are only now beginning to become important issues in saga studies. This book offers a new perspective by relating these topics to one another and to aspects of textual production and dissemination in the medieval period that call into question our sense of a text's own identity. In doing so, the book reflects, but also takes in new directions, some of the concerns of my own research on medieval Icelandic literature over the last twenty years. I see this research as part of the "theoretical turn" taken by saga studies in recent decades (Ármann and Sverrir Jakobsson 2017: 2–3). In this book, I offer a fresh account of the sagas by relating them to some of the questions addressed by postcolonial studies, feminist and queer theory, and ecocriticism, approaches that are currently more familiar in other areas of literary study than in the study of Old Norse–Icelandic literature.

In chapter 1, I argue that the world of the sagas is alien but also strikingly familiar. This opening chapter describes what an Icelandic saga is and explains the differences between saga genres. Chapter 2 explores relevant historical contexts: the period in which the sagas are set (encompassing the Viking Age, the discovery and settlement of Iceland, and that country's conversion to Christianity), and also the period during which the sagas were composed (including the Sturlung Age of the thirteenth century, which was dominated by conflicts between chieftains and complex relations with Norway). One of the most stimulating aspects of the study of medieval literature is the way in which it defamiliarizes many of one's preconceptions about the nature of literary texts. This second chapter accordingly discusses the oral and literary traditions that nurtured the production of sagas of Icelanders and considers some salient aspects of the preservation of the saga texts: their anonymity, the existence of variant versions, manuscript contexts, the difficulties of dating texts, and the interpretative decisions that inform modern published editions.

Chapter 3 shows how themes of central concern to the genre relate to some of the most prominent preoccupations of contemporary literary criticism. Using examples from many different sagas, this section examines in turn the representation of legal structures and national identity, gender and sexuality, and nature and the supernatural. Chapter 4 then reads a selection of individual major texts, including the most admired and most widely studied examples of the genre, in more detail. This fourth chapter offers a "new perspective" by showing how the source traditions discussed in chapter 2 and the thematic concerns examined in chapter 3 come together in narrative explorations of identity.

The sagas of Icelanders have with justice been described as "Iceland's chief contribution to the literature of the world" (Turville-Petre 1953: 230). Many readers around the world now encounter the sagas in English translation, at least initially, and since this book is itself aimed at readers of English (even if some of them are also able to read Old Norse), chapter 5 considers the translation history of the sagas of Icelanders in English. The chapter reveals the importance of the Icelandic sagas to literary culture in the English-speaking world over the last two hundred or more years and also shows how consistently the translation of sagas of Icelanders has been inspired by, and undertaken in accordance with, beliefs about identity. After a conclusion that draws together the different chapters, the book ends with a glossary and other reference materials.

Throughout this book, references for quotations from the sagas are by chapter rather than page number: chapters are generally quite short and although chapter divisions are not entirely uniform across all editions and translations, this seems the most reliable way of enabling readers to locate quotations in whichever editions of the Norse texts or English translations they have access to. Quotations in Old Norse–Icelandic are taken from the standard scholarly editions in the Íslenzk fornrit series.[2] Except where stated otherwise, English translations are from the five-volume collection of *The Complete Sagas of Icelanders* (1997); to illustrate particular points, I have on occasion supplied my own translations (indicated by "my trans."). Further details of the editions and translations are provided in the Table of Sagas of Icelanders and the bibliography at the end of the book.

ACKNOWLEDGMENTS

I was delighted to be asked to contribute to the series New Perspectives on Medieval Literature by its editors, Tison Pugh and Barton Palmer, and I have been inspired by reading the excellent volumes already published in the series. Completion of my manuscript was delayed by heavy administrative burdens of the kind that impede research and scholarship for so many academics in the United Kingdom today; I am grateful to Tison and Barton for their patience in awaiting delivery of the book. Staff at the University Press of Florida, notably including the acquisitions editor Stephanye Hunter and project editor Valerie Melina, have been highly skillful and extremely efficient. I am also grateful to Penelope Cray for her careful copy editing of the book. It is a pleasure to acknowledge the stimulus to fresh thinking and new perspectives presented by my students during two decades of teaching at Cardiff University. The sections on *Egils saga* and *Njáls saga* in chapter 4 include some phrasing and material adapted from my entries on those texts in the online *Literary Encyclopedia* (www.litencyc.com), and I am grateful for permission to draw on that work here. Svanhildur Óskarsdóttir (Árni Magnússon Institute for Icelandic Studies, Reykjavík) provided valuable advice on possible cover illustrations. I am indebted to Mark Llewellyn at Cardiff and Greg Walker of the University of Edinburgh for reading and commenting on the complete first draft of the book, which Tison Pugh also read with an attention to detail and helpfulness well beyond what one might reasonably expect of a series editor. The two reviewers for the University Press of Florida waived their anonymity, enabling me to thank Chris Abram and Alison Finlay here for their helpful and very encouraging reports. Any remaining errors and infelicities are, of course, entirely my own responsibility.

This book is dedicated to Heather O'Donoghue, an inspiring and unfailingly supportive scholar and teacher of the sagas.

A NOTE ON NAMES AND PRONUNCIATION

Published English translations of the sagas usually Anglicize personal and place-names to a greater or lesser extent. Because there are a variety of ways of doing this (and because not all translators do it), I will normally use the Old Norse/Old Icelandic forms of personal names and place-names in this book (the terms "Old Norse" and "Old Icelandic" are used more or less interchangeably for the language of the sagas: see the discussion in chapter 1 below). The Icelandic alphabet includes a few letters not used in modern English, but these are quickly mastered. Although it is possible to reconstruct the pronunciation of Old Norse in, say, the thirteenth century, the language is today usually pronounced as if it were modern Icelandic. For modern Icelanders who can read saga prose with little difficulty, this is eminently sensible, but in fact the pronunciation is the one aspect of the language that has changed most since the medieval period.

The following *very* rough guide to modern Icelandic pronunciation may help with the pronunciation of names in this book (for more accurate and detailed accounts of both reconstructed and modern pronunciations, see Barnes 2008: 8–21):

´	indicates a long vowel (which in a couple of cases has become a diphthong in modern Icelandic pronunciation)
á	is pronounced like *ow* in English *owl*
é	is pronounced like *ye* in English *yes*
í	is pronounced like *ee* in English *keen*

ó	is pronounced like English *oh*
ú	is pronounced like *oo* in English *moon*
ý	is pronounced like *ee* in English *keen*

au	is pronounced like the vowel sound in French *oeil* (a little like *oy* in English *boy*)
ei	is pronounced like *ei* in English *eight*

æ	is pronounced like English *eye*
ǫ ø ö	are all pronounced like German ö (a bit like English *er* but without an "r" sound)

ll	is pronounced like English *tl*
nn	is pronounced like English *tn*
ð	is pronounced like *th* in English *them* (replaced by "d" in many English translations); the uppercase form is Ð
þ	is pronounced like *th* in English *thin* (replaced by "th" in many English translations); the uppercase form is Þ.

A couple of further points about Icelandic names may help to prevent confusion. Old Norse/Old Icelandic and Modern Icelandic are more highly inflected languages than modern English, so words often change their endings to indicate grammatical function. Except when quoting texts that follow a different convention, this book follows the common scholarly practice of always writing Icelandic names in their nominative form (the form they have when they are the grammatical subject of a sentence in the original language).[1]

Because published English translations adopt a variety of different titles for individual sagas, I generally refer to sagas by their Icelandic names in this book (a list of the English titles used in the *Complete Sagas of Icelanders* translation is provided in the Table of Sagas of Icelanders on pp. 170–74). Note that many sagas are named for prominent individuals in the narrative and in such titles the character's name takes a slightly different form to indicate that it is the saga *of* X (genitive case). So, for example, Hrafnkell is the nominative form but the saga named after him is called

Hrafnkels saga in Icelandic, where the nominative ending -l is replaced with the genitive ending -s. Published English translations typically Anglicize the name as Hrafnkel by dropping the nominative ending and the saga then becomes *Hrafnkel's Saga*.

With the exception of very few families who now have hereditary surnames, both medieval and modern Icelanders have patronymics rather than family names: thus, Ármann Jakobsson is the son of Jakob; Björk Gudmundsdóttir is the daughter of Guðmundur Gunnarsson. Like most scholarship on the sagas today, this book follows Icelandic practice in referring to Icelanders by their first or full name and listing them by first name, not by patronymic, in the bibliography (but Sigurður and Guðrún Nordal do have a surname and are treated accordingly).

ABBREVIATIONS

AM   Den arnamagnæanske håndskriftsamling, Det arnamagnæanske institut, Copenhagen, and Stofnun Árna Magnússonar í íslenskum fræðum, Reykjavík [= The Árni Magnússon manuscript collection at the Arnamagnæan Institute, Copenhagen, and the Árni Magnússon Institute for Icelandic Studies, Reykjavík]

CS   *The Complete Sagas of Icelanders, Including 49 Tales.* Ed. Viðar Hreinsson 5 vols. Reykjavík: Leifur Eiríksson, 1997

GKS   Den gamle kongelige samling, Det kongelige bibliotek, Copenhagen, and Stofnun Árna Magnússonar í íslenskum fræðum, Reykjavík [= The Old Royal Collection in the Royal Library, Copenhagen, and the Árni Magnússon Institute for Icelandic Studies, Reykjavík]

ÍF   Íslenzk fornrit series

SI   *The Sagas of Icelanders: A Selection.* With an Introduction by Robert Kellogg. London: Viking Penguin, 2000

CHRONOLOGY

Many dates are necessarily approximate. For discussion of the dating of the sagas of Icelanders themselves see pp. 49–51 below.

793	Viking raid on Lindisfarne, Northumbria
ca. 800–ca. 1080	The Viking Age
ca. 850	Beginning of Viking settlement in England
ca. 860	Discovery of Iceland
ca. 870–930	Settlement of Iceland
ca. 885	Haraldr hárfagri becomes king in Norway
930	Althing (national assembly) established in Iceland
ca. 930–ca. 1030	The Saga Age (period during which most events in the sagas of Icelanders took place)
ca. 965	Iceland divided into quarters for administrative and legal purposes
ca. 985	Beginning of Norse settlement of Greenland
990–995	Óláfr Tryggvason king of Norway
999/1000	Official conversion of Iceland to Christianity by agreement at the Althing
ca. 1000	Discovery of North America by Norse-speakers
ca. 1005	Fifth Court established in Iceland
1014	Battle of Clontarf, Ireland
1015–1028	St Óláfr Haraldsson king of Norway
1030	Óláfr Haraldsson returns to Norway from exile and is killed at the battle of Stiklarstaðir

1056	Ísleifr Gizurarson of Skálholt becomes the first native Icelandic bishop (to 1080)
1067/8	Ari Þorgilsson born; died 1148
1081–1118	Gizurr Ísleifsson bishop at Skálholt
1096	Tithe law introduced in Iceland
1106	Jón Ǫgmundsson becomes the first bishop of the northern Icelandic diocese of Hólar
1117–1118	Icelandic laws first written down
1122–1133	Ari Þorgilsson's *Íslendingabók* compiled
1133	First Icelandic monastery established at Þingeyrar
ca. 1150	Date of the earliest surviving Icelandic manuscript fragments
1153	Archbishopric established at Niðaróss (Trondheim), Norway
1178/9	Snorri Sturluson born
Late twelfth century–ca. 1300	The great age of saga writing
ca. 1220	Snorri Sturluson's *Prose Edda* composed
1241	Snorri Sturluson killed on September 23
ca. 1250	Earliest surviving manuscript fragment of a saga of Icelanders (*Egils saga Skallagrímssonar*)
1261	Greenland comes under Norwegian rule
1262–1264	Icelanders acknowledge the Norwegian king as king of Iceland
1271	*Járnsíða* law code is introduced to Iceland from Norway
1281	*Jónsbók* law code supersedes *Járnsíða*
ca. 1330–1370	Möðruvallabók manuscript written
1380	Personal union of the kingdoms of Norway (including Iceland) and Denmark
1397	Kalmar union of kingdoms of Norway, Denmark, and Sweden
1492	Christopher Columbus "discovers" the Americas
1497	John Cabot "discovers" the North American mainland
ca. 1500	Norse colony in Greenland dies out
1523	End of the Kalmar Union when Gustav Vasa becomes

	King of Sweden; Iceland remains under the Danish-Norwegian crown
1550	Reformation in Iceland; martyrdom of the last Catholic bishop
1663–1730	Árni Magnússon, most important collector of medieval Icelandic manuscripts
1814	Kingdom of Norway united with Sweden by the Treaty of Kiel, but Iceland remains under the Danish crown Sir Walter Scott publishes an abstract of *Eyrbyggja saga*
1861	George Webbe Dasent's translation of *Njáls saga* (*Burnt Njal*) published
1869	William Morris and Eiríkr Magnússon publish their first saga translation: *Grettis Saga: The Story of Grettir the Strong*
1899	Muriel Press's translation of *Laxdœla saga* published
1904	Home rule for Iceland
1918	Independence for Iceland under the Danish crown
1930	E. R. Eddison's translation of *Egils saga* published
1933–1991	Publication of Íslenzk fornrit editions of the sagas of Icelanders in thirteen volumes (now the standard scholarly editions of the Norse-Icelandic texts)
1944	Iceland becomes an independent republic
1960	Magnus Magnusson and Hermann Pálsson's translation of *Njál's Saga* inaugurates a series of saga translations in Penguin Classics
1961	Gwyn Jones's translation *Erik the Red and Other Sagas*
1997	Publication of *The Complete Sagas of Icelanders, including 49 Tales* in five volumes

1

ENCOUNTERING THE SAGAS

The sagas of Icelanders are the most distinctive, and today the most widely read and admired, of the many different kinds of text produced in medieval Iceland. Between the twelfth and fifteenth centuries, Icelanders produced as rich, varied, and extensive a vernacular literature as was produced anywhere in medieval Europe. That literature has ever since been central to Icelandic cultural identity. It has also played a prominent role in the formation of national identity in Denmark, Norway, and Sweden since the sixteenth century, as well as in nineteenth- and twentieth-century Germany, where it was valued for the insights it was believed to offer into a shared Germanic past. Medieval Icelandic literature has also inspired many notable writers in English since the eighteenth century, including Sir Walter Scott, William Morris, J. R. R. Tolkien, W. H. Auden, and A. S. Byatt, among many others.

Medieval Iceland became the main repository of legendary and mythological material once shared by speakers of Germanic languages across northern Europe. It also preserved a corpus of uniquely intricate verse known as skaldic (or scaldic) poetry (see further ch. 2 below). Skaldic poetry was in turn one of several source traditions for a body of prose narratives set in the past for which there is no parallel elsewhere in the period. These narratives are known throughout the world by their originally Icelandic name as sagas. There are several different kinds of Icelandic saga, but the most widely read and appreciated today are the sagas of Icelanders, the subject of this book.

Here is a passage from one of these sagas; it is translated fairly literally to reflect stylistic features that are often obscured in more idiomatic published translations, such as the vacillation between past and present verb tenses:

> It happened that a bull which Karlsefni and his company owned ran out of the wood and it bellows loudly. This frightened the Skrælings and they run to their boats and then rowed south from the land. There was then no sign of them for three weeks. But when that time had passed, they saw a great company of Skrælings traveling from the south like a stream. Their poles were then all being swung withershins and they all howl very loudly. Then Karlsefni and his men took up their red shields and carried them against them.
>
> The Skrælings ran from their ships and then they went together and fought. The battle became fierce because the Skrælings had war-slings. Karlsefni and his men saw that the Skrælings raised up a very big ball on a pole, almost as big as a sheep's stomach, and it was rather black in appearance, and they threw it from the pole up onto the land and over Karlsefni's company, and it made a hideous noise when it came down.
>
> At that, great fear came over Karlsefni and all his company, so that no one wanted anything other than to flee and they keep to the river because it seemed to them that the company of Skrælings were driving all their force at them and they do not stop until they come to some rocks and there they offered hard resistance.
>
> Freydís came out and saw that Karlsefni and his men were fleeing and she called out: "Why are such worthy men as you running away from these detestable men, such that it seems to me that you could be slaughtered like cattle? If I had a weapon it seems to me I should fight better than anyone of you."
>
> They paid no attention to her words. Freydís wanted to follow them and became slow because she was pregnant [literally "not well"]. Then she went after them into the wood, but the Skrælings attacked her. She found in front of her a dead man. That was Þorbrandr Snorrason and he stood with a stone slab in his head. His sword lay drawn beside him. She picked it up and prepared to defend herself. Then the Skrælings came at her. Then she pulled out

a breast from under clothes and slapped it with the sword. The Skrælings took fright at that and ran down to their ships and rowed away. Karlsefni and his men find her and praise her good luck.

Two of Karlsefni's men died and many of the Skrælings. Karlsefni and his men had faced an overwhelming force and they now went back home to their dwellings and bound their wounds and considered what that multitude of men had been which attacked them from inland. It seemed to them now that there must have been the one company which came from the boats and the (other) people must have been illusions.

The Skrælings found a dead man and an axe lay beside him. One of them picked up the axe and cuts a tree with it, and then each after the other does this, and it seemed to them to be a treasure and to cut well. Then one of them struck a stone with it and so broke the axe and then it seemed to them to be of no use, as it could not withstand stone, and they threw it down.

It now seemed to Karlsefni and his men that although the quality of the land was good there would always be fear and conflict on account of those who already lived there. Then they prepared to leave and intended to return to their land and they sailed north along the coast. (*Eiríks saga rauða* ch. 11; my trans.)

Such a passage may prompt a number of questions for readers new to the genre. Does this excerpt come from a historical or a fictional text? How realistic is this narrative? How ought one to make sense of the apparently unrealistic aspects? What is their narrative effect? Who are the Skrælings? What does the passage reveal about gender roles and relations between men and women? Why do the verb tenses shift between present and past?

The excerpt comes from a thirteenth-century Icelandic text that we will look at in more detail in chapter 4 below; it is known as *Eiríks saga rauða*, the *Saga of Eiríkr (Eric) the Red* (i.e., red-headed). *Eiríks saga* is one of several medieval texts that tell of the discovery of North America by Norse-speakers during the Viking Age, roughly five centuries before Christopher Columbus landed in the Caribbean; the Skrælings in the passage we have just looked at are Native Americans or First Nation people.

The saga was written at least two hundred years after the events that it purports to describe would have taken place, so although it may have some basis in history, it mixes historical fact with what we would call fiction (we shall see that its writer may not have made quite the same distinction between those types of discourse as we do). Both the vacillation between past and present verb tenses and the preference for linking clauses and sentences by parataxis (with "and" or "but") are characteristic of saga narrative and may be a legacy of oral storytelling traditions. At this point in the story, Eiríkr the Red's son Leifr has been blown off course from Greenland (where his father lives) and discovered a land to the west, which was given the name Vínland. A character called Þorfinnr Karlsefni has set out from Greenland to explore Vínland, and he and his crew (including Freydís, the illegitimate daughter of Eiríkr the Red) have wintered at a place called Hóp, where they encounter the native population in the passage quoted above. Cultural differences between the Norse-speakers and the indigenous people are encapsulated in the anecdote about the axe, which indicates that the Skrælings were unfamiliar with iron. Freydís's words and behavior express ideals of gendered behavior (from which the men fall short) at the same time as she subverts those expectations by bravely confronting the attackers. Kirsten Wolf has argued that Freydís takes on an Amazonian aspect in this episode, especially in the variant reading of a seventeenth-century manuscript in which she does not just slap her breast with the sword but actually cuts it off and throws it back at the attackers (Wolf 1996: 481–85).

The sagas of Icelanders genre is pervasively concerned with issues of identity: national, religious, social, and personal. This passage from *Eiríks saga* is about an encounter with the "other," with an alien and unfamiliar people and culture. It hinges on beliefs—and anxieties—about ethnic, perhaps even racial, identity. But it is also informed by understandings of social and personal identity, notably in the way that Freydís articulates an ideology of gender roles. The bull's awareness of what is occurring at the start of the passage and the settlers' mysterious delusion that they are being attacked by two armies point to a blurring of the boundaries between animal and human and between the natural and the supernatural that is characteristic of many sagas; identity can be brought into question by this kind of blurring of boundaries, as we shall explore in more detail later in this book.

The modern reader of an Icelandic saga can be thought of as encountering otherness in a manner somewhat analogous to the encounter between Norse-speakers and Skrælings in *Eiríks saga*. Much about the sagas is familiar and readily accessible to a modern reader, but much is also excitingly different or uncomfortably alien. When faced with that which is different, human beings all too often retreat into fear and hatred. The encounter between Karlsefni's people and the Skrælings is one of violent conflict and misunderstanding, and a similar failure to appreciate what people have in common with those who are different from them is evident in the recent adoption of a Vínland myth by white supremacists (see the preface above). Encounters with the unfamiliar or different—including between the modern reader and a medieval text—can, however, lead to a fruitful and enriching dialogue.

Later in *Eiríks saga*, Karlsefni's crew sail farther south and capture two boys. Here I give the original Norse-Icelandic text before my fairly literal translation of the passage:

> Sveina þessa tvá hǫfðu þeir með sér. Þeir kenndu þeim mál, ok váru skírðir. Þeir nefndu móður sína Vethildi ok fǫður Óvægi. Þeir sǫgðu, at konungar stjórnuðu Skrælingum, ok hét annarr þeira Avaldamon, en annarr Avaldidida. Þeir kváðu þar engin hús; lágu menn þar í hellum eða holum. [. . .] Nú kómu þeir til Grœnlands ok eru með Eiríki rauða um vetrinn. (ch. 12)

> They kept these two boys with them. They taught them their language and they were baptized. They [i.e., the boys] named their mother Vethildi and their father Óvægi. They said that kings ruled the Skrælings, and one of them was called Avaldamon and the other Avaldidida. They said that there were no houses there. People there lived in caves or holes. [. . .] Now they came to Greenland and are with Eiríkr the Red during the winter.

There is a coercive aspect to this encounter that echoes colonialist aggression in many other places and periods: the boys are captured, removed from their families, and forced to become Christian (a reminder of the importance of religion to personal and social identity). Nevertheless, by learning to speak Norse, the boys become able to converse with Karlsefni's crew, and dialogue and understanding become possible.

Learning to read Old Norse provides modern readers with access to aspects of the Icelandic sagas that cannot be conveyed in even the best translations. Most published translations, for example, smooth over the shift of tense in the last sentence of the above quotation, putting both verbs in the past tense, although such vacillation of tenses is a characteristic feature of saga style. Yet, highly desirable though it certainly is, it is not absolutely necessary to learn the language in order to be enriched by an encounter with medieval Icelandic literature.[1] What is certainly helpful, whether one is reading sagas in the original or in translation, is some knowledge of the historical, social, and cultural contexts in which medieval Icelandic literature was produced: such knowledge enables the reader to sustain a much more fruitful dialogue with the world of the sagas, as chapter 2 will demonstrate.

The sense of identity of a person or community is constructed on the basis of perceived similarities with and differences from others, whether in terms of ethnicity, nationality, gender, religion, or other factors. As shared stories about the past of their island, the sagas embodied and affirmed Icelanders' beliefs about identity. But the very same texts also reveal how blurred key distinctions and perceived differences can be. By exposing the contingent nature of beliefs about identity the texts provide a site for their possible contestation. The relationship between text and reality is thus a dialogic one in which the text confirms, and at the time reveals the inadequacy of, constructions of identity on the basis of difference. But before we examine these issues in more detail in the following chapters, we need to examine more closely what we mean by the term "sagas of Icelanders."

Kinds of Saga

All sagas of Icelanders are Icelandic sagas, but not all Icelandic sagas are sagas of Icelanders. Nor are sagas the only kind of text produced in medieval Iceland.[2] "Saga" is an Icelandic noun related to the verb *segja*, "to speak, to tell." The word "saga" thus means "something said" or more narrowly "a story, a narrative" (the modern Icelandic plural of *saga* is *sögur*). The term need not imply anything about the historicity of the narrative in question. In modern Icelandic, the word "saga" may be used equally of a novel or of a scholarly piece of historical writing. All sagas are at least purportedly concerned with the past, but they vary greatly in historicity; as one Victorian translator remarked, "There are many kinds of Sagas, of all degrees of truth" (Dasent 1861: v). Whereas in most of Europe in the twelfth and thirteenth centuries, verse was the default medium for extensive narratives, the medieval Icelandic narratives known as sagas are essentially a prose form. Many (though not all) of the sagas incorporate some poetry, however, in widely varying proportions to the prose. The sagas are thus often thought of as prosimetric: a mixed verse-and-prose form. Sagas vary considerably in length: one of the shortest, *Hrafnkels saga*, is twenty pages long in the Complete Sagas of Icelanders translation, whereas the longest, *Njáls saga*, runs to 220 pages. The average length of a saga is forty-seven pages (Rowe 2017: 157), but the four longest—*Laxdæla saga*, *Grettis saga*, *Egils saga*, and *Njáls saga*—are each of novel-like length; they happen also to be the most highly valued and widely read today.

In modern scholarship sagas are conventionally classified according to their subject matter. The sagas of Icelanders are concerned with events in Iceland in the period from the beginning of the Norse settlement in the 870s until around 1030, by which time the island was fully settled, its legal institutions were established, and its inhabitants had officially converted to Christianity. These sagas are, in other words, narratives about the formative period in the creation of a new polity. The century following the establishment in 930 of the national assembly, or Althing (Icelandic: Alþingi), is known as the Saga Age: it is the period during which most of the events in the sagas of Icelanders are supposed to have taken place. But the Saga Age is not the period in which the sagas were written down: the written texts date from the late twelfth century onward (we will return to the question of the dating of texts in chapter 2 below). There are roughly forty sagas of Icelanders, adding up to approximately 2,500 pages in the five volumes of a complete translation of the corpus into English (see the complete list in reference materials below, pp. 170–74). The sa-

gas of Icelanders are also known in English as Family Sagas, and many of
them do indeed trace events affecting several generations of one or more
families. But others are more tightly focused on a single individual's life or
on a region rather than a family, and so this book prefers the term "sagas
of Icelanders," which is a literal translation of the modern Icelandic term
"Íslendinga sögur."[3]

Although the focus in this book is primarily on the sagas of Icelanders,
other kinds of Icelandic saga will occasionally be mentioned. The kings'
sagas (known in Icelandic as *konungasögur*) are concerned with the history of the kings of Norway; there is also a saga of the kings of Denmark
(*Knýtlinga saga*). Bishops' sagas (*biskupa sögur*) recount the lives of Icelandic bishops, including two bishops recognized as saints (Þorlákr and
Jón); lives of non-Icelandic saints are known as saints' sagas (*heilagra
manna sögur*). The *fornaldarsögur*, sagas of ancient times or legendary sagas, are set in the more distant past, before the settlement of Iceland, and
although they are preserved in Icelandic manuscripts, they are concerned
with the legendary history of mainland Scandinavia. The *riddarasögur*,
or sagas of knights, are romances: they include both translations from
French (including, for example, three versions of romances by Chrétien
de Troyes and a saga based on Thomas of Britain's *Tristram*) and original
texts that follow the same generic conventions. Finally, the *samtíðarsögur*,
or contemporary sagas, deal with Icelandic history much closer to the period of composition in the thirteenth century than the events described in
the sagas of Icelanders. They provide valuable information on the period
during which many of the sagas of Icelanders were written. Some kings'
sagas and contemporary sagas are attributed to named authors; most
other sagas, and all the sagas of Icelanders, are anonymous.

These categories are all but universally adopted in saga scholarship,
but the rough and ready nature of this taxonomy may already be apparent.[4] Not only sagas of Icelanders but also bishops' sagas and contemporary sagas deal with Icelandic history, for example. For this reason, some
scholars have begun to prefer the term "sagas of early Icelanders" to make
clear the distinction from "contemporary sagas" that deal with Icelanders
of the thirteenth century (see, e.g., Andersson 2006 and Mundal 2013). In
Eiríks saga rauða, we have already encountered a so-called saga of Iceland-

ers that, although featuring characters of Icelandic origin, is largely set in Greenland and North America. There are also sagas that do not seem to fit into any of the accepted categories. *Orkneyinga saga* is an account of the earls, rather than the kings, of Orkney, but it has much in common with the kings' sagas and tends to be lumped with them—as does *Færeyinga saga*, even though that saga might more appropriately be thought of as an *Íslendinga saga* that happens to be about Faroe islanders rather than Icelanders. *Kristni saga* recounts the history of the conversion of Iceland to Christianity, an event that is treated more briefly in many sagas of Icelanders, but it is usually excluded from the sagas of Icelanders genre and sometimes grouped instead with the bishops' sagas (where it sits uneasily since, although it features non-Icelandic bishops active in Iceland, it is primarily about the period before either of the Icelandic sees was established).

The Icelandic names for the saga genres are frequently encountered in modern scholarship and criticism, but they must not mislead the reader into thinking that the terminology is medieval: almost all the names for the genres are modern, rather than medieval, Icelandic terms (exceptions are *konungasögur* and *riddarasögur*, which do occur in medieval manuscripts). But while medieval Icelanders appear not to have directed attention to classifying their prose or prosimetric narratives, they may implicitly have recognized the groupings adopted in modern scholarship: they did, after all, write texts similar enough to each other for modern scholars to recognize their family resemblances. Moreover, the sagas of Icelanders are often preserved in manuscripts alongside other sagas of Icelanders: this again suggests that although they might not have had a label for the genre, medieval Icelanders thought of sagas dealing with events in Iceland in the period up to about 1030 as forming a recognizable family of texts. A particularly important manuscript collection is Möðruvallabók (AM 132 fol.), copied between 1330 and 1370: this is the only manuscript to contain full texts of *Kormáks saga*, *Droplaugarsona saga*, and *Víga-Glúms saga*, as well as what are in most cases the best surviving texts of many other sagas of Icelanders: *Njáls saga*, *Egils saga*, *Finnboga saga*, *Bandamanna saga*, *Hallfreðar saga*, *Laxdœla saga*, and *Fóstbrœðra saga*.

Another group of texts is frequently associated with the sagas of Icelanders in modern scholarship: these are the *Íslendingaþættir*, "short stories" or "tales" of Icelanders (the singular of *þættir* is *þáttr*, literally a "thread"). Like the sagas of Icelanders, these shorter tales are concerned with the deeds of Icelanders, though in the *þættir* the protagonists are often away from Iceland, raiding, trading, or serving (often as poets) at foreign royal courts. Although their subject matter associates the *þættir* with the sagas of Icelanders, they are preserved as more or less independent short narratives within kings' sagas, usually incorporated into the account of the reign of the relevant Norwegian king. Extracted from their kings' saga manuscript contexts, *þættir* of Icelanders have been included with sagas of Icelanders in the standard scholarly Íslenzk fornrit edition and in the English translation of the Complete Sagas of Icelanders.

It is impossible (and undesirable) to dissociate the sagas of Icelanders entirely from other kinds of writing in medieval Iceland, including legal texts, homilies, and various kinds of learned treatise. Pre-Christian mythological and legendary material was also preserved in both verse and prose. A collection of anonymous mythological and legendary poems known as the *Poetic Edda* survives in a manuscript of the 1270s, the Codex Regius (GKS 2365 4to). Norwegian court poetry from the ninth century onward and other skaldic poetry employing the same extraordinarily complex verse forms by Norwegians, Icelanders, and Orcadians is almost without exception preserved only in Icelandic sagas. Both eddaic and skaldic verse provided source material for the *(Prose) Edda* (ca. 1220) by Snorri Sturluson (1178/9–1241), a prominent figure in historical events of the thirteenth century and the outstanding named author of medieval Iceland. In the course of this handbook for poets, Snorri provides the most comprehensive surviving account of pre-Christian Norse mythology, though it is filtered through his thirteenth-century Christian perspective.

Mythological texts—the *Poetic* and *Prose Eddas* and some skaldic verse—have, perhaps understandably, attracted a disproportionate amount of popular and scholarly attention: such texts constitute a very small proportion of surviving medieval Icelandic literature (somewhat larger, admittedly, if one adds the legendary material found in the *fornaldarsögur*). The myths did, however, have what Margaret Clunies Ross (1994; 1998) has happily called "prolonged echoes": in addition to their continuing survival in the diction of skaldic verse, the pre-Christian myths appear also to have influenced some apparently realistic or historical narratives composed well after the conversion to Christianity, including some material we find in sagas of Icelanders.[5]

The Language of the Sagas: Old Norse or Old Icelandic?

Iceland was discovered by Scandinavian seafarers during the Viking Age and was settled from around 870 onward, mainly by families of Norwegian origin, though many settlers spent time en route in Orkney, the Hebrides, or Ireland and there acquired Celtic-speaking wives, concubines, or slaves. Medieval Icelanders, like mainland Scandinavians of the period, spoke and wrote a Germanic language that they usually referred to as *dǫnsk tunga*, the "Danish tongue," but modern scholars call Old Norse. This language is the parent of modern Danish and Swedish (descended from Old East Norse dialects) and modern Norwegian, Icelandic, and Faroese (descended from Old West Norse). Icelandic has changed very little in its passage from Old to Modern, and Icelanders today can read saga prose with little difficulty. The Danish, Norwegian, and Swedish languages have diverged much farther from Old Norse while remaining close enough to each other for a level of mutual comprehension. The vast majority of surviving medieval texts in Old Norse—and very nearly all those of literary interest—were preserved in Iceland, and so for many purposes Old Norse and Old Icelandic may be regarded as synonymous. Modern scholarship often uses the terms interchangeably, but anxiety that "Norse" might be taken to mean "Norwegian" has led to increasing use of the ungainly but more precise term "Old Norse–Icelandic."

From the ninth century onward, Norse-speaking Vikings settled in parts of England alongside speakers of Old English, a related and probably more or less mutually intelligible Germanic language (see Townend 2002). Though Norse eventually died out in England, many Norse words were borrowed into English and survive in the language today. A few notable examples include: law, sky, take, they, their, window. The genetic, cultural, and linguistic inheritance that Britain derived from the Vikings provided a major stimulus to British scholarly and popular interest in medieval Scandinavia and Iceland from the eighteenth century onward. In a similar manner, American interest in Norse literature and culture, particularly among descendants of immigrants from Scandinavia, was stimulated by Icelandic sagas describing the Norse discovery of North America. (The reception and influence of medieval Icelandic culture in the English-speaking world will be examined in more detail in chapter 5 below.) Having introduced the sagas in this chapter, we will now look in more detail at the historical context for their writing in medieval Iceland.

2

TRADITIONS IN TIME

The sagas of Icelanders are texts with a history, set in the past. They were mostly first written in the thirteenth and fourteenth centuries, but they are set in the period between about 870 and about 1030. The texts can therefore be read in relation to two different Icelandic historical contexts: (i) the period that the sagas depict, encompassing the Viking Age, the discovery and settlement of Iceland, the establishment of the island's legal and social structures, and its conversion to Christianity, and (ii) the period during which the sagas were composed, including the so-called Sturlung Age of the thirteenth century, dominated by conflicts between chieftains and complex relations with Norway, especially with the Norwegian King Hákon Hákonarson (r. 1204–1263), leading eventually to Iceland's submission to the Norwegian monarchy. The first section of this chapter explores these historical contexts. The next section provides a sense of the variety of source traditions that nourished the writing of sagas of Icelanders: oral storytelling, skaldic verse, possible Irish influences, and European literary genres such as hagiography and romance. Finally, the chapter pursues some of the implications of the state in which saga texts have been preserved in manuscripts: their anonymity, the existence of variant versions, the difficulties of dating texts, and the interpretative decisions that inform modern published editions. The chapter shows that the texts do not have single fixed identities but are constituted through a complex process of oral and literary creation, re-creation, and conservation.

I: Historical Contexts

Settlement

Vague references to Scandinavia appear in classical writers, but it was with the beginning of the Viking Age, from around 800 C.E. onward, that the peoples of Scandinavia forced themselves upon the consciousness of other Europeans. That same period of Scandinavian exploration and expansion overseas saw the discovery and settlement of Iceland.[1]

The causes of the Viking expansion remain to some extent unclear, but there were a number of contributory factors. Medieval Scandinavians would not have been able to undertake their voyages of exploration and trading, or their overseas raids, had they not first made technological advances in the art of ship-building. They developed clinker-built ships with hulls built of over-lapping planks, a technique also known as lapstrake. These ships were equipped with both sails and oars that ensured they were highly maneuverable yet also capable of enduring inclement conditions on the ocean. Population pressures have often been seen as impelling a search for new land by Scandinavians unable to expand further in their relatively infertile homelands, a more convincing explanation for Norwegian Viking activity than for Danish and Swedish. Some historians have suggested that Viking raids were provoked by a perceived threat from Charlemagne's strong and aggressive European empire; others, conversely, have suggested that the Vikings took advantage of conflict among Charlemagne's successors. Icelandic sources, written down long after the end of the Viking Age it must be remembered, attribute the settling of Iceland to dissatisfaction with King Haraldr hárfagri's unification of (much of) Norway under his personal rule following the Battle of Hafrsfjǫrðr in 872 (though settlement probably began very slightly before that date).

Iceland is unique in Europe for being a society with origins in recorded history. Before the arrival of Norse-speaking settlers in the late ninth century, the island had no permanent human population. A few Irish hermits, intent on seeking God in solitude, seem to have come to Iceland before the Norse settlement. The Irish scholar Dicuil, writing in 825 in Frankia, refers to hermits spending the summer in Thule, by which he may mean Iceland (Dicuil 1967: 74–75).[2] Although there is no archaeological evidence to support this statement, the presence of Irish monks on Iceland is independently confirmed by the earliest Icelandic written sources centuries later and, probably, by a number of place-names recorded in Iceland containing the element *papar* (from Latin *papa* [father, pope], via Old Irish). Inevitably, men vowed to celibacy could not (and indeed did not wish to) establish a permanent population; medieval Icelandic sources record that the Irish left once their solitude was compromised by the appearance of Norse settlers.

The sources for early Icelandic history are primarily narratives written down some centuries later in Iceland, including the sagas of Icelanders themselves. Any attempt to use these texts to reconstruct the early history of the island must begin by recognizing that these narratives reveal what Icelanders from the twelfth century onward believed (or wanted to believe) about the history of their island. They may have inherited reliable traditions about their past, but our only access to those traditions is via the written texts of the twelfth and later centuries.

The earliest known historical writing in Iceland no longer survives. Sæmundr Sigfússon (1056–1133) is cited as an authoritative historian in later texts (see Turville-Petre 1953: 84–87). Since Snorri Sturluson claims in the early thirteenth century that Ari Þorgilsson (1068–1148) was the first to write history in Icelandic (Faulkes and Finlay 2011–2015: I, 4), it is assumed that his predecessor Sæmundr, who had been educated in France, wrote his now lost history of the kings of Norway in Latin.

Ari Þorgilsson's *Íslendingabók* (*Book of Icelanders*) is the earliest vernacular history of Iceland and the earliest extant prose narrative in Old Norse. It survives only in two seventeenth-century copies of a now lost twelfth-century manuscript but is thought to have been written between 1122 and 1133. The surviving text covers the history of Iceland during the formative period between the beginning of the settlement and the first writing down of the Icelandic laws, so circa 870–1118. It is a short text—just twelve pages in Grønlie's translation (2006). Allusions to Ari's work in later medieval texts suggest that what survives may be an abbreviated revision of an originally longer text, or possibly that Ari wrote other works that no longer survive (or both). Ari is, for example, cited as an authority on the history of the kings of Norway as well as Icelandic history in various kings' sagas and in *Laxdæla saga* (chs. 4, 78), *Eyrbyggja saga* (ch. 7), *Njáls saga* (ch. 114), and elsewhere. Ari is scrupulous in informing the reader of his oral informants and their proximity to the events they recalled, information that reinforces the historical value of his account. Hermann Pálsson writes, "An essential purpose of Ari the Learned and other early Icelandic historians appears to have been to find the right answer to the crucial question: Who are we?" (1999: 18). This continues to be a central concern in the sagas of Icelanders, different in form and style from Ari's history though those sagas are.

Accepting the claim of the compiler of the fourteenth-century Hauksbók manuscript that he used a version of the text of *Landnámabók* (*The Book of Settlements*) compiled by Ari Þorgilsson and Kolskeggr Ásbjarnarson, many scholars from the seventeenth century onward have maintained that Ari was involved in the original production of *Landnámabók* in the early twelfth century. The five surviving variant versions of that text date, however, from the thirteenth to seventeenth centuries.[3] All descend from a lost version known as Styrmisbók. One or more versions earlier than those that survive are thought to have been used as sources for several sagas of Icelanders, but sagas in turn supplied material that is now incorporated in the surviving texts of *Landnámabók*. As its title (*The Book of Settlements*) suggests, *Landnámabók* names about 420 of the settlers of Iceland and provides genealogies and information on where they settled; it is concerned primarily with independent (male) settlers rather than with their wives, slaves, or dependents, so it names perhaps as few as 5 percent of the first settlers. It is typically a terse account but occasionally breaks out into slightly more expansive anecdote.

The Þórðarbók redaction includes the following comment on the purpose of *Landnámabók*:

> People often say that writing about the Settlements is irrelevant learning, but we think we can better meet the criticism of foreigners when they accuse us of being descended from slaves and scoundrels, if we know for certain the truth about our ancestry. And for those who want to know ancient lore and how to trace genealogies, it is better to start at the beginning than to come in at the middle. Anyway, all civilized nations want to know about the origin of their

own society and the beginnings of their own race. (*Book of Settlements* 1972: 6)

Similar sentiments must inform the writing and preservation of the sagas of Icelanders, which are set in the period during which Iceland was settled and its society established.

Medieval Icelandic sources refer to a number of pioneering temporary visitors to Iceland from the 860s onward. *Landnámabók* mentions a Norwegian called Naddoðr, blown off course to Iceland, a Swede called Garðarr whose ship drifted there, and another Norwegian, Flóki, who made a failed attempt at settling Iceland and, having fallen foul of the inhospitable climate, gave the island its lasting name (*Landnámabók* ÍF 1: 34–39; *Book of Settlements* 1972: 16–18) This trio of pioneers and some details of the account (such as three ravens sent out by Flóki to find land in a scene reminiscent of the story of Noah's Ark) indicate that we are dealing here with more or less legendary traditions about the nation's origins. Ari Þorgilsson's *Íslendingabók* begins not with these supposed discoverers of the island but with the first permanent settler: Ingólfr Arnarson, who came from western Norway to live in the area around the modern Icelandic capital of Reykjavík circa 870 (874 is the traditional date). Like Ingólfr, most of the settlers came from western Norway, but *Landnámabók* and some of the sagas of Icelanders indicate that some came via the British and Irish Isles (including Orkney, Shetland, the Hebrides, and Ireland), where some of the men acquired Celtic-speaking wives, slaves, or concubines; a number of prominent individuals in the sagas of Icelanders bear names of Irish origin (e.g., Kjartan, Kormákr, and Njáll). In this respect, the written sources have been corroborated by recent DNA studies of the current population in Iceland, which have indicated that perhaps as many as 50 percent of female and 20 percent of male settlers came from the British and Irish isles (Gísli Sigurðsson 2000: ii, 35–40). One strand of scholarship on the origins of saga writing argues that Irish models may have influenced the development of the Icelandic saga.

The period of settlement lasted about sixty years, circa 870–930 (a period known in Icelandic as the *landnámsöld*, the age of land-taking). The date of its beginning is confirmed by archaeological evidence, the earliest evidence of human settlement appearing in close proximity to a layer of volcanic ash known from analysis of the Greenlandic ice sheet to have been deposited in 871. The settlement period ended with the establishment in 930 of a national legislative and judicial assembly known as the Althing (*Alþingi*), an event inaugurating what is often referred to as the period of the Free State or Commonwealth. By this time, the population of the island may have been somewhere between ten and twenty thousand. In circa 927, Úlfljótr was sent to Norway to obtain a law code, which he modeled on the Gulaþing law of western districts of Norway and which was formally adopted in 930. For a little over three hundred years from that date, Iceland was an anomaly in Western Europe: a nation without a king. Icelanders (and others) were well aware of this anomalous status, and their awareness must have fostered a particular sense of national identity and difference. The kings of Norway, however, pursued a policy of intervention in Icelandic affairs that led, eventually, to Iceland accepting rule by the Norwegian king in a series of assembly decisions between 1262 and 1264. When Norway in turn came under the Danish monarchy in 1397, so did Iceland; the island continued to be ruled by the Danish king after Norway united with the kingdom of Sweden in 1814. Iceland regained its full independence only in 1944.

Seventeen of the forty or so sagas of Icelanders begin with events before or at the time of the settlement of the island.[4] Although they thus often begin with events during the sixty years of the *landnámsöld*, the sagas of Icelanders tell mainly of events set in the first century of the Free State, that is, from circa 930 to circa 1030.[5] Scholars often refer to this century as the Saga Age (Icelandic: *sagaöld*), but the term is potentially confusing: this is the period during which the sagas are set, not the period during which they were written. The period is bisected by an event of enormous cultural significance for the island: its conversion to Christianity in the year 999 or 1000.

Conversion

According to the sagas, there were some (at least nominal) Christians among the earliest settlers in Iceland and certainly some settlers would have encountered Christianity in Britain or Ireland on their way to Iceland. *Landnámabók* famously tells of the early settler Helgi the Lean:

"Helgi's faith was very much mixed: he believed in Christ but invoked Thor when it came to voyages and difficult times" (*Book of Settlements* 1972: 97). Nevertheless, Christians can have been only a small minority, and, if their faith was not in fact the pious invention of later Icelanders, they were probably quickly assimilated to the pagan religion of the majority (no Christian graves earlier than the eleventh century have been found). Later Icelanders encountered Christianity on their travels abroad: *Egils saga* (ch. 50) tells how Egill Skallagrímsson received prime-signing in England so that he could interact socially with the Christian people of that kingdom (prime-signing—being marked with the sign of the cross—was a preliminary to baptism, enabling the recipient to associate with Christians). Like so many aspects of early Icelandic history, the island's conversion to Christianity took place in a unique fashion, by a decision of its legislative assembly, the Althing. The earliest surviving account of the Conversion is in Ari's *Íslendingabók*, where indeed it is of central importance; the fullest accounts of the earliest missionary period (ca. 981–985) are found in the thirteenth-century *Þorvalds þáttr víðfǫrla* and *Kristni saga*. According to these texts, the Icelander Þorvaldr Konráðsson accepts the new faith in Germany and then returns to convert his compatriots in Iceland with Bishop Friðrekr, who had baptized him. They become the subject of obscene insults, which lead Þorvaldr to kill rather than turn the other cheek, and not surprisingly the mission ends in failure. Another Icelander, Stefnir Þorgilsson, meets with a similar lack of success when he is sent as a missionary to Iceland by the Norwegian king, Óláfr Tryggvason, in 996. Again, his predilection for violence—destroying temples and idols—creates enemies rather than converts and he returns to Norway the following year. Sagas of Icelanders record how Óláfr Tryggvason, who labored for the conversion of Norway and its satellites, obtained the conversion of several Icelanders while they were resident in Norway, prominent among them Kjartan Óláfsson and Bolli Þorleiksson (in *Laxdæla saga*) and the poet Hallfreðr vandræðaskáld, whose saga offers a fascinating insight into an individual's conversion (see Whaley 2003). In 997, Óláfr sent another missionary to Iceland, a German priest called Þangbrandr. Ari recounts that he converted several chieftains, but he also killed two or three men who slandered him and his mission enjoyed limited success;

later sagas, including *Kristni saga* (chs. 5, 7–9) and *Njáls saga* (chs. 100–104), offer more detailed and more colorful versions of Þangbrandr's escapades. There is a pattern here of failure by successive missionaries who took vengeance for insults: Gabriel Turville-Petre plausibly suggests that the stories of Þorvaldr and Þangbrandr may both have been shaped by the monk Gunnlaugr Leifsson, whom we know to have written a Latin life of Óláfr Tryggvason that survives only in fragments translated into Norse-Icelandic and incorporated in sagas of the king (Turville-Petre 1953: 67).

Ari gives a vivid account of the final conversion by decision of the Althing in June 1000 (or 999). Icelanders Gizurr inn hvíti (the White) and Hjalti Skeggjason promise King Óláfr Tryggvason of Norway that they will work to bring about Iceland's conversion. They present their case eloquently at the Althing but are not able to convince everyone: "Ok sǫgðusk hvárir ýr lǫgum við aðra, enir kristnu men ok enir heiðnu, ok gingu síðan frá lǫgbergi" (ch. 7; "Each side, the Christians and the heathens, declared itself under separate laws from the other, and they then left the Law-Rock" [Grønlie 2006: 8]). The Christians ask the Lawspeaker, Þorgeirr Þorkelsson, to determine which faith the island will follow, even though he is at that point still heathen. He spends all day and night under his cloak and then emerges to argue that the land must have only one religion, not on theological grounds, but on the basis that unity of religion is necessary to preserve peace: "ok hǫfum allir ein lǫg ok einn sið. Þat mon verða satt, es vér slítum í sundr login, at vér monum slíta ok friðinn" (ch. 7; "let us all have the same law and the same religion. It will prove true that if we tear apart the law, we will also tear apart the peace" [Grønlie 2006: 9]). When both sides agree to accept his decision, "it was then proclaimed in the laws that all people should be Christian." Some concessions are made, temporarily, to allow certain pre-Christian practices to continue, but as Ari presents it, "the ease and unanimity with which the Icelanders accepted Christianity is remarkable" (Turville-Petre 1953: 68). Whether or not it happened as smoothly or as quickly as Ari maintains, Icelanders of the twelfth and following centuries believed that their ancestors had changed religion in a unique way and to preserve their distinctive legal institutions. The conversion is of enormous literary importance, because the new religion brought the technology of manuscript production to Iceland

and also acquainted Icelanders with the established literary traditions of Christian Europe.[6]

The consecration of Ísleifr Gizurarson as the first native bishop in Iceland (1056–1080) marked another important stage in establishing the nation.[7] Having been educated abroad, he played a pivotal role in the introduction of European learning to the island, establishing an influential school at Skálholt. His son Gizurr succeeded him as bishop in 1081 and consolidated the church's position by donating the farm at Skálholt to be the permanent seat of the bishopric. Several events of importance to the development of a literate culture in Iceland took place during Gizurr's episcopate: his introduction of the tithe law in 1096 was a spur to administrative record-keeping, and at the end of his life the Althing resolved to have the hitherto orally transmitted laws written down. According to Ari (*Íslendingabók* ch. 10), laws were first transcribed during the winter of 1117–1118. Historical writing also began around this time, with the now lost history of the kings of Norway written by Sæmundr Sigfússon at Oddi in southern Iceland (like Skálholt, this farm would go on to be an influential center of learning).

The Sturlung Age

As references above to the sagas as historical sources imply, much of what we "know" about Saga Age Iceland depends on what Icelanders of the thirteenth century thought they knew about it. From circa 1200 onward, Icelanders wrote saga narratives about the period from circa 870 to circa 1030. Remarkably few surviving texts deal with events from the next century or so (1030–1130), but there is again a sizeable group of texts dealing with "contemporary" history from circa 1120 into the fourteenth century. These *samtíðarsögur* (contemporary sagas) are the main sources for the period during which the sagas of Icelanders were written, a period of conflict and change in Iceland that likely prompted many islanders to reflect on their past.

During the twelfth century, power that had been distributed among nearly forty *goðar* ("chieftains"; singular *goði*) became concentrated in fewer and fewer hands, as a small number of families took over more and more of the chieftaincies: by circa 1220, ten *goðar* held large geographi-

cal domains. One of these leading families, the Sturlungs (Icelandic: Stur-
lungar), have given their name to the period circa 1220–1262: the Age of
the Sturlungs. This period is characterized by conflict between (and often
within) the leading families and by interventions from abroad by the King
of Norway, who sought to extend his control over the island and played
rival Icelandic *goðar* off against each other. The two most powerful families, the Sturlungs and the Oddi family, sided with opposing factions in
Norway. The conflicts described in sagas of Icelanders, though they strike
modern readers as very violent, are seen to be restrained by unwritten
rules of feuding in comparison to the unbridled violence of the contemporary sagas, which has been appropriately described as "mindless maim-
ing and mutilation, pillaging, arson and limitless butchery" (Helgi Þorláksson 2005: 150). The Icelanders eventually decided that the way to find
peace was to submit to the Norwegian king, as each quarter assembly did
between 1262 and 1264.[8]

Two members of the Sturlung family who were deeply involved in
international and national affairs at this time were Snorri Sturluson and
his nephew Sturla Þórðarson. Sturla's lengthy *Íslendinga saga* ("Saga of
the Icelanders") is a contemporary saga rather than a saga of Icelanders
in the generic sense and is preserved as part of the *Sturlunga saga* collection of contemporary sagas. It covers the period 1183–1242 and is almost
the sole source for events of the period 1213–1241. Sturla also wrote sagas
of the two Norwegian kings who involved themselves in Icelandic affairs
at this time and received the island's submission: Hákon Hákonarson (r.
1217–1263) and Magnús lagabætir ("law-mender" r. 1263–1280; only a brief
fragment of this saga survives).

Why Iceland?

For readers of the sagas of Icelanders, knowledge of Iceland's early history
not only supplies essential context for understanding the events and institutions represented in the sagas but also provides possible answers to
the question why saga-writing developed only in Iceland. Why did this
island produce such a wealth of realistic prose narrative quite unlike anything produced anywhere else in medieval Europe? Why, for example, did
Norwegians, who shared a language and so much of their culture with

Icelanders, not produce a comparable saga literature (cf. Gísli Sigurðsson 2004, 3)?

The answers must be related to aspects of twelfth- and thirteenth-century Iceland that set it apart from other contemporary societies. Power was more widely distributed in the first centuries after the settlement than it was elsewhere in Europe. It is stretching the meaning of the term to claim that early Iceland was "democratic" exactly, but it can still be maintained that, as Hermann Pálsson (1999: 67) carefully puts it, "the society that was created in Iceland by the original settlers and their immediate descendants early in the tenth century was more democratic than any other community in medieval Europe." Decisions were made at the Althing by the chieftains: while this might be fewer than forty people (men, in fact), this nevertheless represents a wider distribution of power than in medieval monarchies. A related point is that there was no royal (or even aristocratic) court in early Iceland, so courtly institutions of literary patronage that were of seminal importance elsewhere in Europe had no influence on the development of native writing. Nor was there any urban culture on the island. The literature that was produced was written in the context of quite different institutions of literary patronage and production than existed elsewhere in Europe, and this must have conditioned the kinds of text produced. The one national institution, the Althing, also played a role, bringing Icelanders from all over the island together each June, thereby unifying the country and providing an occasion for the sharing of stories. In the absence of royal and aristocratic courts or cities, the institutions that fostered medieval Icelandic literary culture were the monasteries and certain farms that became centers of learning.

In the pagan period, the role of *goði* or chieftain combined both political and religious leadership; hence some English translations render the term as "priest." After the conversion to Christianity, sons of prominent families often received a clerical education, and some were ordained.[9] Schools and centers of native scholarship became established at some of the leading farms, including those at the episcopal sees (Skálholt and Hólar) and also Oddi and Haukadalr in the south, Reykholt in the west, and Möðruvellir in the north. Sæmundr the Learned taught at Oddi; later alumni of the school there included Bishop St Þorlákr and Snorri Sturluson. Ari Þorgilsson was educated at Haukadalr. These learned farmsteads had no equivalent elsewhere in Europe, and they no doubt imbued Icelandic learning and literature with a distinctive ethos and set of preoccupations.

The first Icelandic monastery was founded at Þingeyrar in 1133. Its monks played a key role in the early development of Icelandic literary culture, with both Oddr Snorrason and Gunnlaugr Leifsson writing lives of King Óláfr Tryggvason of Norway in Latin (though these survive now only in Old Icelandic translation), and Abbot Karl Jónsson writing (at least part of) *Sverris saga*, an account of the life of King Sverrir Sigurðarson. It is possible that sagas of Icelanders set in the area around Þingeyrar (such as *Vatnsdœla saga*) may have been written at the monastery. The next monastery to be founded, also a Benedictine foundation and also in northern Iceland, was established at Þverá in Eyjafjǫrðr in 1155. It too was a center of literary culture: its first abbot, Nikulás Bergþórsson (d. 1159), wrote a guide for Icelandic pilgrims to the Holy Land. *Víga-Glúms saga*, which tells of events in the area of Munka-Þverá (as the monastery-farm was known) may be linked to the monastery. *Eyrbyggja saga* and *Laxdœla saga* both tell of events at Helgafell on the Snæfellsnes peninsula in the west of Iceland, and it is possible that they were written at the monastery of Augustinian canons established there in 1184.

In this section, we have examined historical factors that shaped the sagas of Icelanders. The next section considers a variety of oral and literary source traditions on which saga-writers drew.

II. Source Traditions: Oral and Literary

Much scholarly and critical discussion of the sagas of Icelanders has been devoted to assessing their value as historical sources. Are they best thought of as history (however inaccurate or unreliable) or as fiction? Or are those very categories misleadingly anachronistic? The lack of other written sources for the early history of Iceland means that it is often impossible to judge the saga accounts against other versions of events. This absence of alternative evidence enabled early saga scholars to see the sagas as what they wanted them to be: reliable sources for the early history of Iceland. The realistic narrative mode of the sagas also made it easy for scholars to believe that they were trustworthy, and the historicity of the sagas was not seriously questioned until well into the nineteenth century. The eminent Icelandic scholar Finnur Jónsson was still defending this long-standing view of the sagas vigorously in 1921, writing, "I will maintain and defend the sagas' trustworthiness [. . .] until I am forced to lay down my pen" (quoted and translated in Andersson 1964: 45). Nevertheless, apparent plausibility and lack of an alternative version of events are no guarantee of reliability, and the pendulum of scholarly opinion swung from an implicit acceptance of the sagas as history in the nineteenth century to extreme skepticism as to their historical reliability by the mid-twentieth century. This shift coincided with, and in part enabled, a focus on literary analysis and appreciation of the sagas in ways that had scarcely been possible while they were valued primarily as historical sources. In more recent decades, it has become axiomatic that in judging the historical value of the sagas of Icelanders, it is necessary to make an important distinction: whatever their utility for reconstructing events in the tenth and eleventh centuries, they certainly have value as sources for what thirteenth- and fourteenth-century writers thought about the past. To that extent, the sagas of Icelanders retain exceptional importance as historical sources for the beliefs and ideological positions of Icelanders of the period in which the texts were written: not only beliefs about what happened in the past and what life in Iceland was like then but also contemporary beliefs about such things as national identity, gender, sexuality, and the supernatural. Such beliefs inevitably, if often unconsciously, informed the saga writers' work. Insofar as their later copying is indicative of continuing resonance with subsequent readers, the sagas can also tell us something about later Icelandic beliefs.

The inclusion of material that strikes many modern readers as improbable or impossible (supernatural beings, magic, prophetic dreams, miracles, etc.) does not in itself mean that the sagas were not conceived as history by medieval Icelanders. On the contrary, it seems clear that however imperfectly they may conform to modern conceptions of historical writing, the sagas of Icelanders were regarded as plausible records of what had happened. On the other hand, it is also important to appreciate that medieval, in contrast to modern, ideas of historical writing held it appropriate, indeed desirable, for writers to employ their imagination in, for example, writing speeches of which there was no verbatim record. Such creativity was seen as enhancing rather than compromising the historical "truth" of a narrative. Thus, the inclusion of material that may seem, from a modern perspective, to be incapable of being true often reflects differences between medieval and modern understandings of historiography rather than indicating that the saga-writer was writing fiction rather than history.

Recognizing that the sagas offer a more dependable insight into beliefs of the thirteenth and fourteenth centuries than into events of the tenth and early eleventh, an influential approach to the historicity of the sagas of Icelanders in recent decades has been to see them as portraying a society consistently across the genre, to recognize that this portrait of "saga Iceland" was what thirteenth- and fourteenth-century Icelanders believed about their island's past, and to leave somewhat to one side the question of the relation of this consistent picture to the realities of the period between 870 and 1030.

The Content of the Past: Oral Traditions

Whatever value the sagas might have as sources for the period in which they are set depends upon the reliability of the traditions with which the writers were working. Where saga writers were drawing on earlier written texts of the twelfth century (such as Ari's *Íslendingabók*, or some version of *Landnámabók*), the historical value of those texts likewise depends upon the quality of the oral traditions upon which their writers depended. Scholars who have trusted in the historical reliability of the sagas have had simultaneously to believe in the reliability of oral traditions that sustained memories about the past until the moment when they were first written down. On the other hand, even those scholars who have been most skeptical about the historical reliability of the sagas have recognized that the authors did not simply invent all their content from scratch. There is no doubt that writers of sagas of Icelanders drew on unwritten stories and beliefs about the past: what is (and has long been) at issue is the scope of those oral sources and their reliability.

Debate about the origins of the sagas of Icelanders has revolved around the relative importance of oral and written sources.[10] The two extreme positions in this debate were labelled by Andreas Heusler in 1913 as *Buchprosa* and *Freiprosa*, terms opaquely translated in English as "book prose" and "free prose." Heusler, with the Norwegian Knut Liestøl, was a proponent of the free prose position, which maintained (despite the label) that texts circulated in fixed and therefore dependable oral form from soon after the events they recounted until they were written down two hundred or so years later. This view dominated scholarship of the early twentieth century but was challenged from the middle of the century by proponents of the "book prose" theory, whose origins can be traced back to the work of the German scholar Konrad Maurer in the 1870s. Without denying that material from oral traditions found its way into the sagas, the book prose position maintained that sagas were written compositions by individual authors of the thirteenth century; it ascribed much greater agency to those authors than the mere transcribing of tradition. Book prose was particularly associated with the so-called Icelandic school and especially with two prolific and influential Icelanders, Einar Ólafur Sveinsson and Sigurður Nordal. These and other scholars emphasized the creativity of medieval Icelandic writers, though at the same time they argued for the use of multiple written, rather than oral, sources in many of the sagas. Such an approach informs the lengthy introductions to the standard modern edition of the sagas in the Íslenzk fornrit series and ensured that for some decades little attention was paid to possible oral traditions behind the sagas.

More recently, "oral tradition" has regained some of its credibility but with a shift of emphasis away from the old free prose concept of fixed "oral sagas" toward a better informed appreciation of the oral roots of saga writing (Gísli Sigurðsson 2004: xiv). Work on living oral traditions in the twentieth century revealed that, at least as far as lengthy narratives are concerned, such traditions do not pass on fixed texts but involve the recomposition of texts in performance. Research also confirmed that the verbatim written transcription of an oral performance is impossible without modern sound-recording technology. The old idea of a verbally fixed "oral saga" finding its way onto parchment is thus at odds with what we now know of the mechanics of oral tradition, but this does not mean that the first writers of sagas did not draw on material that had been passed on in oral tradition.[11]

In an influential article published in 1986, Carol Clover argues, on comparative evidence and in light of the existence of the short written stories known as *þættir*, that oral stories preceding the writing down of sagas would have been short narrative episodes that the audience would have recognized as belonging to larger narratives, even though they would never have heard the whole of such a larger narrative performed. With the writing down of sagas, larger narratives were created by linking orally transmitted episodes and thus realizing the hitherto "immanent" stories of which they formed part.

Theodore Andersson has, on the other hand, offered reasons for thinking that longer as well as shorter narratives may have existed in oral form: narrative devices such as dilation, retardation, and gradual buildup are ubiquitous in sagas but cannot have developed in oral short stories since they are inherently suited only to longer, more leisurely tales (Andersson 2006: 12; see also Andersson 2002).

Although the book prose/free prose debate sometimes appeared to be pitting historically reliable oral tradition against literary fiction, more recent work on Icelandic oral tradition has recognized that "an oral tale can be every bit as creative, artistic, and historically unreliable as a piece of written fiction made up by a specific, named author" (Gísli Sigurðsson 2004: 21). Investigating whether a saga draws on oral tradition or not is therefore not the same as assessing its historical reliability: though a thirteenth-century text cannot tell us anything reliable about the tenth century unless an oral tradition preserved information accurately during the intervening time, proving that a saga is historically unreliable does not prove that it did not draw on oral tradition, which could itself have been unreliable.

Memory is as essential to communal identity as it is to an individual's. As members of a fledgling polity established in a formerly uninhabited land, Icelanders recounted their past as a way of affirming, interrogating, and understanding their present identity. Arguably, all historical writing is at least as much about the present in which it is produced as about the past it portrays; certainly in oral cultures, what is remembered and passed on is what the present values. In his classic account of the shift from orality to literacy, Walter Ong writes that "oral societies live very much in a present which keeps itself in equilibrium or homeostasis by sloughing off memories which no longer have present relevance" (1982: 46). Referring to anthropological fieldwork in Nigeria that showed that genealogies were adjusted in an oral society to fit with present social realities, Ong notes, "The integrity of the past was subordinate to the integrity of the present" (1982: 48), or as he phrases it later in the book, "Narrators narrate what audiences call for or will tolerate. [. . .] When the market for an oral genealogy disappears, so does the genealogy itself, utterly" (Ong 1982: 67). Moreover, in a preliterate community, narrative performs the role of organizing knowledge that in literate societies is performed by abstract categories: oral cultures "use stories of human action to store, organize, and communicate much of what they know" (Ong 1982: 140).

Evidence for the vitality of Icelandic oral tradition comes from two mainland Scandinavian historians writing in Latin who acknowledge their debt to stories told by Icelanders: Theodoricus monachus in Norway (McDougall and McDougall 1998: 5) and Saxo Grammaticus in Denmark (Friis-Jensen and Fisher 2015: 6–7). There are also a number of episodes in medieval Icelandic texts that represent a moment of oral storytelling or performance. These episodes include, among others: a much-discussed episode in the contemporary saga Þorgils saga ok Hafliða, chapter 10, which features the performance of legendary sagas at a wedding at Reykjahólar in 1119;[12] Gunnarr Lambason's account of the burning of Njáll in chapter 155 of Njáls saga (which is memorably cut short when he is decapitated by the avenging Kári Sǫlmundarson); and Egils saga, chapter 78, which shows how oral material including verses might be transmitted at the Althing.

One of the þættir of Icelanders presents a particularly appealing vision of oral storytelling. The Story of the Saga-Wise Icelander (Íslendings þáttr sǫgufróða) is one of the shortest of the þættir, and a closely literal translation can be given here in full:

It happened one summer that a young and sprightly Icelandic man came to the king and asked for his support. The king asked if he knew any lore and he claimed that he knew stories. Then the king said that he would take him in but that he would in return have always to entertain anyone who wanted him to whenever he asked him. And he does so and he is popular among the king's men and they give him clothes and the king gives him weapons. And so it goes until Christmas.

Then the Icelander becomes unhappy and the king asks him why that happened. He said it was his changeable mood.

"That won't be it," says the king, "and I will guess the reason. I guess," he says, "that all your stories are used up. You have always entertained everyone who has asked you this winter. You don't want to fail at Christmas."

"It is exactly as you guess," he says. "There is only one story left and I dare not tell it here because it is the story of your own travels."

The king said: "That is also the story that I most want to hear and you must now not entertain until Christmas, as people are now working. But on Christmas day you shall begin this story and tell a short piece of it and I will so arrange things for you that the story will last as long as the Christmas season. Now there is much drinking at Christmas and little time to sit and listen to stories and you will not be able to discover while you are speaking whether it pleases me or not."

Now it is that the Icelander tells the story. He begins on Christmas Day and speaks for a time and the king soon asks him to stop. People start to drink and many discuss how daring it is that the Icelander tells this story and whether the king would value it. It seems to some that he tells it well, but some thought less well of it. It goes on in this way throughout Christmas.

The king ensured that it was listened to well and it happened with the king's management that the story and the Christmas season ended together. And on the thirteenth evening [i.e., Twelfth Night] when the story had ended earlier in the day, the king said: "Are you not curious, Icelander," he says, "to know how the story pleases me?"

"I am afraid about that, sire," he says.

The king said: "It seems very good to me and no worse than the subject matter is. Who taught you the story?"

He answers: "It was my custom out in my country that I went each summer to the assembly and I learned something of the story each summer from Halldórr Snorrason."

"Then it is not strange," says the king, "that you know it well. And your luck will be with you and you are welcome to stay with me and you will be given whatever you want." The king gave him fine wares and he became a prosperous man. (my trans.)

This þáttr not only tells how stories could be passed on orally at assemblies in Iceland but also makes claims about the trustworthiness of such traditions. The king confirms the accuracy of the story about himself that the Icelander has learned from another Icelander. This story would, of course, be of the kind that would be written down in the kings' sagas, rather than the sagas of Icelanders, but the process of oral transmission would not have been very different.

In narratives such as this, we see the truth of Walter Ong's observation that "the spoken word forms human beings into close-knit communities" (1982: 74). This was the case in preliterate Iceland, in which storytelling at the Althing played a crucial role in binding the island together, but it remained true when written sagas were read aloud to communities gathered in farmhouses. On Icelandic farms, nightly reading aloud from manuscripts during the winter months continued into the nineteenth century in a performance tradition known as *kvöldvaka*.

Besides narratives about past events, a number of other originally oral source traditions, such as genealogies and folk etymological explanations of place-names, also fed into the composition of the sagas of Icelanders. For nearly two hundred years after the establishment of the Althing, the island's laws were transmitted orally rather than in written form, and the law was central both to the establishment of a working polity in the newly settled land and to the narrative content of many of the sagas.

Perhaps the most important, and certainly the most immediately obvious, of the sagas' source traditions is skaldic verse. Many, but not all, of the sagas of Icelanders incorporate poetry that is said by the narrator either to have been uttered by a character in the saga (two hundred or more years earlier) or sometimes composed by a poet in the period between the events recounted in the saga and the writing of the text.

The verse incorporated in sagas of Icelanders is of the kind known to scholars as "skaldic" or "scaldic," a word derived from the Norse word for poet, "skáld" (usually anglicized to "skald").[13] As we noted in chapter 1, such verse employs a variety of exceptionally complex meters and stanza patterns and is almost without exception preserved only within saga narratives: manuscript anthologies of skaldic verse, if any were ever produced, have not survived. About five-sixths of the surviving corpus of skaldic verse is composed in a meter known as *dróttkvætt*, or "court meter." Each *dróttkvætt* strophe has eight lines, each of six syllables (of which the last two of each line form a trochee). The eight lines divide into two half-strophes of four lines each (known as *helmingar*; singular *helmingr*). Within the stanza, lines are linked in pairs and each couplet is held together by alliteration: two syllables in each odd-numbered line alliterate with the first syllable in the following even-numbered line (all vowels are regarded as alliterating together). There is also internal rhyme within each line: the penultimate syllable of each line rhymes with an earlier syllable in the line, often the first. In the strictest form of *dróttkvætt*, this rhyme is full rhyme in even-numbered lines, involving a vowel and following consonant(s); in odd-numbered lines the rhyme is half-rhyme involving only the postvocalic consonant(s). To accommodate all these rules, the poet takes liberties with the normal word order. This is easier in a relatively highly inflected language like Old Norse than in modern English, but it makes translation challenging, and even editions aimed primarily at modern Icelanders offer help in understanding the verses by providing notes in which the words are rearranged in their prose word order. Skaldic verse also employs specifically poetic vocabulary not encountered in prose, including many synonyms (*heiti*) and a form of periphrastic metaphor called a kenning in which a thing is called by the name of something else, qualified in such a way as to make it poetically appropriate. So, for example, "bows' hail" is a kenning for "arrows." Skaldic kennings employ elements relating to the natural world (as in the example just given) and from pre-Christian mythology and heroic legend.

To illustrate these features of skaldic verse, here is a verse attributed to Gunnlaugr ormstunga (verse 13 in *Gunnlaugs saga*), in which he complains of the marriage of his beloved Helga to his rival Hrafn. Alliteration is here marked in bold, full rhyme by underlining, and half-rhyme by italics. The verse is followed by a rearrangement of the words of the poem into prose word order, and then by a translation into English:

Ormst*ung*u varð *eng*i
allr dagr und sal fj<u>all</u>a
hæ*gr*, síz **H**elga en *fagr*a
Hr<u>afn</u>s kvánar réð n<u>afn</u>i;
lítt sá h<u>ọ</u>lðr enn **h**v*í*ti
hjọr**þ**<u>ey</u>s, faðir m<u>ey</u>jar,
gefin vas *Eir* til *aur*a
<u>**u**ng</u>, við minni t<u>ung</u>u.

With the words rearranged in prose word order:

Ormstungu varð engi dagr allr hœgr und sal fjalla, síz Helga en fagra réð nafni Hrafns kvánar; enn hvíti hjọrþeys họldr, faðir meyjar, sá lítt við tungu minni; ung Eir vas gefin til aura.

A literal translation:

For Serpent-tongue no whole day was easy under the hall of the mountains since Helga the Fair had the name of Hrafn's wife. The white man of the sword-thaw, the girl's father, paid little attention to my tongue: Eir was married young for money.

The following phrases in this verse are kennings: "hall of the mountains" (meaning "sky") and "man of the sword-thaw" ("sword-thaw" = battle; "man of battle" = Þorsteinn [Helga's father]; he is "white" either because he is white-haired or because he is cowardly [or both]). "Eir" is the name of a goddess; as is usual in skaldic verse, any god's name can refer to any man and any goddess's to any woman, so Eir here is Helga. A paraphrase might thus run something like this: "I, Gunnlaugr, have been distressed ever since Helga the Fair married Hrafn; her father paid little attention to my words [Gunnlaugr had promised to return to Iceland to marry her]; she was married for money."

Guðrún Nordal has drawn attention to patterns in the amount of verse in a saga that lead to a division of sagas of Icelanders into six groups (2007: 222–23; 2013: 198–203). Sagas about court poets (the skalds' sagas), other sagas in which the main protagonist is a poet, and sagas in which verse is integral to the narrative even though "there is no principal poet" contain a lot of skaldic verse, whereas sagas with a strongly royal or courtly emphasis, sagas dated to the fourteenth century with a "learned" interest in the past, or sagas dealing with events in the Eastfjords and the northeast of Iceland include little or no such verse. Roughly half of the sagas of Icelanders are interlaced with verses. The other half have fewer than five stanzas per saga, with sixteen sagas containing no verse, though the number of verses in any given saga can vary between manuscripts (Guðrún Nordal 2007: 220).

Why are verses of this kind included in the sagas of Icelanders? The question becomes all the more pressing when it is realized that the verses in sagas "are not the primary carrier of the main body of the narrative: they are secondary to the prose, fulfilling either a corroborative or an ornamental role" (O'Donoghue 2005: 3). Indeed, skaldic verse itself is, generally, descriptive rather than narrative.

As court poetry, skaldic verse was initially associated with the praise or entertainment of princes, and in the ninth and tenth centuries its primary patrons were the kings of Norway. Verse in saga narrative appears first in kings' sagas that began to be written a little before the first sagas of Icelanders. In kings' sagas, the verses primarily (though not exclusively) function as source citations, comparable to modern scholarly footnotes. They are thus intended to guarantee the historical reliability of the narrative of the ruler commemorated in the verse. The combination of verse and prose employed in the kings' sagas became an expected convention of extended narrative in Icelandic and so was adopted by the writers of sagas of Icelanders.

It is helpful to distinguish between two different kinds of use of verse in Icelandic prosimetric narratives, to which scholars have given a variety of names.[14] I shall follow Diana Whaley and others in distinguishing between "authenticating verses," cited by the narrator as corroboration of the narrative, and "situational verses," spoken by a character within the narrative (Whaley 1993: 252). Joseph Harris prefers the terms "evidential" and "dramatic," while O'Donoghue refers to the two uses of verse as "documentation and dialogue" (Harris 1997: 142; O'Donoghue 2005: 77).

The basic distinction can be made clearer with examples. Authenticating verses are quoted in sagas to corroborate the content of the narrative; this implies that the verses are the writer's source for the immediately preceding material. Such verses are usually introduced by the phrases *svá kvað N* ("thus said N") or *svá segir N* ("so says N"). An example occurs in chapter 12 of *Gunnlaugs saga ormstungu* when an incident in the narrative is corroborated by a verse from a poem about Gunnlaugr by Þórðr Kolbeinsson. Situational verses are spoken by a character or characters within the saga-narrative: the stanza attributed to Gunnlaugr that was used to illustrate the *dróttkvætt* meter above is an example of such a verse. Situational verses are often introduced with phrases such as *þá kvað N þetta* ("then N said this . . .").

Medieval Icelanders regarded the complex metrical form of skaldic verse as securing its value as a dependable historical source. The prologue to the kings' saga collection, *Heimskringla*, states:

Með Haraldi konungi váru skáld, ok kunna menn enn kvæði þeira ok allra konunga kvæði, þeira er síðan hafa verit í Nóregi, ok tókum vér þar mest dœmi af, þat er sagt er í þeim kvæðum, er kveðin váru fyrir sjálfum hǫfðingjunum eða sonum þeira. Tǫkum vér þat allt fyrir satt, er í þeim kvæðum finnsk um ferðir þeira eða orrostur. En þat er háttr skálda at lofa þann mest, er þá eru fyrir, en engi myndi at þora at segja sjálfum honum þau verk hans, er allir þeir, er heyrði, vissi, at hégómi væri ok skrǫk, ok svá sjálfr hann. Þat væri þá háð, en eigi lof. (Bjarni Aðalbjarnarson 1941–1951, I: 5).

There were skalds with King Haraldr [hárfagri], and even now people know their poems and the poems about all the kings which there have been since then in Norway, and we follow most closely what is said in those poems which were recited in front of the chieftains themselves or their sons. We take all that for true which is found in those poems about their journeys or their battles. It is the custom of skalds to praise him most before whom they stand, but no one would dare to tell a man about deeds of his which all those who heard, and not least he himself, knew to be falsehood and invention. That would then be mockery and not praise. (my trans.)

The writer, usually taken to be Snorri Sturluson, then claims, "En kvæðin þykkja mér sízt ór stað fœrð, ef þau eru rétt kveðin ok skynsamliga upp tekin" (Bjarni Aðalbjarnarson 1941–1951, I: 7; "But those poems seem to me least corrupted which are correctly composed and can be plausibly interpreted"). In the longer version of this prologue attached to Snorri's *Separate Saga of St Óláfr*, there is an additional statement:

Þau orð, er í kveðskap standa, eru in sǫmu sem í fyrstu váru, ef rétt er kveðit, þótt hverr maðr hafi síðan numit at ǫðrum, ok má því ekki breyta. (Bjarni Aðalbjarnarson 1941–1951, II: 422)

The words in poetry are the same as were originally there if it is correctly recited, even though each man has later learned it [by heart] from others, and thus it cannot be changed.

Like many modern scholars, Snorri here expresses the belief that the extreme complexity of skaldic verse forms such as *dróttkvætt* ensures accurate transmission over long periods of time because any corruption to the text would spoil the meter and so be immediately apparent.

The authenticity of the skaldic verses in sagas has been one of the most debated topics in saga scholarship for many decades. In any given case a number of possibilities exist: a verse spoken by a character in a saga may authentically derive from the poet to whom it is attributed and may have been passed on orally more or less accurately across the intervening centuries; or a thirteenth-century saga writer may have composed a verse and put it into the mouth of one of his characters (just as he invented the characters' prose dialogue); or the saga-writer may use a verse that he had received and believed to be authentic but that does not go back to the speaker to whom it is attributed in the saga and was rather composed by a poet in the period between the date at which the events in the saga are presumed to have taken place and the writing of the text. It is often not possible for a modern scholar to be sure which of these scenarios is most likely in any given case, but the variety of possibilities makes it sensible to proceed on a case-by-case basis and assess each use of verse in a saga separately. Linguistic and metrical features of the verse can be used to date it (though often leaving room for disagreement), and discrepancies between the content of the verse and the prose narrative are likely to indicate that the verse was not composed by the prose-writer, though this need only mean that the verse existed before the prose, not that it dates back to the period in which the narrative is set.[15]

In some recent work on verse in the sagas, critical attention has shifted from determining the authenticity of verses to what Heather O'Donoghue calls "the aesthetic contribution of the poetry in saga narratives, that is, the role of verse in the poetics of saga composition" (O'Donoghue 2005: 4). The juxtaposition of verse and prose in sagas creates a profound stylistic contrast between the characteristically "plain" narrative prose style and the metrically intricate and lexically prodigious skaldic verse. Though several sagas, such as *Hrafnkels saga Freysgoða*, contain no verse, the stylistic contrast between verse and prose in the sagas is one of the most characteristic formal features of the genre as a whole.

Besides authentication, ornamentation, and stylistic contrast, verses in Icelandic sagas produce a number of other narrative effects. One of these is variation in narrative pace. As O'Donoghue puts it, "The virtue of simple contrast between two such different media leads to the possibility of verses being used to pace a narrative, to create tense climaxes or halt the inexorable flow of narrative cause and effect" (O'Donoghue 2005: 6). The change from prose to verse in sagas also sometimes enables a change of register appropriate for the heightened expression of emotions. (Romantic love is, for example, a prominent feature of the *skáldsögur*, sagas about Icelandic poets to which we will return in chapter 4.) Skaldic verses thus sometimes function like soliloquies that reveal emotions at psychologically significant moments. O'Donoghue writes, "The expression of personal and deeply felt emotion in a skaldic strophe may provide a dimension to the men and women in a saga narrative which the saga prose, typically functioning as externally focalized narrative, does not" (O'Donoghue 2005: 6).

The inclusion of skaldic verse in sagas thus creates richly polyphonic narratives in which different voices can be heard in dialogue with one another. Insofar as skaldic verse has been (or is believed to have been) transmitted from the Saga Age, its inclusion in a saga ensures, as Preben Meulengracht Sørensen argues (2001), that voices from the past (or those believed to be from the past) are heard again in the present.

(Possible) Irish Influence

Although there are no other medieval texts quite like the Icelandic sagas, it is striking that Iceland and Ireland, two island cultures of northwestern Europe connected by Norse trading and raiding in Ireland and Irish/Celtic settlement in Iceland, were both precocious in developing extended vernacular narrative forms in prose (both sometimes mixing prose with verse). Such texts in both languages are now known in English as sagas, an originally Icelandic term that has been applied to Irish texts by analogy. Since the nineteenth century, a number of scholars have argued that Irish storytelling traditions may have influenced those of Iceland, helping to account for the fact that Iceland developed a vernacular literary culture unlike anything produced in mainland Scandinavia. The development of this view in the late nineteenth century by Guðbrandur Vigfússon and Sophus Bugge led to its more systematic presentation by Alexander Bugge in the early twentieth century. It met, however, with considerable opposition, and it cannot be denied that (quite apart from a chronological gap of several centuries between the beginnings of Irish and Icelandic saga writing) the two kinds of saga differ profoundly in style and mode, despite the common modern nomenclature. Andreas Heusler, for instance, emphasizes that "the Icelandic saga is sober and realistic, the Irish fantastic" (see Andersson 1964: 59). By "Icelandic saga," he is referring here primarily to the kings' sagas and sagas of Icelanders; the legendary *fornaldarsögur* are closer in spirit to Irish sagas. Still, comparison of Icelandic and Irish sagas may, in the end, lead modern readers to appreciate more clearly how unique the sagas of Icelanders are in a medieval European context.

There is, however, another area of possible influence. Both Irish and skaldic verse rely on syllable-counting and indulge in extremely complex metrical forms (unlike anything found in early Germanic literatures other than Icelandic). This similarity led Gabriel Turville-Petre, among others, to canvas the possibility of Irish influence on skaldic poetics (Turville-Petre 1972; see also Tranter 1997).

In his overview of research on Irish influence on Icelandic literature, Gísli Sigurðsson argues that Irish influence can more clearly be seen in some of the *fornaldarsögur* and Norse mythological texts than in the sagas of Icelanders, but he suggests that "sagas [of Icelanders] which came from the west of Iceland (e.g., *Laxdœla saga* and *Kjalnesinga saga*) where Gaels or people from the Gaelic world were among the named settlers, show more signs of Gaelic influence than others" (2000: 86–87). The case for Irish influence on Icelandic storytelling traditions remains open to question after more than a hundred years of debate on the issue, an indicator of the difficulties involved in reconstructing lost oral traditions behind the surviving written texts.

Models for Shaping the Past: Hagiography and Romance

Oral tradition, including skaldic verse, provided some of the content of sagas of Icelanders. Literary traditions provide a different kind of "source": formal models that shaped how sagas were written, providing examples of sustained literary narrative from which saga-writers could learn how to deploy and organize their material.

Whatever oral tales may have existed before the conversion of Iceland, Icelanders began to write down their narratives of the past only after they became Christians. A form of writing, runes, was used by pre-Christian Scandinavians but not (as far as surviving inscriptions reveal) for the recording of extended narrative texts. Runic inscriptions, of which there are many in mainland Scandinavia but few in Iceland, typically recorded ownership of an artefact or memorialized an individual on a gravestone. Only one complete skaldic stanza is preserved on a runic monument, on a rune stone from circa 1000 at Karlevi on the Swedish island of Öland (other brief praise poems in a simpler meter more like that of eddaic poetry occur on Swedish rune stones circa 970–1100). The runic script was designed for carving; the technology of manuscript production was brought to Scandinavia and Iceland with Christianity. The peoples of northern Europe did not write books until they became Christians.

Sometime in the mid-twelfth century, and thus shortly before the first of the sagas of Icelanders were written, the anonymous writer of an account of the Icelandic language of the period, known to modern scholars as the *First Grammatical Treatise*, listed the kinds of text then available in Icelandic, singling out genealogies, laws, and interpretations of sacred writings.[16] As the writer of this treatise indicates, Christian religious texts are among the earliest surviving texts from medieval Iceland. A collection of Icelandic sermons or homilies, now known as the Stockholm Homily Book because it is preserved in the Royal Library at Stockholm, dates from circa 1200 and is therefore one of the oldest surviving Icelandic manuscripts. Many of the more than fifty homilies it contains are older in origin than the surviving copy. A large number of lives and acts of the apostles were translated from Latin into Icelandic and survive in manuscripts from circa 1220 onward. Likewise, a life of the Virgin Mary, *Maríu saga*, has traditionally been ascribed to Kygri-Bjǫrn Hjaltason and would therefore date from before his death in 1237/8.

Given that saga-writing became possible only with the introduction of the techniques of book production brought to Iceland with Christianity, and given the centrality of books (including the Scriptures and the liturgy) to the Christian religion, it should not be surprising that several scholars argue that the learned literature of Christianity provided models for Icelanders who sought to create sustained written narratives. The most prolific and widespread of narrative genres throughout medieval Europe was hagiography, written lives of saints. The sagas of Icelanders are certainly in many ways very unlike saints' lives, but a prominent strand of saga scholarship argues that saints' lives provided Icelanders with a model for how to construct a narrative. In Gabriel Turville-Petre's frequently quoted words, "The learned literature did not teach the Icelanders what to think or what to say, but it taught them how to say it. It is unlikely that the sagas of kings and of Icelanders, or even the sagas of ancient heroes, would have developed as they did unless several generations of Icelanders had first been trained in hagiographic narrative" (Turville-Petre 1953: 142). Turville-Petre's claim has been broadly supported, though also modified, in subsequent work by scholars such as Peter Foote (1994), Birte Carlé (1985), and the present author (2007, esp. ch. 6).[17]

Hagiography influenced not only the origins or the merely formal characteristics of saga-writing. It also continued to exert some influence on the content of the genre in its later history (as we shall see in some of the discussions of individual sagas in chapter 4; see also Grønlie 2017). One of the most striking examples of hagiographic influence on saga content occurs in the probably early-fourteenth-century *Flóamanna saga*. Chapter 20 of the saga tells how Þorgils was one of the first converts when Christianity came to Iceland. He dreams that the pagan god Thor threatens to punish him for betrayal, but Þorgils expresses confidence in the Christian God's assistance. Thor kills some of Þorgils's animals and fights him one night. Shortly afterward, Þorgils decides to move to Greenland to join Eiríkr rauði there. Thor appears to him again in a dream and threatens to wreck his ship. Þorgils forbids his crew to pray to Thor, and in another dream Þorgils maintains that "Þótt ek taka aldri höfn [. . .] þá skal ek þér ekki gott gera" (ch. 21; "Even if I never reach harbor [. . .] I will never worship you"). The ship is wrecked, but they make it ashore in the ship's boat. That winter, sickness kills many of the company; they return as ghosts to haunt Þorgils until he is able to burn their bodies. After a short trip away, Þorgils returns to find his wife dead and their baby boy suckling the dead body. Þorgils fears that the boy will die but then cuts his own nipples: "Fór fyrst út blóð, síðan blanda, ok lét eigi fyrr af en ór fór mjólk, ok þar fæddist sveinninn upp við þat" (ch. 23; "First blood came out, and then a mixed fluid, but he did not stop until milk came out, and he nursed the boy with it"). This miraculous male lactation is a hagiographic motif that fits the saga's broader theme of struggle between paganism and Christianity, imagined as a contest between Thor and the Christian God.[18]

If hagiography was the most widespread and prestigious genre of religious narrative, its secular equivalent in medieval Europe was romance. The two genres have much in common: both prominently feature the supernatural and center on heroes who exemplify (either religious or secular) ideals. Continental romance became influential in Norse literary culture from the 1220s, when King Hákon Hákonarson of Norway commissioned the translation of French courtly romances into Old Norse, including Thomas of Britain's *Tristram* (translated as *Tristrams saga Ísǫndar*) and a collection of lais (short narrative poems) by Marie de France and other anonymous writers rendered into Old Norse prose in *Strengleikar*.

Translations of French romances became known in Iceland and were copied and imitated there: both translations and original Icelandic romances are known as *riddarasögur,* "sagas of knights." Besides Icelandic romances as such, the influence of the romance genre can also be seen in several of the sagas of Icelanders, as we shall see in the discussions of individual sagas in chapter 4.

Saga Style

European literary models, such as hagiography and the apocryphal acts of apostles, combined with oral storytelling traditions in the development of the characteristic stylistic features we find in sagas of Icelanders, the so-called saga style. By definition, the sagas of Icelanders belong to a (partly) literate culture, but unless one realizes that the transition from orality to literacy is a gradual one—and that residual orality persists long after the introduction of writing—one will fail to appreciate many features of the sagas. Whatever the extent of the contribution of oral traditions to the content of sagas of Icelanders, the sagas are the products of a period of transition from oral to written culture, as is encapsulated in the very name for the written prose genre, "saga," derived as it is from the verb *segja,* "to say, speak, tell." Just as the earliest printed books in the fifteenth century deliberately resembled manuscripts, so early written texts resembled the oral narratives with which audiences were already familiar and that provided them with models of what they expected a narrative to be like.

Ong notes that in an oral culture thought and expression tend to be "Additive rather than subordinative" (1982: 37) and both the paratactic sentence construction so characteristic of saga prose and the concatenation of episodes to produce lengthy narratives may be seen as literate echoes of this tendency of oral storytelling. But apart from stylistic features, certain larger characteristics of the sagas may also reflect this relation to oral narratives. Another feature of oral culture is that it is "Agonistically toned [. . .] Orality situates knowledge within a context of struggle" (Ong 1982: 43). This in part accounts for the fact that "enthusiastic description of physical violence often marks oral narrative" (Ong 1982: 43), as it still does in the written saga narratives indebted to oral storytelling traditions. Memorable examples include Gunnlaugr chopping off Hrafn's leg in a duel in *Gunn-*

laugs saga, chapter 12: "Hrafn fell þó eigi at heldr ok hnekkði þá at stofni einum ok studdi þar á stúfinum" ("Yet Hrafn did not collapse completely, but dragged back to a tree stump and rested the stump of his leg on it"); or a drunken Egill Skallagrímsson in *Egils saga* (chs. 72, 73), who vomits over the Norwegian farmer Ármóðr and then "krœkði hann fingurinum í augat, svá at úti lá á kinninni" ("gouged out one of his eyes with his finger, leaving it hanging on his cheek").

Although there is variety both within and between sagas of Icelanders, their stylistic homogeneity justifies use of the term "saga style" to refer to a common set of features found across the genre (and in the kings' sagas). The style represents a fusion of oral storytelling traditions with conventions of written prose composition. Key features of saga style include:

- a relatively restricted vocabulary, at least as far as the narrative prose is concerned; the skaldic verses incorporated in many sagas are lexically richer;
- brief syntactical units, often linked to each other by parataxis and relatively rarely by subordination;
- vacillation between past and present tenses, often for no obvious reason, though sometimes the present tense gives greater immediacy to the narrative, and some verbs more often appear in one tense or the other;
- changes from indirect to direct speech (and vice versa) within a single speech;
- apparently objective narrative, with few obvious value judgments on characters or events by the narrator.

Stylistically, the sagas of Icelanders are therefore typically concise, lexically and syntactically straightforward, and sparing with rhetorical devices. The narrative is externally focalized, with characters' inner thoughts and feelings almost never revealed, and the narratorial voice is restrained, with judgments on characters and events typically given in terms of "what people say" rather than as the view of the narrator. Dialogue is important and often constitutes a high percentage of the text, averaging at 30 percent across the corpus as a whole (Vésteinn Ólason 1998: 113), but it is usually pithy, even lapidary: characters usually say no more than they need to. Understatement also characterizes saga narrators and their characters: much of the humor in the sagas finds expression in such understatement.[19]

In this section, we have seen how saga writers draw on oral traditions (including skaldic verse) and on literary models: both the sagas and the characteristic style in which they are written are products of the coming together of these oral and literate traditions. In the final part of this chapter, we will reflect on some aspects of the transmission of saga texts *after* they were written.

III: Textual Traditions

The composition of a saga can be seen as the end point at which a number of contributory elements converge: oral traditions including skaldic verse, memorable anecdotes, folk etymologies, and genealogies, as well as literary models such as hagiography, chronicle, and romance. It is, however, equally true that the first writing down of a saga marks the beginning of a new process of textual transmission and development. In recent decades, medievalists in general, including many scholars of Old Norse–Icelandic literature, have become newly sensitive to the material forms in which texts from the period were preserved. In this final section of the chapter, we will consider some salient aspects of the preservation of saga texts: their anonymity, the existence of variant versions, the contexts of manuscript preservation, the difficulties of dating texts, and the interpretative decisions that inform modern published editions.

About 750 manuscripts survive from medieval Iceland, dating from the mid-twelfth century to the mid-sixteenth century.[20] Few of these are undamaged and most of the earliest are mere fragments; the earliest such fragment from a saga of Icelanders is from *Egils saga Skallagrímssonar* and dates from about 1250. Medieval manuscripts have had to survive many hazards to endure until the present, and we know of many texts that no longer survive. The Icelandic climate is not particularly conducive to the preservation of manuscripts, and the conditions in which texts were kept in farmhouses were far from ideal. The sagas were also victims of their own popularity: many medieval manuscripts must simply have been destroyed by use. Some sagas are known to have been lost without trace except for a reference in another text.

With the rise of Scandinavian antiquarian interest in Iceland's literature in the seventeenth and eighteenth centuries, many Icelandic manuscripts were saved by being exported to major libraries in Denmark and Sweden. However, they were not always safe even there, and some important manuscripts collected by Árni Magnússon were destroyed when fire ravaged his library in Copenhagen in 1728. Such losses are in part offset by the survival of thousands of postmedieval manuscripts of sagas, written on paper from the sixteenth century onward. A more or less continuous tradition of copying sagas by hand in Iceland, even after the introduction of printing, means that many texts are preserved more extensively in postmedieval copies than in medieval manuscripts.[21]

Just over a hundred Icelandic manuscripts survive from before about 1300; roughly three times that many survive from the fourteenth century, including the earliest complete manuscripts of most sagas of Icelanders (some survive only in even later manuscripts). Where datable earlier fragments are extant, they provide a *terminus ante quem* for dating the composition of the text and offer valuable evidence for editing the saga, but we are largely reliant on copies of the sagas that date from a century or more after the likely composition of the texts. The number of surviving medieval manuscripts for each saga varies: while some sagas survive in only a single copy, there are twenty-one medieval manuscripts of *Njáls saga*, the most of any saga of Icelanders. There are thirteen of *Egils saga*, though most of these are fragmentary, and seven of at least part of *Laxdœla saga*. It is striking that the sagas that survive in the most medieval copies are among those most highly regarded by modern readers. Insofar as the number of surviving copies can be taken as indicative of popularity in the medieval period, this intriguingly suggests that medieval and modern value judgments here coincide. In a few cases, parts of a saga are preserved and incorporated into manuscripts of other texts. For example, some chapters of *Laxdœla saga* are interpolated at appropriate points in later versions of the sagas of Kings Óláfr Tryggvason and St Óláfr Haraldsson of Norway.

In a manuscript culture, copying of texts by hand means that no two copies of a text are ever exactly identical in content and layout: as Matthew Driscoll notes, "instability (Variance) is a fundamental feature of chirographically transmitted literature" (2010: 90). This means that surviving copies—and therefore modern printed or electronic editions based on them—are inevitably at some remove from the (lost) earliest written form of a text. Such a state of affairs is typical for the earliest literature in many languages but differs radically from the situation familiar from more recent periods in which authors have overseen the publication of their writings in print, producing multiple identical copies.

A few specific examples may make the situation clearer. *Heiðarvíga saga* is often regarded as one of the earliest sagas of Icelanders to have been written down, perhaps circa 1200. The text we read today is, however, something of a Frankenstein's monster: the second part of the saga survives in a manuscript from ca. 1300 now in Stockholm, but the first third of that text of the saga was destroyed by fire in Copenhagen in 1728, where it had been on loan. For the first part of the saga, we are therefore reliant now on the reconstruction of the missing text by an Icelander, Jón Ólafsson, who read the text before the fire and rewrote it from memory after its destruction.

The process of manuscript copying has led to several sagas being preserved in two or more substantially different versions. One of the most striking examples of this is *Fóstbrœðra saga*. Versions preserved in both Flateyjarbók and Möðruvallabók contain numerous digressions in uncharacteristically flamboyant style that are missing from the text of the saga preserved in Hauksbók. Tellingly, scholarly opinion as to whether the digressions are later interpolations or were present in the first written version and later removed has fluctuated back and forth.[22]

The editing of premodern texts has traditionally sought to arrive at the "best" possible text by comparing and collating all (or as many as possible) of the surviving witnesses and working out (on the basis, for example, of shared errors) the likely relationships between the surviving texts. This enables the editor to construct a "family tree" of the manuscripts, known as a "stemma," and so identify the surviving copies closest to the original. He or she is then able to produce an edition that gives weight to variant readings in proportion to their place in the history of textual transmission. Recent decades have seen growing dissatisfaction with this approach, though the impact of such dissatisfaction has not yet been seen as clearly in Old Norse–Icelandic studies as in some other areas of medieval textual scholarship.[23]

The traditional approach to editing is liable to produce a printed text that differs from all the surviving manuscripts. The editor may attempt to produce a text that might reasonably be posited to lie behind all the surviving texts, though it may still be some distance, textually, from the first written version of the saga, in which case it may differ considerably from all the surviving manuscript versions. But even if the editor decides to follow only the version that analysis has revealed is closest to the text that preceded all surviving versions, he or she will still draw on readings from other manuscripts to correct the base text where it does not make sense or can be shown otherwise to be inaccurate.

There are reasons to feel uncomfortable with two aspects of this traditional approach. One may question the value of producing a text that not only demonstrably differs (perhaps only in small details) from all surviving copies but also may not be identical to any copy that ever did exist and in any case may still represent a text several removes from the first written form of a saga. In addition, there is increasing recognition that the attempt to produce a "best" text radically misrepresents the very nature of medieval manuscript culture. *Hallfreðar saga vandræðaskálds*, for example, survives in an abbreviated version in Möðruvallabók, in a fuller text that is split up and woven into a saga of Óláfr Tryggvason, and in a version in the Flateyjarbók manuscript that conflates the two other redactions, leading Russell Poole to write that "when we say 'Hallfreðar saga' this name is in reality a loose designation for a motley array of differing redactions, the general heterogeneity of which is veiled in the various translations and even to some degree in standard editions such as Íslenzk fornrit" (Poole 2001: 127). Scholars have come to recognize that textual variation is of the very essence of medieval literary culture: that because texts existed in variant forms, it might be more appropriate to think of a saga as the sum total of all this variance rather than to try to reduce the variation to a single "best" text. In the influential formulation of Bernard Cerquiglini, "medieval writing does not produce variants; it *is* variance" (1993: 77–78). Such a recognition takes more seriously the experience of the medieval reader, who encountered a saga in a particular variant form in a particular manuscript and engaged with the text in that form. As yet, most of the published editions of sagas with which scholars and critics work do not reflect adequately the complexity and variance of the manuscript tradition, though with the increasing use of computers to produce digital editions, we may expect that future editing projects will do this. As Judy Quinn puts it, "we are still on the cusp between traditional editorial practices and 'e-philology,' without a clear protocol for editing such complex vernacular textual traditions as that of Old Norse, though with exciting possibilities provided by ever more sophisticated technological developments" (2010: 24).

Quinn goes so far as to assert that modern readers of the sagas "are, for the most part, reading editorial creations, creations which over the decades of the twentieth century rooted themselves into critical scholarship and medieval literary history" (Quinn 2010: 19). Very few readers today are in a position to do anything other than rely on the editions that are available. Nevertheless, though one may not at present be able to do much about it, it is worth being aware of the extent to which editors are responsible for the texts of the sagas of Icelanders that we read. In a sense, the continual process of textual change characteristic of medieval literary culture is ongoing and includes modern editors alongside medieval scribes.

A number of related points emerge from the state of preservation of the sagas of Icelanders to which it is worth drawing attention. For the reader more accustomed to modern textual culture, it is striking that the sagas of Icelanders are anonymous. There was a period in saga scholarship when the hunting down of possible authors for individual texts among the known named Icelanders of the thirteenth century was a popular sport, but with only one or two exceptions—above all, the ascription of *Egils saga* to Snorri Sturluson—the various arguments have won little acceptance. Indeed, the anonymity of the texts usefully reminds us that although a specific individual will have been responsible for the first written form of a saga (though in at least some cases, they may have dictated the text to a scribe rather than actually written it down themselves), that moment of textual production is merely one point on a continuum. A variety of source materials feeds into the saga, and as soon as another copy is made the process of textual variation begins. The anonymity of the sagas may indeed have facilitated textual change, as scribes may have been less constrained than if they had been copying texts attributed to named individuals. There is a sense in which the sagas can be thought of as communal products at least as much as the works of individual authors.

These features of saga textuality lead us to a final key issue arising from the mode of preservation of the saga texts: dating. Paleographers and codicologists are able to date most saga manuscripts quite accurately. But, as we have seen, many sagas survive complete only in copies of considerably later date than the earliest surviving fragments, and all the sagas are preserved in manuscripts of a later date than the period when scholars think that they were first composed. How, then, do we date a saga? And, even more fundamentally, what do we mean by the date of a saga? It might seem obvious that the date of a saga is the date it was first written down, but if all the surviving manuscripts of a text descend from a copy made considerably later than the first written version, to what extent is it helpful to date the saga earlier than the earliest version that can now be reconstructed? Given that no two manuscript texts will be identical and that the later copying of a text provides evidence of its continuing interest and resonance for a later period, perhaps it is more meaningful to talk about the dates of (surviving) versions, rather than of some "original" now accessible to us only through those later versions. And given the reliance of saga writers on a variety of earlier oral and written traditions, one might argue that the first writing down of a saga is in some important respects not the origin of the text. Thus, the question of dating, like serious attention to the variance inherent in manuscript preservation and dissemination, calls into question the nature of the text, its stability, and its supposed moment of origin.

Although the meaning and usefulness of dating sagas is thus open to question, scholars have understandably tried to find ways of dating the original composition of sagas of Icelanders. Such datings are essential for constructing a literary history of Iceland and have important implications for the questions relating to historical reliability that we examined earlier in this chapter.

Whereas there was a tendency in the latter part of the twentieth century to argue for a slightly later start for the beginnings of the sagas of Icelanders genre (from the 1230s or 1240s), recent work (such as Andersson 2006 and the contributors to Mundal 2013, especially Mundal and Andersson) has reverted to a date of circa 1200 for the start of the genre. Comparison of the dates of composition proposed by the editors of the Íslenzk fornrit editions of sagas of Icelanders (only one volume of which was published later than the period 1933–1959) with those suggested in the translation of the *Complete Sagas of Icelanders* (1997) shows a clear shift in the second half of the twentieth century toward later dates for most sagas (see the table in Reference Material below pp. 170–74).

A brief but influential account of the issues and evaluation of the different kinds of evidence is in Einar Ólafur Sveinsson's *Dating the Icelandic Sagas*, published in 1958 and described by its translator, Gabriel Turville-Petre, as "pioneering work" that provided the first general account of the issue "since modern methods have been applied" (Einar Ólafur Sveinsson 1958: vii). Einar Ólafur emphasized the importance of the surviving manuscript evidence and assessed the value of references to saga-writing or specific sagas in other texts, anachronisms and references to events or people after the period in which the saga is set, intertextual relations with other texts, linguistic evidence, and more subjective criteria such as artistic competence and a perceived decline in realism and literary quality late in the genre's history. Despite the varied evidence available, dating the sagas remains, in his words, an "exceedingly treacherous" enterprise (Einar Ólafur Sveinsson 1958: 1).

Recently, an edited collection of essays with a title (*Dating the Sagas: Reviews and Revisions*) that deliberately evokes Einar Ólafur Sveinsson's work has revisited the principles and methods used to date sagas in the light of scholarly and critical work produced in the last half century. One common theme that emerges from both Einar Ólafur Sveinsson's monograph and Else Mundal's collection is that the evidence for dating each individual saga has to be considered separately. Where appropriate, reference will be made to debates about saga datings in the chapters that follow: there remains scholarly disagreement about particular datings and, given the nature and state of the evidence, there may always be. Uncertainties about the dates of individual sagas have, however, two consequences worth signaling here. They make interpreting any text in the context of historical events contemporaneous with its composition problematic, and they make a literary history of the genre, an account of its historical development as a genre, a difficult task. Indeed, in the past there have been viciously circular arguments whereby sagas have been dated, in part, in accordance with a view of the development of the genre (e.g., that poorly structured primitive texts preceded artistically sophisticated narratives, or that realism gave way to a regrettable preference for romance) and the resulting dates for sagas have then been taken as demonstrating that the genre developed in that way.

A recent attempt at a literary history of the first hundred years of saga writing (Andersson 2006) does not entirely avoid linking dates to notions of the "development" of saga-writing and to value judgments associated with that development: *Heiðarvíga saga*, for example, is said to demonstrate "a real narrative advance" on its predecessors *such* that it "ranks high among the early sagas" (2006: 73). Nevertheless, Andersson tries to focus on sagas (both kings' sagas and sagas of Icelanders) with relatively secure datings, though he is forced to admit that even several of these datings are disputed. Andersson charts the growth of saga writing from early sagas about Kings Óláfr Tryggvason and St Óláfr of Norway, through early sagas of Icelanders in which the actions of protagonists are expressions of their personalities, to *Egils saga*, *Laxdœla saga*, and shorter sagas with a strong thematic emphasis, culminating in *Njáls saga*. Grounded in some beautiful close reading of texts, it is probably as convincing a narrative of development as uncertainty about saga dating allows.

In the remaining chapters of this book, I will not seek to provide such a history of the development of the genre but will instead pursue a more thematic approach to the corpus in the next chapter and will then turn to examine selected individual texts in chapter 4. In both chapters, as throughout this book, I offer a fresh perspective by focusing on how sources of the kind we have examined in this chapter were molded into narratives that not only entertained but also expressed, and enabled writers to explore, beliefs about identity.

3

ICELANDIC IDENTITIES

In writing about their past—especially the period in which their island was settled, its legal and social institutions were established, and it chose to become part of Christendom—medieval Icelanders were exploring their identities, answering the questions "Who are we?" and "Where did we come from?" The sagas thus performed what is sometimes called "ideological work": they gave expression to the common memories and ideals of a community, and they strengthened bonds within that community through the shared activity of reading the stories or hearing them read.

In reading the sagas of Icelanders as narrative explorations of identity, this book maintains not only that they are wonderfully entertaining and involving stories but also that (like all stories, in fact) they give expression to shared beliefs, assumptions, and ideals—in a word, ideologies. Stories do not simply reflect contemporary ideology; they also help to construct and confirm it by presenting as "natural" and inescapable what could in fact be different. Because they are commonly associated with unequal power relations (between, for example, men and women, heterosexual people and sexual minorities, or humans and other animals), ideologies attempt to make other possible ways of looking at the world "unthinkable." Even when not written specifically to promote particular ideologies, texts inevitably bear witness to shared assumptions of their time and place of writing. In recent decades, critical and cultural theory have given us a heightened awareness that the textual construction of beliefs and aspirations as "natural" or inescapable—obscuring their contingent and historically located nature—involves a sort of sleight of hand. Careful reading of texts can reveal the contingency of, and contradictions inherent in, the ideological positions they subscribe to. This in turn opens up the possibility of resisting dominant ideologies; readers can use texts to explore potential alternative ways of understanding identities.

In the next chapter, we will look in detail at some of the most widely read and studied sagas, but, before doing so, we will here look at the ways in which sagas of Icelanders engage with and explore three broad aspects of identity: nationality, gender and sexuality, and the distinction between human and nonhuman. Sagas are not about only these three topics, and these subjects are not necessarily the most important issues addressed in all sagas of Icelanders. They do, however, resonate with some of the most prominent concerns of contemporary literary studies. Bringing the sagas into dialogue with approaches more familiar from the study of other periods and other literatures will shed new light on the sagas and on thinking about identity today.

Law and Nation

The sagas of Icelanders both reflect and contribute to constructing a shared Icelandic identity. The sense Icelanders had of themselves as distinct and distinctive was nourished by their unique legal and sociopolitical institutions. As Hermann Pálsson writes, "With the absence of a monarch, the national law played a much more significant role in early Icelandic society than in Norway and neighbouring countries" (1999: 91).[1] In the late eleventh century, Adam of Bremen elegantly made a similar point: "Apud illos non est rex; nisi tantum lex" (IV.36 scholia; Adam of Bremen 2000: 486; "Among them [the Icelanders] there is no king, except the law" [my trans.]). The anthropologist Kirsten Hastrup argues that *vár lǫg* ("our law"), as centered on the national assembly of the Althing, "defined the community of the Icelanders vis-á-vis the outside world: the society was primarily a legal unit" (Hastrup 1990: 34). The crucial role of the law is memorably encapsulated in one of the most famous speeches in all the sagas of Icelanders, when Njáll Þorgeirsson remarks that "með lǫgum skal land várt byggja, en með ólǫgum eyða" ("with law our land shall rise, but it will perish with lawlessness"; *Njáls saga*, ch. 70).

It is today commonly claimed that nations, and so national identity, are a modern phenomenon, inapplicable to the Middle Ages. It can also plausibly be maintained that, given its lack of an executive, medieval Iceland was even less like a modern nation-state than most other European countries at the time. Benedict Anderson among others has influentially maintained (1983/2016) that both nationalism—a belief that each nation should have its own state—and the full apparatus of the modern nation-state developed only from the eighteenth century onward. It nevertheless seems justifiable to refer to medieval Iceland as a "nation," without claiming that it was fully a nation-state in the modern sense.[2] The historian David Cannadine maintains that "national identity relies on a shared narrated memory and sense of geographical belonging, reinforced by a common language and culture and state power" (2013: 4); of these elements, only the last, state power, is lacking in medieval Iceland. As an island with a single legal code, a common language, and a shared religion (changed in 999/1000 by common consent), Iceland was geographically and legally distinct, in possession of a unifying culture, and aware that this was the case.[3] There were certainly strong regional identities, as we perhaps see manifested in the desire for a separate diocese in the north of the island, and most sagas of Icelanders confine themselves mainly to events in a relatively small part of the island. Nevertheless, the very fact that sagas survive that are set in each of the four quarters into which the island was divided is evidence of a shared literary culture across the whole island. Saga-writing was a "national institution" insofar as it was practiced across the island (and, with the exception of a few kings' sagas and *riddarasögur* produced in Norway, not practiced outside Iceland).

It is true that, unlike when the island converted to Christianity, when Iceland submitted to the Norwegian monarchy it did so not as a whole but quarter by quarter over a two-year period. Nevertheless, Iceland had in the Althing a national institution that brought people together from across the island each year to make decisions applicable to the whole island. As Hastrup points out, a national assembly superior to local things had no parallel in Norway, where there was no legal assembly above the local things (Hastrup 1990: 72). We saw in the previous chapter the important role that the Althing played in the sharing of stories that contributed to a shared memory of the past and so to a common identity.

Like nationalism and the concept of the modern nation-state, race and racism are, in the precise forms with which we are sadly familiar today, modern rather than medieval concepts. Beliefs and prejudices of a similar kind—what Richard Cole (2015) calls "proto-racial" thinking—are, however, evident in medieval literature, including in Icelandic sagas.[4] Some of the Celtic speakers brought to Iceland in the settlement period were slaves, and this leaves some bias in the sagas against dark complexions and black hair, which surviving texts suggest Icelanders associated with Celtic populations (Jochens 1999a). We saw in the previous chapter that the Þórðarbók redaction of *Landnámabók* betrays some anxiety or embarrassment about the place of slaves in Iceland's early history and the claims made by foreigners regarding their contribution to the Icelandic population.

The transition from oral to written storytelling created new perspectives on national identity, as Gísli Sigurðsson suggests: "The writing of *Íslendingabók* and *Landnámabók* doubtless promoted a kind of community of spirit among the inhabitants and opened up previously unknown ways of uniting the people and their origins in a single place—recorded for perpetuity in a book" (2004: 56). *Landnámabók* and several sagas of Icelanders agree in maintaining that early settlers of Iceland fled Norway because they wished to escape the tyranny of King Haraldr hárfagri (see especially *Vatnsdœla saga, Eyrbyggja saga, Egils saga, Laxdœla saga, Grettis saga, Gísla saga*). Bruce Lincoln (2014) has recently argued that texts treat the story of Haraldr hárfagri rather differently depending on whether they were intended for Norwegian, Icelandic, or mixed readerships. Texts aimed at a Norwegian audience, such as the kings' saga *Fagrskinna*, offer a formation myth for the Norwegian state, whereas in Icelandic texts the heroes of the foundation story are those who emigrated and thereby "created a polity where law, rather than king, kingship, nation, or state, was the central institution" (Lincoln 2014: 103). The most critical accounts of Haraldr are Icelandic texts, including sagas of Icelanders.

It is clear, however, that Icelanders felt ambivalent about their relationship to Norway. The sense of a separate Icelandic identity conflicted with an awareness of strong links with mainland Scandinavia. Alongside saga narratives of separation, with settlers fleeing Haraldr hárfagri's tyranny, we find an acknowledgment in Ari's *Íslendingabók* (ch. 2) that Úlfljótr was sent to Norway to obtain laws for the newly settled island. We read, too, of Icelanders working at the Norwegian royal court as court poets. St Óláfr's grant of special privileges to Icelanders in Norway in a treaty of circa 1025 (preserved in *Grágás* in the form confirmed in 1085) also indicates that they were not considered as foreign as other nationals, and while this may say more about Norwegian designs on the island than about Icelandic identity, Icelanders were content to take advantage of the privileges they acquired. And Iceland eventually did submit to Norwegian rule. Even as the saga narratives express a sense of separateness, they also bear witness to common ties that might justify the events of 1262–1264.

Medieval Icelanders were also aware of other international links that are reflected in the sagas of Icelanders. Large parts of many of the sagas are set abroad, with Icelandic characters trading, raiding, or otherwise engaged in Scandinavia, Britain, and Ireland especially, but also more widely from North America to Byzantium (as in, for example, *Egils saga*, *Njáls saga*, and the Vínland and poets' sagas). A sense of belonging to Iceland would not have precluded Icelanders from also claiming other kinds of identity, some of which may have seemed more important to them: as Linda Colley has neatly expressed it in a related context, "Identities are not like hats. Human beings can and do put on several at a time" (Colley 1992: 6). In particular, after their conversion, Icelanders were aware of belonging to Christendom, a supranational allegiance embodied in Iceland's being part of the archdiocese of Hamburg-Bremen, then of Lund from 1104, and eventually of Trondheim from 1152/3.

Lacking the institutions that other European polities relied on (such as a monarchy and royal court), Icelandic identity became invested in the island's unique legal system. Law-making assemblies and courts were places where people from across the island met, they fostered community, and they gave expression to the shared values of the island's inhabitants through the laws that they enacted and the sentences that they pronounced. The sagas of Icelanders reflect the centrality of the law to Icelandic identity: the law features in some way in almost every text but is especially prominent in *Bandamanna saga*, *Eyrbyggja saga*, *Hœnsa-Þóris saga*, *Ljósvetninga saga*, *Valla-Ljóts saga*, *Víga-Glúms saga*, and *Njáls saga*.

During the period in which the sagas of Icelanders are set, the law was preserved orally and it was the duty of the island's lawspeaker (*lǫgsǫgumaðr*) to recite one-third of the law from memory each year at the Althing. The laws were, however, among the first Icelandic texts to be written down, and the saga-writers themselves were familiar with written law codes, sometimes anachronistically conceiving historical disputes in terms of later written laws with which they were familiar (and thus providing evidence for the dating of some sagas). It is likely that the tithe laws were written down from their institution in 1096–1097. Ari Þorgilsson gives an account of how, following a decision of the Althing, the laws as a whole were first written down during the winter of 1117–1118 at Breiðabólstaðr in Vesturhóp in northern Iceland (*Íslendingabók*, ch. 10). This earliest text of the laws, known after Hafliði Másson as *Hafliðaskrá*, does not survive, but much of its content was probably incorporated into the surviving Commonwealth-period legal text known as *Grágás*.

The earliest surviving manuscript fragments of *Grágás* (literally "Gray Goose," a name of uncertain relevance) date from circa 1200, but two nearly complete manuscripts, with considerable differences between them, date from the mid- to late thirteenth century: *Konungsbók* (GKS 1157 fol.) and the slightly later *Staðarhólsbók* (AM 334 fol.). These fine manuscripts both "contain illuminations of great artistic merit" (Jónas Kristjánsson 1993: 56), and this is indicative of the value that Icelanders set upon their laws. By contrast, manuscripts of sagas of Icelanders rarely contain illustrations (the damaged mid-fourteenth-century Kálfalækjarbók being a notable exception).

After the Icelanders' submission to the Norwegian crown, they were given a law-code known as *Járnsíða* in 1271. This code was much disliked for its failure to take account of existing Icelandic law and was soon replaced in 1281 by the code known as *Jónsbók*, after the Icelandic lawyer Jón Einarsson who brought it from Norway. *Jónsbók*, much of which derived directly from *Grágás*, formed the basis of Icelandic law for the next several centuries and survives in more than 260 manuscripts, more than any other early Icelandic text; these copies are also often beautifully illustrated.

Not only the laws but also the institutions that promulgated and pronounced on them were central to early Icelandic society, to the Icelanders' sense of their identity, and to the development of their literature. Scholars have traditionally reconstructed the early Icelandic constitution and its institutions primarily from the law in *Grágás*. The constitution established with the introduction of Ulfljótr's law code in 830 had twelve local assemblies across the island, to each of which belonged three chieftains or *goðar* (singular *goði*), yielding thirty-six *goðar* in total. In the pre-Christian period, a *goðorð*, or chieftaincy, had both sacred and secular aspects, and so English translations of the sagas sometimes render the term *goði* as "priest." But with the conversion to Christianity, the *goðar* ceased to exercise priestly functions unless they happened also to be ordained. Þórðr gellir introduced reforms in 965 whereby the island was divided into four "quarters" (*fjórðungar*), each of which had three local assemblies with three *goðar* each, except that the northern quarter had four assemblies with three *goðar* each, increasing the total number of chieftains from thirty-six to thirty-nine. These *goðar*, with three "extra" chieftains from each of the three quarters that had only nine *goðar* each to ensure parity with the Northern Quarter, were the voting members of the *lǫgrétta* or law council, where they were each joined by two þingmenn ("assembly men") as nonvoting advisors and (after the establishment of the two dioceses) by the Icelandic bishops, as well as the lawspeaker: a legislative body of 147 men, though only the forty-eight *goðar* could vote. If one turns from the legal texts to the sagas of Icelanders, there appears to be a higher number of chieftaincies than allowed for in the surviving legislation. Jón Víðar Sigurðsson (1999) has argued that this saga evidence deserves to be taken more seriously than it was in the past. He concludes that "we may work on the assumption that there were 50–60 chieftaincies at any one time" in the Saga Age (1999: 55).

A *goðorð* could be inherited, shared, bought, or loaned, and it was by these means that—however many chieftains there once were—a small number of families gradually acquired all the chieftaincies toward the end of the Free State period. During the Age of the Sturlungs in the first half of the thirteenth century, there were just a handful of *stórgoðar* ("great chieftains"), who between them had accrued all the island's chieftaincies.

Legal disputes had first to be brought to the appropriate local assembly, which met in the spring (*várþing*). If resolution was not possible there, then the case was taken to the national assembly or *Alþingi* (Althing), which met at Þingvellir in the southwest of the island for two weeks each June. After the reforms of 965, the Althing comprised two bodies: the *lǫgrétta*, which created and interpreted laws, and the four *fjórðungs-dómar* or Quarter Courts (one for each quarter of the island), at which juries appointed by the *goðar* decided legal disputes. In or after 1004/5, an additional Fifth Court (*fimmtardómr*) was established as an appeals court.[5]

Two main kinds of punishment could be handed out by the courts: fines or outlawry. If a man was sentenced to lesser outlawry (*fjǫrbaugsgarðr*), he had to leave Iceland for three years; if he had not left within three years, he became a full outlaw. Full outlawry (*skóggangr*) was effectively a death sentence, as it meant that the convicted person could be killed with impunity and was denied all assistance in Iceland. The legislative assembly could allow a full outlaw, *skógarmaðr*, to go into exile abroad for the rest of his life, but he would lose all the rights of an Icelander abroad.

It is not possible to understand the society portrayed in sagas of Icelanders unless one realizes that there was no state body for enforcing the decisions of courts, no equivalent of a national police force or army. It was therefore up to the wronged party to ensure that the sentence of the court was carried out. If a man sentenced to outlawry refused to go abroad, it was up to the party he had wronged to try to kill him, and if they did not dare or were unable to do so, there was no reason why he might not carry on life as normal.

Conflict of some kind powers narrative, and in the sagas of Icelanders such conflict typically takes the form of feud: "The bloodfeud informs every aspect of Icelandic political and legal life" in the period in which the sagas are set (Miller 1990: 179). The prominence of feud in the sagas can be attributed to the lack of an executive power that could enforce legal decisions. In such a society, people seek ways of limiting violence and the conventions of feud enable this; as Jesse Byock writes, "The dominant concern of this society—to channel violence into accepted patterns of feud and to regulate conflict—is reflected in saga narrative" (1982: 1).

Thus, although to a modern reader the sagas portray a bloody and violent society, the texts in fact explore ways in which society sought to limit and control violence within certain "rules." Writers and readers during the turbulent decades toward the end of the Commonwealth period may well have looked back to the relatively restrained feuding of the tenth century as a golden age in comparison with the indiscriminate bloodshed of their own days.

In his *Bloodtaking and Peacemaking: Feud, Law, and Society in Early Iceland*, William Ian Miller usefully distinguishes feud from other kinds of violence (1990: 180–81). Feud is a hostile relationship between groups, not just individuals, and the groups involved are based on affinities such as kinship, vicinage, household, or clientage. Feud is conducted on a smaller scale than war. Disputes in the sagas are relatively mundane: there are no wars in early Iceland and no foreign invasions. Because feud is between groups, "the target need not be the actual wrongdoer, nor, for that matter, need the vengeance-taker be the person most wronged" (Miller 1990: 180). The controlled nature of feud is seen most clearly in the way that it proceeds in a tit-for-tat process of attack and retribution and is governed by a sense that responses should be roughly proportionate: if you kill my brother, I would be justified in killing one of your relatives in return, but not in wiping out your entire family. "Cross-culturally, there appears to be a correlation between the existence of feud and a culture of honor" (Miller 1990: 181), and honor is, as Peter Hallberg states, "ethically the key concept in the world of the Icelandic sagas" (Hallberg 1962: 99).

In theory, what Miller calls the "my-turn/your-turn" rhythm of feud would mean that disputes ended only when one group had killed all members of the opposing group. The concern of early Icelanders to limit and control violence meant, however, that other ways of resolving feuds were available involving arbitration and compensation.

Feud is not merely a central theme in the sagas of Icelanders; it also structures their narratives, so there is a direct link between social practices and literary structures. In 1967, Theodore M. Andersson published a broadly structuralist account of the sagas of Icelanders in *The Icelandic Family Saga: An Analytic Reading*. As Vladimir Propp identified

common elements and structures in the Russian folktale in his seminal
Morphology of the Folktale (1928/1958), so Andersson identifies a basic
structure common to the sagas of Icelanders: Introduction–Conflict–
Climax–Revenge–Resolution. As the analyses Andersson provides indicate, however, his pattern fits some sagas better than others and can
on occasion distort the relative importance of episodes within a saga,
sometimes overemphasizing the climax element (and maintaining that
there should be only one per saga). One might also ask whether this
model is much more than a sophisticated way of saying that sagas have
beginnings, middles, and ends: it certainly risks reducing richly individual works to a uniform pattern.

A similar, though more flexible, account of *Feud in the Icelandic Saga*
was published by Jesse Byock in 1982. Byock coins a term, "feudeme," for
the smallest meaningful element of a feud narrative. The term is modeled on concepts from structuralist linguistics such as phoneme and
morpheme and so resonates with Propp's use of "morphology." These
feudemes are of three types: conflict, advocacy, and resolution. Conflict
may be over material goods or over nonmaterial issues such as honor or
status. Advocacy may involve brokerage, self-advocacy, arbitration, goading, or information passing: in these ways private hostility may become
the concern of a community. Resolution may be achieved by third-party
arbitration or by direct resolution by the parties involved, or attempted
resolution may be rejected. Byock argues that although sagas are often
thought to be characterized by conflict, they are at least as much about
resolution.

Unlike the elements of Andersson's feud structure, which follow a set
order, Byock's feudemes appear in clusters to form what he calls "feud
chains." Feudemes or feudeme clusters can be preceded or followed by
other narrative elements such as travel or units of information, and in this
way clusters can be separated by shifts of location, character, season, or
time. The model is thus a flexible one, allowing for a variety of possible
narrative structures within the conventions of feud.

As an especially clear example of the importance of feud and the role of
distinctively Icelandic legal institutions in the sagas of Icelanders, we will
now look in some detail at *Hrafnkels saga*.

Hrafnkels saga Freysgoða

Hrafnkels saga Freysgoða (*The Saga of Hrafnkel Frey's Goði*) is one of the shortest sagas of Icelanders and one of those most often read.[6] Its elegant construction is widely praised, with Gabriel Turville-Petre describing it as the "most perfect of the shorter sagas, in structure and character drawing" (1953: 240–41) and Sigurður Nordal claiming that it is "the most coherent and neatly constructed of all the Icelandic sagas" (1958: 34). What turn out to be crucial details or key characters are carefully prepared in advance rather than suddenly introduced, and little echoes or parallels between events and characters bind the text together so that, for example, both Hrafnkell and Sámr are attacked early in the morning while still in bed and both Eyvindr and Þorkell have been in the service of the Byzantine emperor abroad. One reason for the saga's popularity with readers new to the genre is its comparatively economical cast list: it has only twenty-five named characters, and only eight of those play an important part in the story.

The saga is set in the first half of the tenth century and begins with the settlement in Iceland of Hrafnkell's father, Hallfreðr, during the reign of Haraldr hárfagri of Norway, whose colorful genealogy begins the story. Hrafnkell is a boy of fifteen when he emigrates with his father. He grows up to become a chieftain at Aðalból in the east of Iceland and acquires the nickname Freysgoði because of his special devotion to the god Freyr. He builds a temple to the god and dedicates a favorite horse, called Freyfaxi, to him, forbidding anyone to ride the stallion on pain of death. Hrafnkell is said to behave unfairly toward people (ch. 2).

A man called Einarr becomes a shepherd in Hrafnkell's service. When some of the sheep go missing, Einarr ignores the clear warning Hrafnkell had given him and rides Freyfaxi in search of them. The horse alerts Hrafnkell to this sacrilege by returning to the farm dirty and sweaty; Hrafnkell feels obliged by his vow to kill Einarr but offers Einarr's father, Þorbjǫrn, compensation, something he has always been too arrogant to condescend to pay when he has previously killed men. The generosity of his offer indicates a sense of regret over the killing: he offers between ten and twenty times what Þorbjǫrn could expect to receive from an arbitrated settlement

(Miller 2017: 88). Þorbjǫrn, however, displays pride of his own in refusing the offer and asking instead for a third-party to arbitrate between them. Hrafnkell refuses this on the grounds that it would involve recognizing Þorbjǫrn as his equal. After his brother refuses to support him, Þorbjǫrn seeks the assistance of his nephew Sámr in bringing Hrafnkell to court, something Sámr agrees to unwillingly and only because of the duties of kinship.

At the Althing, Sámr is unable to secure the required support from chieftains because they recognize no obligation to him and Þorbjǫrn that justifies their opposing Hrafnkell. Eventually, though, he secures help from two brothers, Þorkell and Þorgeirr, from the West Fjords. They come from the other side of the island from Sámr and Hrafnkell and so are perhaps more willing than nearer chieftains to oppose Hrafnkell, but Þorkell is also motivated by a sense of justice: he tells Sámr that "Mér þykkir œrin nauðsyn til at mæla eptir náskyldan mann" (ÍF ch. 4; "I think it necessary to bring a suit after the slaying of a close relative" CS ch. 8) and he later persuades his brother to help.

With the support of the brothers, Sámr obtains a sentence of outlawry against Hrafnkell. He surprises Hrafnkell at home early one morning while he is still in bed, confiscates the chieftain's property, strings him up by his heels, and—against his supporters' advice—offers him a choice between death and surrendering all his property and his goðorð to Sámr (ÍF ch. 5/CS ch. 11). Hrafnkell chooses not to die (for the sake, he says, of his sons) and leaves the farm to Sámr. The brothers from the West Fjords give Sámr advice on how to be a good chieftain and then have Freyfaxi killed and Hrafnkell's temple burned (ÍF ch. 6/CS ch. 12).

When Hrafnkell learns of his stallion's death and the destruction of his temple, he declares that "'Ek hygg þat hégóma at trúa á goð'—ok sagðisk hann þaðan af aldri skyldu á goð trúa" (ÍF ch. 7; "He considered it vanity to believe in gods and said that from that time onwards he would never believe in them" CS ch. 13). He appears to have learned some lessons from the experience, and in his new home he becomes prosperous again, but a kinder and more restrained man and a more popular leader than he had been at Aðalból. He does not, however, become reconciled to his situation. Six years later, when Sámr's brother, Eyvindr, returns to Iceland from abroad, Hrafnkell attacks the innocent man and kills him in revenge for the humiliation he has suffered (ÍF ch. 8/CS ch. 14). Sámr plans to take revenge but is still in bed early the next morning when Hrafnkell's men attack Aðalból. Hrafnkell offers Sámr a choice between death or surrender like that which he had earlier been offered; Hrafnkell declares that his killing of Eyvindr is equivalent to the hardships he has endured and that he therefore owes Sámr no compensation. Like Hrafnkell, Sámr opts to live on humiliated and is forced to give up the farm at Aðalból and the chieftaincy (ÍF ch. 9/CS ch. 15). He appeals in vain for further help from Þorkell and Þorgeirr, who refuse on the grounds that Aðalból is too far from the West Fjords and point out that he ignored their earlier advice to kill Hrafnkell and so has only himself to blame for his misfortune.

Although a short text, *Hrafnkels saga* has attracted a large amount of commentary, much of it devoted to assessing the narrative's historicity.[7] In the nineteenth century, it was regarded as one of the most historically reliable sagas and was thought to have been written down early. It was noted that Hrafnkell appears as a chieftain in the Eastern Quarter in other sources, including *Landnámabók* and *Njáls saga*. The absence of "fantastic" deeds and creatures was taken as signifying its reliability, and the writer's strong interest in place-names and their origins also appeared to ground the narrative in history, though some of the etymologies offered in the saga have been shown to be incorrect.

An article by E. V. Gordon published in 1939 and a short book by Sigurður Nordal, which appeared in Icelandic in 1940 and in English translation in 1958, demolished belief in the historical reliability of *Hrafnkels saga*. They noted that the saga does not refer to oral traditions and contains no verse that might have been handed down from the period in which the narrative was set. There is no evidence from other sources for the existence of the brothers who help Sámr, and some of the legal material is anachronistic. The case for the slaying of Einarr should have gone first to a local thing at this period, not straight to the Althing, for example. The title Freysgoði is not attached to Hrafnkell outside this saga, and the god Freyr appears to have attracted little devotion in pre-Christian Iceland (only three Icelandic place-names refer to him). The realistic tone of the saga and its descriptive and explanatory detail have created a misleading impression of reliability. Following Nordal's work, it became customary to regard *Hrafnkels saga* as historical fiction. Recently, however, Tommy Danielsson (2002) has argued that rather than fiction the saga is better thought of as a literary reworking of narrative materials from oral tradition.

Hrafnkels saga was dated by Sigurður Nordal to after the end of the Free State and the introduction of new laws in 1271; recent scholarship has accepted a date of circa 1280 (Andersson 2006: 162n1) or circa 1290 (Miller 2017: xiv). There are, however, some grounds for thinking that the saga may be of later date and the earliest manuscript fragment (AM 162 I fol.) is from as late as circa 1500. The oldest complete manuscript of the saga, AM 551 c 4to, dates from circa 1640. Four versions survive and this accounts for some differences among published editions and translations (including variant chapter divisions). The D version translated in Hermann Pálsson 1971 is about three hundred words longer than the A version translated and analyzed in Miller 2017. Andersson sees the saga, along with *Hænsa-Þóris saga* and *Bandamanna saga*, as one of a group of mid-to-late-thirteenth-century sagas that "share a new skepticism about governance" (Andersson 2006: 162) and especially about the reliability of chieftains. It is not surprising to find such skepticism at a time when the legal and political structures of the Free State had collapsed and been replaced by Norwegian monarchy.

When criticism of *Hrafnkels saga* has not been preoccupied with the text's historicity, it has tended to focus on judging the main characters in the saga and on explicating its moral system. There is, however, no consensus on whether Hrafnkell is a morally flawed chieftain who is punished and then reforms or a skillful politician who displays resilience in recovering his losses after a temporary setback. Moral readings of the saga also bring out the connection between character and religion. On such readings, Hrafnkell's fall is precipitated not only by his arrogant pride but also by his devotion to the pagan god Freyr; when he loses his farm and hears that Sámr has had Freyfaxi killed, he abandons belief in the god who has so obviously failed his devotee. Hrafnkell learns his lesson and, although he dies before the conversion to Christianity, his rejection of Freyr coincides with his moral reformation and he goes on to become a popular and successful chieftain. It is, however, alternatively possible to see Hrafnkell as admirable in terms of a pagan moral system or, perhaps, a late-thir-teenth-century vision of what living by a pagan morality might have been like.

Miller has recently expressed dissatisfaction with criticism on the saga that tries to read the text as promoting simple views of complex moral and political issues: "The author meant to ask difficult questions with no easy answers" (Miller 2017: 5). I want here to emphasize how, in its exploration of those difficult questions, *Hrafnkels saga* depends on—and so exempli-fies—several characteristics of feud as it appears in the sagas of Icelanders. The saga shows how aggrieved parties have recourse to the law but is also clear about the need for influential support, rather than merely the justice of one's cause, to win in court. The characters share a belief in equivalence between fines and killings or physical injuries, even when they disagree about the appropriate level of compensation in a particular case. When Hrafnkell kills Eyvindr, he is justified insofar as the conventions of feud allow one to take vengeance against any of one's opponent's family or fol-lowers. Hrafnkell's act is also strategic, as it removes in advance the close relative who would be obliged to take vengeance if Hrafnkell killed or in-jured Sámr. The arrogance and pride of those with wealth and power is assuredly not peculiar to early Iceland, but conflict in *Hrafnkels saga* takes place within very specifically Icelandic socio-legal structures.

Gender and Sexuality

Hrafnkels saga is set in "a firmly male political world" (SI p. 436). Only one woman, a servant, is accorded any direct speech in the whole saga. Like most literature from the past, the sagas of Icelanders are products of a profoundly patriarchal culture and reflect, indeed perpetuate, the gender ideology of that culture—though women appear to have had higher status and more legal rights in medieval Iceland than elsewhere in Europe at the time. No saga of Icelanders is named after a female character and, largely because their capacity for actions of the kind narrated in these sagas was so limited, women are very rarely main characters in a saga, though, as we will see in the next chapter, Guðríðr Þorbjarnardóttir is the connecting link between episodes in *Eiríks saga rauða* and Guðrún Ósvífrsdóttir is in many ways the most compelling character in *Laxdœla saga*.

Nevertheless, the sagas of Icelanders present memorable portraits of several formidable women, including Freydís, whom we met in chapter 1; the sagas also include some fascinatingly frank accounts of aspects of sexuality. Gender and sexuality have become central topics in literary research in recent decades, but scholars in Old Norse–Icelandic studies have rather lagged behind other fields in this respect. Although some fine work on women in the sagas has been published during the last few decades, it is only more recently that related approaches such as masculinity studies and queer theory have begun to make an impact in the field. In this section, I will examine representative examples of gender roles, relations between men and women in love, marriage, and the law, and accusations of male same-sex intercourse.[8]

We can begin with that sole female speaking-character in *Hrafnkels saga*. Tellingly, in this saga of power relations between men, she is both anonymous and a mere servant. She is, in a sense, further anonymized by fulfilling a stock role: she is one of many women in the sagas of Icelanders whose words incite a man to violence. When the newly returned Eyvindr is riding to his brother Sámr's farm, a servant woman washing linen sees Eyvindr go by and rushes indoors to tell Hrafnkell; he has not even risen from bed yet. The woman's speech, a paragraph long as presented in modern texts, goads Hrafnkell into violent action by implying that he is less manly than Eyvindr:

"Verðr sú litil virðing, sem snimma leggsk á, ef maðr lætr síðan sjálfr af með ósóma ok hefir eigi traust til at reka þess réttar nǫkkurt sinni, ok eru slík mikil undr um þann mann, sem hraustr hefir verit. Nú er annan veg þeira lífi, er upp vaxa með fǫður sínum, ok þykkja yðr einskis háttar hjá yðr, en þá er þeir eru frumvaxta, fara land af landi ok þykkja þar mestháttar, sem þá koma þeir, koma við þat út ok þykkjask þá hǫfðingjum meiri. Eyvindr Bjarnason reið hér yfir á á Skálavaði með svá fagran skjǫld, at ljómaði af. Er hann svá menntr, at hefnd væri í honum." Lætr griðkonan ganga af kappi. (ÍF ch. 8)

"The respect a man receives early in life isn't worth much if he later loses it through dishonour and hasn't got the self-confidence to go off and rescue his rights. And it's a particularly big surprise in those men who have been made out to be courageous. Now these people who grew up with their fathers, their lives are different. You think nothing of them compared with yourselves, but then they grow up and they go from country to country [as Eyvindr has done] and are thought of as being terribly important wherever they travel. And then they come back home and they're thought of as being greater than chieftains. Eyvind Bjarnason, who just rode over the river at Skalavad with a shield so beautiful that it shone, is so accomplished that he'd make a worthy object for revenge."

The servant woman went on relentlessly. (CS ch. 14)

Hrafnkell is duly provoked and sets off to kill Eyvindr. The woman's speech says as much about masculinity as about women's roles: Hrafnkell is incited by the suggestion that a worthy chieftain (he has in fact lost his *goðorð* to Sámr at this point) would not let an opportunity such as this go to waste and that in appearing to accept his loss of status he is acquiescing in his own dishonor. The comparison with Eyvindr's dashing figure, bearing a beautiful shield he has acquired along with an enhanced reputation on his foreign travels, draws attention to differences between the two men that Hrafnkell rightly perceives do not reflect well on him.

In saga Iceland, violent feud is the province of men, not of women, who must rely on men to avenge them if wronged. Nevertheless, women frequently exert limited agency in feuds through the role of inciter, goader, or, as it is sometimes called, whetter. Rolf Heller's foundational study of this figure identified at least fifty-one women who incite men to violence in the sagas of Icelanders (Heller 1958: ch. 3). Sometimes, as in this example from *Hrafnkels saga*, the woman's motivation seems primarily to be concern for the reputation and honor of the man she is goading; in other examples, though, a woman incites a man to violent acts against his will in order to achieve her own ends. One of the most memorable goading scenes occurs when Hildigunnr Starkaðardóttir incites her kinsman Flosi Þórðarson to avenge her dead husband, Hǫskuldr Hvitanessgoði, in *Njáls saga* chapter 116. She does so not only with words but also by placing on Flosi the cloak in which Hǫskuldr had been killed, so that "the dried blood poured down all over him." Carol Clover (2002) draws on comparative evidence from other Norse texts and other cultures to argue that Hildigunnr's acts constitute a widow's lament as well as a call to action by Flosi.

Flosi's bitter response to Hildigunnr's goading is to remark that "eru köld kvenna ráð" ("cold are women's counsels"). The proverb has been seen as encapsulating the (misogynist) image of women presented in the sagas of Icelanders, though it occurs only three times in the corpus (this once in *Njáls saga* and twice in *Gísla saga*: see Harris *Concordance*). Critical use of the proverb has, however, reduced and misrepresented the full range of female roles in the sagas: several saga women give good, rather than cold, counsel. While the role of inciting men to violence is prominent in the sagas of Icelanders and represents the main way in which women involve themselves in the feuds that are central to the genre, Jóhanna Katrín Friðriksdóttir (2013) has recently made the important point that other female roles, especially that of the wise female peacemaker, are more important in other kinds of Old Icelandic saga, such as the *fornaldarsögur*, or legendary sagas. Sensitivity to the full range of female characters presented to medieval Icelandic audiences not only enables us to see the inciter as characteristic of the sagas of Icelanders (and some of the heroic poetry in the *Poetic Edda*), rather than of Old Norse literature more generally, but also brings other female figures in the sagas who may be more attractive to modern readers into prominence. As Jóhanna Katrín Friðriksdóttir notes, there are examples of wise, peace-promoting women in the sagas of Icelanders, including Unnr djúpúðga and Jórunn Bjarnardóttir, in *Laxdæla saga*, and Þorfinna the wife of Þorsteinn Kuggason, in *Bjarnar saga Hítdœlakappa* (see Jóhanna Katrín Friðriksdóttir 2013: 25–45).

The extent to which women could exercise agency or exert power is brought sharply into focus by the institution that must have affected their lives more than any other: marriage. Here the situation portrayed in the sagas is, at least sometimes, different from what we might expect elsewhere in Europe at the time and, to an extent, is at odds with what the surviving laws suggest was desirable to the powerful in Icelandic society. So in *Kormáks saga*, for example, although Steingerðr is married to Bersi against her will, she seizes the opportunity to divorce him after he has his buttocks cut off in a duel. She later accepts marriage with Þorvaldr tinteinn and further decides not to abandon him in favor of the poet Kormákr, who has been in love with her throughout the saga. Such a narrative surprises the modern reader accustomed to thinking of early medieval women as having no say in marriages arranged for them and no possibility of obtaining a divorce.

From the middle of the twelfth century, the Western Church taught that marriage was valid only if the woman consented to it. This doctrine was known in Iceland by the late 1180s at the latest, though not written into Icelandic law until 1275 (Bandlien 2005: 165, 187). In some of the sagas of Icelanders, however, tenth-century women are portrayed as having a say in their marriage, and, in other cases, marriages in which the bride was not consulted go badly wrong. While it is possible to argue that the saga authors read back into the past the customs and attitudes of their own thirteenth-century situation (whether unthinkingly, or deliberately to promote the church's doctrine), it is not necessary to assume that there was no historical basis at all for the saga episodes. A relative scarcity of women in Saga Age Iceland might very well create a situation in which women obtained some say in their marriages, even if legally they were at the disposal of their father or other male guardian.

The sagas of Icelanders refer to twelve divorces, of which nine are initiated by women, with a further five threatened divorces all made by women (Frank 1973, Clover 1990: 124). Widowhood seems also, in the sagas, to endow women with increased agency, though as we will see in the discussion of *Laxdœla saga* in chapter 4, saga characters can take different views about this.

Various ways of interpreting the relationship of strong saga women to social reality emerge. Noting that the agency that women sometimes exercise in the sagas of Icelanders is at odds with what *Grágás* and the contemporary sagas collected in *Sturlunga saga* have to say about the status and power of women, Jenny Jochens has seen the strong female characters of the sagas of Icelanders more as products of male fantasy than as reflections of reality (Jochens 1986a, 1986b, 1995, 1996). Insofar as women incite men to violence against their more peaceful instincts, one could read them as being blamed by misogynist male writers for perpetuating outdated and disruptive models of dealing with conflict; the female whetter in this way "served as a convenient scapegoat for male misdeeds that threatened the existence of the present society" (Jochens 1996: 211). In at least some instances, there is likely to be an element of truth in this interpretation, though previous scholarship has not registered as strongly as it might the possibility that, even if such portraits were designed to associate women with violence in a negative way, some female readers or hearers of the sagas reading against the grain of the narrative could have found such instances of female agency attractive and even empowering.

Carol Clover, on the other hand, has argued that strong female figures such as we find in the sagas of Icelanders arise in societies where there is a sex imbalance because of a preponderance of men among pioneer settlers. Moreover, this situation is coupled with selective female infanticide, for which there is some evidence in the sagas (e.g., *Gunnlaugs saga ormstungu*, ch. 3), though most instances of (attempted) saga infanticide involve male children.[9] Clover notes that a high sex ratio of men to women typically aligns with institutionalized male violence, male competition for women, and easy divorce and remarriage (Clover 1990: 123). In Clover's reading, the mismatch between the legal status of women (with no allowance in *Grágás* for divorce and remarriage, as opposed to annulment and separation) and the ease with which women acquire divorces and remarry in the sagas of Icelanders could reflect a disparity between what (male) lawmakers wished were the case and what women empowered by their scarcity were, at least sometimes, able to achieve (Clover 1990: 126).

In another highly influential article, Carol Clover argues that the sagas of Icelanders reveal a "sex-gender system rather different from our own, and indeed rather different from that of the Christian Middle Ages" (1993: 364). Her analysis of the sagas suggests that rather than think in terms of masculinity and femininity or male and female, medieval Icelanders distinguished between people (able-bodied men and a few exceptional women) who were *hvatr* and others (most women, children, and old or disabled men) who were *blauðr*. *Hvatr* literally means "brisk, vigorous" and *blauðr* "soft, weak." Rather than take these as metaphorically equivalent to male and female or masculine and feminine, Clover prefers to think in terms of a "one-gender" system in which people either possess or lack the quality of being *hvatr*, but—importantly—can also acquire or lose it: "Although the ideal man is *hvatr* and the typical woman is *blauðr*, neither is necessarily so; and each can, and does, slip into the territory of the other" (1993: 377). Clover's analysis works well for the sagas of Icelanders she discusses and has been extended by other scholars, sometimes rather uncritically, to other Old Norse texts (and even to other early Germanic literatures). Nevertheless, as insightful as it is, the model is not entirely unproblematic. It can be argued that the terms *hvatr* and *blauðr* come close to being little more than synonyms for masculine and feminine, and Clover herself is arguably not always successful in avoiding this.

Although one might have thought that expectations about gendered behavior in the Middle Ages were rigidly fixed, and that there was little room for resistance to hegemonic ideology, Clover's analysis of gender in the sagas draws attention to examples of men performing gender in ways associated primarily with women and vice versa. While witnessing to dominant beliefs and values, these episodes also reveal the contingency and potential fluidity of gender roles. The same can be said of some episodes in which men are seen to lose masculinity in old age. The serving woman who incites Hrafnkell in *Hrafnkels saga* remarks that "svá ergisk hverr sem eldisk," rendered by Sayers (2007: 393) as "Age unmans a man." One aspect of what the servant means can be illustrated from *Egils saga*. In chapter 85 of the saga, the elderly Egill, now physically frail and partially deaf and blind, has become an object of amusement to the women of the household, who laugh at him when he falls over. Grímr Svertingsson comments that "Miðr hæddu konur at okkr, þá er vit várum yngri" ("Women made less fun of us when we were younger"), and Egill then speaks a verse in which he reflects on his physical deterioration in terms that relate directly to Grímr's gendered view of their situation:

> Vals hefk vǫfur helsis;
> váfallr em ek skalla;
> blautr erum bergis fótar
> borr, en hlust es þorrin.

I have a shaking horse of the collar [= neck]; I am inclined to fall onto my bald head; my borer of the hill of the leg is soft, and my hearing has diminished. (my trans.)

In Egill's lines "Blautr erum bergis fótar / borr" the phrase "bergis fótar borr" is a kenning that has been interpreted in various ways. It might be translated literally as "borer/drill of the hill of the leg/foot." The "hill of the leg" may then be interpreted to mean "head," in which case its borer or drill is the tongue and Egill is confessing an inability to compose verse as fluently as in the past. Alternatively, a more obscene meaning of "hill of the leg" entails that its borer or drill is Egill's penis. Given the skaldic love of double entendre, it is likely that both meanings are intended (for a fuller discussion of this episode, see Phelpstead 2007b: 424–28). In terms of Clover's binary, Egill has moved in old age from being *hvatr* to being *blauðr*: his gendered identity is changeable over time rather than fixed.

We see a different kind of movement across gender boundaries in some saga episodes involving cross-dressing. Anxieties about the potential to resist gender roles are evident in the laws against cross-dressing in *Grágás:*

If women become so deviant that they wear men's clothing, or whatever male fashion they adopt in order to be different, and likewise if men adopt women's fashion, whatever form it takes, then the penalty for that, whichever of them does it, is lesser outlawry. (*Grágás* 2: 69–70)

Notice here how the anxiety is expressed in terms of fear of difference or lack of conformity to society's expectations concerning gendered identity ("in order to be different"). We will consider below an episode in which a man is insulted by an accusation involving female attire, but first we will look here at a well-known example of a female character wearing men's clothes.

Chapter 32 of *Laxdæla saga* introduces a character called Þórðr Ingunnarson—unusually bearing a matronymic rather than patronymic because he "was identified with his mother," perhaps a first hint at the confusion of gender to ensue. He is married to Auðr, "ekki var hon væn kona né gǫrvilig. Þórðr unni henni lítit; hafði hann mjǫk slœgzk til fjár, því at þar stóð auðr mikill saman" ("a woman who was neither good-looking nor exceptional in other ways, and Thord had little affection for her. He had married primarily for wealth, which Aud had brought him in quantity"). Þórðr's lack of affection for his wife contrasts with the warm relationship he builds with another woman, Guðrún Ósvífsdóttir. One day, the pair are riding together and Guðrún asks "hvárt er þat satt, Þórðr, at Auðr, kona þín, er jafnan í brókum, ok setgeiri í, en vafit spjǫrrum mjǫk í skúa niðr?" (ch. 35; "whether the rumour is true, that your wife Aud is often dressed in breeches, with a codpiece and long leggings?"). As the "codpiece" indicates, these are trousers specifically designed for men to wear (a *setgeiri* was a piece of cloth inserted into men's trousers as a gore or gusset where women's trousers had an opening). Þórðr replies that he has not noticed, prompting Guðrún to ask "fyrir hvat skal hon þá heita Bróka-Auðr?" ("what other reason is there then for her being called Breeches-Aud?"). His reply that she cannot have been called that for long hints at the possibility that Guðrún herself has invented the nickname and its explanation. In any case, it provides a pretext for getting Auðr out of the way of the couple:

> Einn dag spurði Þórðr Ingunnarson Guðrúnu, hvat konu varðaði, ef hon væri í brókum jafnan sem karlar. Guðrún svarar: "Slíkt víti á konum at skapa fyrir þat á sitt hóf sem karlmanni, ef hann hefir hǫfuðsmátt svá mikla, at sjái geirvǫrtur hans berar, brautgangssǫk hvárttveggja."
>
> One day [Thord] asked [Gudrun] what consequences it could have for a woman if she wore trousers like men.
>
> Gudrun answered: "If women go about dressed as men, they invite the same treatment as do men who wear shirts cut so low that the nipples of their breasts can be seen—both are grounds for divorce." (ch. 35)

Guðrún had previously divorced her husband after making him a shirt revealing his nipples, at Þórðr's suggestion (such a shirt was clearly conceived as a female garment). Þórðr duly announces his divorce from Auðr "on the grounds that she had taken to wearing breeches with a codpiece like a masculine woman."

Auðr later takes revenge on Þórðr. When she sets off on horseback to do so, the saga informs us that "var hon þá at vísu í brókum" (ch. 35; she was then "dressed in britches to be sure"). She goes to the bed closet where Þórðr is sleeping and wakes him, but he turns over when he sees what he takes to be some man who had come in. Clothing was so closely associated with gender that anyone, male or female, wearing trousers of this kind would be taken to be a man. Auðr strikes Þórðr with a short sword, wounding his right arm and cutting "á báðum geirvǫrtum" ("across both breasts"), the same nipples that a man's shirt should not reveal. She then rides away, but Þórðr dissuades Ósvífr from going in pursuit, saying that "hana slíkt hafa at gǫrt, sem hon átti" (ch. 35; "what Aud had done was only evening the score"). The woman (perhaps wrongly) accused of subverting gender expectations by wearing trousers thus takes on a masculine role and, this time certainly wearing clothing appropriate to the role, exacts vengeance on her former husband. Þórðr recognizes she has justice on her side. and the account suggests a kind of grudging admiration of Auðr's performance of masculinity, strongly contrasting with the shame associated with male cross-dressing in saga narratives.

As this episode from *Laxdœla saga* illustrates, saga accounts of love and marriage focus issues of gender and sexuality in particularly clear ways, and this is especially the case in a subgroup of the sagas of Icelanders genre, the sagas of poets (*skáldasögur*). Most of the poets' sagas revolve around a love triangle involving a poet, the woman he loves, and the man (often also a poet) who succeeds in marrying that woman. Much of the surviving skaldic love poetry is preserved in these poets' sagas and they have been at the heart of a long-running scholarly debate about the possible influence of troubadour poetry from the south of France on that of Iceland. Bjarni Einarsson (1961) influentially argued that skaldic verse expressing male emotion and love longing was influenced by foreign poetic traditions and that four poets' sagas featuring love-triangle plots were modeled on the romance of Tristan, translated into Old Norse in Norway in the 1220s. Our uncertainty concerning the dates of composition of sagas of Icelanders is an issue here. Some of the poets' sagas (e.g., *Kormáks saga*, which Bjarni sees as the entry point of the foreign traditions into Icelandic) are generally regarded as among the earliest sagas of Icelanders and are sometimes dated to before the 1220s, making influence from a Norse version of the Tristan story impossible.

As Alison Finlay has pointed out, there is a circularity to Bjarni's arguments: the need to posit foreign influence is based on a belief that this kind of love poetry was foreign to the Icelandic tradition, and therefore instances of it must show foreign influence (Finlay 1995, see also Finlay 2001). Bjarni also refers loosely to "troubadour" influence while citing examples from the slightly later northern French trouvère tradition. And while there are some similarities between skaldic love poetry and troubadour or trouvère verse, there are also considerable differences: the conventions and constraints of *dróttkvætt* meter ensure that skaldic love poetry is sui generis. Finlay looks in detail at one particular saga episode central to the debate: an account in *Orkneyinga saga* of the visit of Earl Rǫgnvaldr Kali Kolsson of Orkney and Icelandic poets in his entourage to Vicountess Ermengarda of Narbonne, in the south of France, and their subsequent composition of verses about her. Despite the linguistic difficulties involved (a bishop in Rǫgnvaldr's company could speak French but probably not Occitan), this episode provides a possible point of entry for continental love poetry into the Icelandic tradition.

Others have argued that there is no need to posit troubadour or trouvère influence on skaldic poetry. Peter Dronke (1965–1966) deploys love poetry by Kormákr Ǫgmundarson (which he takes to be authentically tenth-century) as evidence, alongside a wide range of material from such diverse sources as Ancient Egypt and twelfth-century Georgia, to argue that the supposed distinguishing features of "courtly love" appear across times and places where there can have been no troubadour influence. He maintains that the novelty of medieval love poetry lies rather in the variety of sophisticated and learned ways in which these universal themes are developed.

As with the status of women, there is something of a mismatch between legal and narrative sources concerning love poetry in early Iceland. The *Grágás* law collection expressly bans love poetry: "If a man composes a love-verse on a woman, then the penalty is full outlawry" (*Grágás* II: 198). The thinking behind such a law seems to be that the consequent damage to the woman's reputation would render her "damaged goods" on the marriage market. It seems again important to remember that laws represent a desired state of affairs that must to an extent diverge from reality: there would otherwise be no need for the law. It is possible, however, that, as Edith Marold has argued, the legal prohibition applied only to a "sub-literary" kind of love-song, rather than to skaldic love poems of the kind preserved in sagas (Marold 2007: 261).

The world of the sagas is, unsurprisingly, a patriarchal one, but women have greater agency than one might expect (whether as whetters, wives, or widows) and gender boundaries can be crossed in either direction. We will see in chapter 4 that strong female characters often play key roles in saga narratives; such episodes bring issues of gender to the fore while also contributing to the overall literary effect of the narrative.

Historically, patriarchal societies have almost always also been strongly heteronormative. Homosexual activity appears most explicitly in sagas of Icelanders in the context of insult and slander.[10] The laws, as well as the sagas, describe a form of sexualized insult known as *níð*. *Tunguníð* was verbal slander; *tréníð* ("wood-níð") involved erecting a pole or carving an insulting image. The typical allegation constituting níð was that a man was *argr* or *ragr*, an adjective related to the noun *ergi* and roughly translatable as "unmanly" in a sense that covered both cowardice and participation in homosexual intercourse, specifically the adoption of the passive role in anal intercourse. The term could also be used of a woman, but in that case it has usually been understood as meaning sex-crazed or nymphomaniacal, without implying any same-sex activity.[11] Another term used in this context is the verb *serða*, "to fuck/bugger," which appears as a past participle *sorðinn* and in the compound *sannsorðinn*, which might be translated as "truly buggered" but has been rendered by Folke Ström as "demonstrably used as a woman" (1974: 6).[12] What that translation, the different meanings of *ergi* when applied to a man or a woman, and the semantic range of male *ergi* to cover cowardice as well as sexual behavior indicate is that sexualized insult was more about transgression of accepted gender roles than about same-sex intercourse per se. It was shameful for a man to perform female roles or to fail to live up to expectations of manly behavior. This also explains why it was specifically the passive role in anal intercourse that was despised.

Accusations of homosexual behavior are levelled against the chieftain Guðmundr inn ríki Eyjólfsson in both *Ljósvetninga saga* and *Ǫlkofra þáttr* (also known as *Ǫlkofra saga*). In *Ǫlkofra þáttr*, when Broddi Bjarnarson informs Guðmundr that he will ride over the Ljósavatn pass, Guðmundr tells him to make sure he keeps his word, to which Broddi replies:

> Efna skal þat, eða ætlar þú, Guðmundr, at verja mér skarðit? Allmjǫk eru þér þá mislagðar hendr, ef þú varðar mér Ljósavatnsskarð, svá at ek mega þar eigi fara með fǫrunautum mínum, en þú varðar þat eigi it litla skarðit, sem er í milli þjóa þér, svá at ámælislaust sé. (ch. 4)
>
> I will keep it, but do you mean, Gudmund, to close the pass to me? It would be a serious mistake on your part if you close Ljosa-vatn pass to me so that I may not travel there with my companions, yet you couldn't keep the little "pass" between your own buttocks decently closed.

It is said that these words became known throughout the Thing: what was at stake in this shame culture was public reputation.

An instance of *tréníð* in *Bjarnar saga Hítdœlakappa* offers evidence of the distinction made between the active and passive partners in anal intercourse, though in this case (unlike in the law codes) some opprobrium is attached to the active partner as well:

> Þess er nú við getit, at hlutr sá fannsk í hafnarmarki Þórðar, er þvígit vinveittligra þótti; þat váru karlar tveir, ok hafði annarr hǫtt blán á hǫfði; þeir stóðu lútir, ok horfði annarr eptir ǫðrum. Þat þótti illr fundr, ok mælti menn, at hvárskis hlutr væri góðr, þeira er þar stóðu, ok enn verri þess, er fyrir stóð.
>
> It is further related that something appeared on Thord's harbor mark which hardly seemed a token of friendship. It represented two men, one of them with a black hat on his head. They were standing bent over, one facing the other's back. It seemed to be an indecent encounter, and people said that the position of neither standing figure was good, and yet that of the one in front was worse. (ch. 17)

Notice again the importance of what "people said": public reputation is what matters most. Both active and passive partner are shamed here, though the passive partner's role is considered worse. An episode in *Gísla saga* (ch. 2) confirms that although a distinction might be made between roles, neither was entirely without opprobrium. Assuming that Kolbjǫrn, his rival for the hand of Þórdís, Gísli's sister, will fail to show up to a duel, Holmgǫngu-Skeggi orders a carving to be made showing Kolbjǫrn and Gísli in a compromising position. His intention is to shame them both, though Gísli does come to fight the duel and so proves himself not to be a coward. As in other instances of *níð*, the suggestion of homosexual activity is a way to comment on cowardice, a symbolic assertion of failure to live up to a manly ideal rather than a literal claim about individuals' sexual habits. Cowardice is similarly the charge implicit in a slightly different form of *tréníð* in chapter 34 of *Vatnsdœla saga* involving a pole and a mare, rather than a carving.

Sexual themes are explored with consummate skill and subtlety in *Njáls saga*, and slander relating to both sexuality and gender occurs at a key turning point in the second half of the saga. The pivotal moment has been prepared for much earlier in the saga. In conversation with some itinerant beggar women, Hallgerðr, the wife of Njáll's close friend Gunnarr, makes fun of Njáll's inability to grow a beard by suggesting that he should have had the sense, since his men were putting dung on his fields to make the hay grow better, to put it instead on his beard

> at hann væri sem aðrir karlmenn, ok kǫllum hann nú karl inn skegglausa, en sonu hans taðskegglinga, ok kveð þú um nǫkkut, Sigmundr.
>
> so that he would be like other men. Let's call him "Old Beardless," and his sons "Dung-beardlings" and you, Sigmund, make up a poem about this. (ch. 44)

Sigmundr obliges with three or four malicious verses that circulate the insult widely, as we see when Flosi Þórdarson refers to Njáll as "Old Beardless" much later in the saga (ch. 123). At that point, a legal settlement has been agreed on for the killing of Hǫskuldr Hvítanessgoði by Njáll's sons, but Flosi, who was incited to take on the case by Hǫskuldr's widow shaking the dried blood from her husband's cloak over him, takes exception to the addition of a cloak to the money that has been agreed. He clearly sees the cloak as an insulting allusion to the whetting by Hildigunnr. When Skarpheðinn Njálsson tauntingly asks who Flosi thinks gave the cloak, Flosi replies:

> Þat er mín ætlan, at til hafi gefit faðir þinn, karl inn skegglausi—því at margir vitu eigi, er hann sjá, hvárt hann er karlmaður eða kona.
>
> It's my guess that your father gave it, Old Beardless, for there are many who can't tell by looking at him whether he's a man or a woman. (ch. 123)

Skarpheðinn defends his father's masculinity in terms of his having fathered sons and goes on to insult Flosi, first by implying that legal arbitration is less manly than vengeance ("Hafa fáir várir frændr legit óbœttir hjá garði, svá at vér hafum eigi hefnt"; "Few of our kinsmen have been buried uncompensated by our wall, without our taking vengeance for them") and then by throwing a pair of trousers at Flosi and declaring that he had more need of them

> Því þá—ef þú ert brúðr Svínfellsáss, sem sagt er, hverja ina níundu nótt ok geri hann þik at konu. (ch. 123)
>
> Because if you are the sweetheart of the troll at Svinafell, as is said, he uses you as a woman every ninth night.

Though the text does not say so, there must be something specifically feminine about these trousers. Jenny Jochens argues that men and women in early Iceland wore different kinds of trousers, those for women having a hole for, as she puts it, "purposes of elimination" (1991: 12); such a hole could equally be put to other purposes by the troll at Svínafell. The accusation of being a woman every ninth night is specifically singled out as an example of defamatory talk in the Norwegian Gulaþing law (quoted in Ström 1974: 7). Weirdly arbitrary as it may seem to the modern reader, the same insistence on the enormity occurring every ninth night appears in the insult levelled at Króka-Refr in chapter 7 of the mid-fourteenth-century *Króka-Refs saga*. Refr is called Refr inn ragi (>*ragr* cf. *ergi*) and mocked for taking a woman's role every ninth night because he is thought to have fled in fright from a polar bear; in fact, he had gone to fetch an axe with which to confront it and he proves his bravery by killing those who slander him.

It has been conventional since publication of the first volume of Michel Foucault's *History of Sexuality* for historians of sexuality to distinguish between homosexual *identities* or orientations (invented in the mid-nineteenth century, according to Foucault) and homosexual *acts*, in which someone might indulge in the medieval and early modern periods without thereby being regarded as a particular kind of person. It would be anachronistic to identify men who are (said to be) *argr* as gay in today's terms: the distinction made between the active and passive partner in medieval Iceland does not, for example, map neatly onto a modern hetero/homosexual binary. The distinction between acts and identities might, though, be less clear-cut than Foucauldian analysis suggests. With a performative theory of gender (of the kind developed in Butler 1999, for example), it is possible to see gendered *identities* in the sagas of Icelanders as constituted by *behavior* (i.e., acts) rather than by any "essential" orientation.

Early Icelandic insults and laws reveal an anxiety about gender roles and a fear of their being transgressed. At the same time as they witness to normative gender behavior expected of all men, the very need to police gender boundaries in this way reveals the contingency of those expectations and the possibility of crossing such boundaries.

As we have seen in examples from *Laxdœla saga* and *Njáls saga*, clothing is an important marker of gendered identity in the sagas of Icelanders (no doubt in part because the island's climate meant that people were generally well wrapped up). Physical appearance and bodies can also, however, signify gendered identity. Hair provides an example of this. In the sagas, women wear their hair long, whereas men have theirs cut short (Jochens 1991: 13). Baldness like Egill Skallagrímsson's is, on the other hand, inextricably linked with losses of mobility, hearing, sight, and sexual potency, and thus of masculinity, in old age (Phelpstead 2013: 6–7). We have seen that in *Njáls saga*, Njáll's inability to grow a beard casts doubt on his masculinity.

The alterity of the past is both a challenge and an attraction of medieval literature. The sagas of Icelanders offer compelling insights into beliefs about gender and sexuality that, by their very difference from our own, expose the historical contingency of all such identities. Sensitivity to such

issues is required to appreciate fully the literary ends to which the treatment of these themes in the sagas is dedicated. In chapter 4, we will look
at some ways in which these themes—alongside others—contribute to
selected individual sagas, but we will end this chapter by looking at one
other thematic area that involves even more fundamental issues of human
identity.

Nature and the Supernatural

As noted above, an individual has not one but multiple identities. Even
more fundamental than nationality or gender is the sense of oneself as
human as distinct from animals and the rest of the natural world, on the
one hand, and from supernatural, or at least superhuman, beings, on the
other. As with other types of identity, though, distinctions that can appear
straightforward and "natural" quickly prove to be less clear-cut on critical
reflection. In this section, we will look at some saga episodes concerning
the relationship of medieval Icelanders to the rest of the natural world and
to the supernatural. The divisions between these categories turn out to be
blurred and permeable.

We can begin by returning to *Hrafnkels saga*. In this text, the sharp distinction between humans and other animals is called into question by the
relationship between Hrafnkell and his stallion, Freyfaxi, especially in the
scene when Freyfaxi gallops back to Hrafnkell's farm after being ridden by
Einar. "When the stallion reached the door, he neighed loudly" (CS ch.
5; "Ok er hestrinn kemr fyrir dyrr, hneggjaði hann þa hátt" ÍF ch. 3) and
when Hrafnkell sees the muddy, sweaty state the horse is in, he talks to
the horse: "Illa þykki mér, at þú ert þann veg til gǫrr, fóstri minn, en heima
hafðir þú vit þitt, er þú sagðir mér til, ok skal þessa hefnt verða. Far þú til
liðs þíns" (ÍF ch. 3; "I don't like the way you've been treated, my foster-
son. But you had your wits about you when you told me of this. It shall be
avenged. Go to your herd" CS ch. 5). In addressing the horse in this way,
calling it his foster-son and suggesting that it has the kind of personal status that justifies the taking of vengeance, Hrafnkell is treating the animal
as if it were a (human) person.

There are two ways of reading this scene. On the one hand, it might be taken as blurring the distinction between humans and other animals, a moment when the mask slips, as it were, and we are reminded of the cultural work involved in maintaining the human/animal boundary. On the other hand, it is possible to see Freyfaxi not as revealing the kinship between humans and all other animals but as an exceptional creature endowed with supernatural faculties through his having been dedicated to the god Freyr. Several critics (among them Fulk 1986–1989, Sayers 2007, and Miller 2017) note that there is something uncanny about many of the animals in *Hrafnkels saga*: not only Freyfaxi but also the mares, who inexplicably avoid being ridden, and the mysteriously disappearing sheep who seem so pleased to see Einar when he finds them. Sayers (2007: 387) suggests that the fact "that the animals become a bit strange shows that Frey accepted Hrafnkel's gift." Such an observation raises the question whether the narrative therefore moves into a fantastic mode, or whether the saga-author might have believed that such supernatural intervention was possible. In the remainder of this chapter, we will pursue these two perspectives more generally, first looking at relations between humans and their natural environment, including other animals, and then returning to the supernatural and the relationship between realism and fantasy.

Iceland's stunning landscape is the star of the show for modern visitors to the island. To that extent, one might say that the Icelandic tourist industry benefits from the Romantic revolution in attitudes to nature, a legacy of the late eighteenth century that still conditions our interaction with our physical surroundings. The medieval sagas of Icelanders, by contrast, show little interest in the Icelandic environment—even in its most unusual features, such as hot springs and volcanoes—and very nearly no sense of aesthetic pleasure to be derived from its observation.[13] Oren Falk notes that although there are a few references to volcanic activity in *Landnámabók*, the bishops' sagas, and Norse poetry, there is no evidence of Icelandic vulcanism in the sagas of Icelanders and only one reference to an Icelandic earthquake (in *Laxdœla saga* ch. 38; Falk 2007: 6–7). The interest shown by saga-writers and characters in the environment is instead typically focused on food production, farming, and animal husbandry, or on how landscape features assist or hinder characters in their (generally violent) interactions with other men and women.

The sagas of Icelanders are unique (at least within Europe) in offering historically grounded narratives of the foundation of a human community in a land previously completely without human inhabitants. The
land itself was a primary attraction of Iceland for the early settlers, as
Grímr Ingjaldsson memorably acknowledges in chapter 10 of *Vatnsdœla
saga*: "Er mér sagt gott frá landkostum, at þar gangi fé sjálfala á vetrum,
en fiskr í hverju vatni, skógar miklir, en frjálsir af ágangi konunga ok ill-
ræðismanna" ("I have heard good things about the land—that livestock
feed themselves during the winters, and that there are fish in every river
and lake, and great forests, and that men are free from the assaults of kings
and criminals"). Chapter 3 of *Eyrbyggja saga* similarly reports of early visitors to the island from Norway that "þeir menn, er kómu af Íslandi, sǫgðu
þar góða landakosti" ("men who returned from Iceland spoke of the good
quality of the land"). Because the barren interior consists of glaciers and
desert, settlement in Iceland has always been confined to a relatively nar-
row band around the coast; those who came to Iceland late in the settlement period of course found that the best land had been taken, as Ǫnundr
Tree-Foot laments in verse in *Grettis saga* (ch. 9). The search for habitable
land was ongoing and stimulated exploration of Greenland and Vínland.
Eiríkr rauði gave the attractively misleading name "Greenland" to the island he discovered to attract settlers there (*Eiríks saga rauða* ch. 2).

Representing the period of earliest settlement as a golden age of plenty
is a common topos in the sagas of Icelanders. In chapter 4 of *Eyrbyggja
saga*, we are told that "þá var gott matar at afla af eyjum ok ǫðru sæfangi"
("there was plenty of food to be had from the islands and the sea"). *Egils saga* (ch. 29) records that in the settlement period "Hvalkvámur váru
þa ok miklar, ok skjóta mátti sem vildi; allt var þar þá kyrrt í veiðistǫð, er
þat var óvant manni" (whales beached on Iceland "in great numbers, and
there was wildlife there for the taking [. . .] the animals were not used to
man and would never flee").

Like all golden ages, this one did not last. Descriptions of a land of
plenty by characters in the sagas mark off the time in which the narrative
is set from the present of those reading or hearing it. The most notorious
environmental consequence of human settlement in Iceland was the island's deforestation. In *Íslendingabók*, Ari Þorgilsson writes of the period

of settlement that "Í þann tíma vas Ísland viði vaxit á miðli fjalls ok fjöru" (p. 5) ("At that time Iceland was covered with trees between the mountains and the shore"; my trans.). "At that time" indicates that this was no longer the case when he wrote in the early twelfth century. The importance of timber as a natural resource becomes very clear in chapter 31 of *Eyrbyggja saga* when it leads to conflict between Snorri goði and Þórólfr bægifótr (lame-foot) and his son Arnkell (see further discussion in Phelpstead 2014: 5–7).

The exceptional moment in the sagas of Icelanders when a character displays an appreciation of the beauty of the landscape occurs in *Njáls saga*. The outlawed Gunnarr Hámundarson falls from his horse as he is setting off to go into exile, looks up at his farm at Hlíðarendi, and fatally declares, "Fǫgr er hlíðin, svá at mér hefir hon aldri jafnfǫgr synzk, bleikir akrar ok slegin tún, ok mun ek ríða heim aptr ok fara hvergi" (ch. 75; "Fair is the slope, so that it has never seemed as fair to me, the pale fields and the mown home-field; I shall ride back and go nowhere"; my trans.). This is "one of the few places in the sagas where landscape is identified as aesthetically beautiful" (Overing and Osborn 1994: 65), and Gunnarr might appear here to be a Romantic landscape lover avant la lettre. But the landscape for which Gunnarr expresses his love is not a natural, wild one, but a man-made agricultural one or, to use a term current in ecocriticsm, a "naturalcultural," rather than purely natural, landscape, one that has been shaped by and has meaning because of human activity.

The backdrop for the sagas' narratives of violent feud is a primarily agricultural world. Saga-authors were aware that the consequences of unusually poor weather and/or poor farm management could be severe. In *Hænsa-Þóris saga*, agricultural problems precipitate the feud at the heart of the saga. Following a failure of crops, Blund-Ketill Geirsson forces Hœnsa-Þórir to sell hay to men who have been less prudent than he, and this leads to conflict and killing.[14]

After Hrafnkell is ejected from his home by Sámr in *Hrafnkels saga*, the care with which he builds up his new farm is stressed: he looks after kids and calves during winter and benefits from rich stocks of fish in the river (cf. Miller 2017: 24). Similarly, the farmer Úlfarr is introduced in chapter 30 of *Eyrbyggja saga* with a relatively rare recognition of the extreme climatic conditions in which Icelandic society was established: "Hann var ok svá fésæll, at fé hans dó aldri af megri eða drephríðum" ("He was so lucky with his livestock that none of his animals ever died from starvation or in blizzards").

Most of the animals encountered in the sagas of Icelanders are domesticated farm animals of one kind or another, and that domestication blurs the simple distinction between humans and animals, insofar as both live together on the farm and are dependent on each other. In the case of a few memorable animals, the distinction is blurred further when individual named animals appear to display humanlike consciousness and communicative abilities. In *Njáls saga*, the consequence of Gunnarr of Hlíðarendi's refusing to go into exile is that he can be killed with impunity. The episode in which that killing takes place furnishes an example of the blurring of the distinction between human and animal to set alongside Hranfkell's Freyfaxi. When Gunnarr's killers approach his farm, they know that they need to try to prevent his dog, Sámr, warning him of their approach. They therefore force a neighboring farmer, Þorkell, whom the dog will trust, to lure it away. When the dog sees the other men with Þorkell and realizes what is going on, he "hleypr á hann Þorkel upp ok grípr í nárann" (ch. 76; "jumped at Thorkel and bit him in the groin" ch. 76). One of the men kills the dog, but before it dies "hundrinn kvað við hátt, svá at þat þótti með ódœmum" (ch. 76; the dog "gave out a loud howl that was like none they had heard before"). This wakes Gunnarr, who remarks that "Sárt ertú leikinn, Sámr fóstri, ok búið svá sé til ætlat, at skammt skyli okkar í meðal" (ch. 77; "You've been cruelly used, my foster-child Sam, and this may mean that our deaths will be close together").[15] The dog has a humanlike understanding of what is happening and the intelligence to attack Þorkell where it hurts. Gunnarr recognizes his affinity with his dog by calling it his "foster-child," the same language that Hrafnkell used of his horse, Freyfaxi.

A different kind of blurring of the divide between human and animal is evident in *Eyrbyggja saga*. A four-year-old bull has acquired a name, Glæsir, and becomes part of a human-animal community. The bull seems to be a reincarnation of Þórólfr bægifótr, having been engendered by the mother cow's consumption of the revenant's ashes, further blurring the human/animal distinction. The farmer Þóroddr decides to kill the bull, but it understands his speech, tosses him in the air, and impales him on one of its horns. As with Freyfaxi, there is an uncanny aspect to the humanlike action of this animal, in this case because of the suggestion that a human has been reborn as an animal.

The agricultural society that both produced and is portrayed in the sagas of Icelanders was one where the interdependence of animals and humans and the reliance of both on landscape, plants, and weather was an inescapable daily reality. Although this reality is only fleetingly the central focus of saga narratives, attention to the moments when it becomes prominent offers insight into medieval Icelandic beliefs about the relationship between humans and their environment—and reveals how permeable the distinction between human and animal could be.

The Supernatural

The sagas of Icelanders are celebrated for their realistic, matter-of-fact rendition of life in early Iceland. This narrative mode has led to comparisons with the modern novel as it developed from the eighteenth century onward. The canonical status of modern realist fiction has perhaps encouraged critics of Old Norse literature to give more attention to the sagas of Icelanders than to genres that seem less realistic to modern readers, such as the legendary sagas and *riddarasögur*. It can come as a surprise, therefore, to realize that roughly three-quarters of the sagas of Icelanders include at least one incident involving either magic or some other form of the supernatural or paranormal. Modern readers can find it difficult to know how to reconcile the sagas' realism (and their appearance of recording history) with content that seems inherently implausible or simply unbelievable. One response has been to think of the sagas as shifting between (or juxtaposing) realism and fantasy. In my opinion, however, the fact that the terms "fantasy" and "fantastic" have been used by theorists and critics in several quite different senses has led to some confusion when the term has been deployed in saga studies.[16]

In particular, not everyone who has cited Tzvetan Todorov's influential study *The Fantastic* (1975) has taken fully on board the distinction between "the fantastic" in its everyday sense and the particular meaning that Todorov gives the term. Todorov defines "the fantastic" as "that hesitation experienced by a person who knows only the laws of nature, confronting an apparently supernatural event" (1975: 25). The fantastic in this sense depends for its effect on the appearance of an initially inexplicable phenomenon in an otherwise realistic context, but the fantastic lasts only as long as uncertainty about that phenomenon. Once we have decided that it is an illusion or that it has taken place despite the laws of nature, Todorov maintains that "we leave the fantastic for a neighboring genre, the uncanny or the marvelous" (1975: 25). Todorov's fantastic is therefore not merely what is impossible because beyond the laws of nature: that would be what he calls "the marvelous." Todorov's fantastic can be experienced only by someone who, in his words, "knows only the laws of nature," and it would therefore be anachronistic to imagine it was experienced by medieval readers for whom what we would call the supernatural was, in fact, at least as real as the natural.

In my fuller discussion of these issues elsewhere (Phelpstead 2012), I have argued in favor of using the terms "fantasy" and "fantastic" with their commonsense rather than Todorovian meanings, echoing Kathryn Hume's statement that "by fantasy I mean the deliberate departure from the limits of what is usually accepted as real" (Hume 1984: xii). To judge whether a given text or episode is fantastic in this sense, one needs to assess its plausibility in terms of what was accepted as real at the time of writing, not what a modern reader might believe to exist. Understanding fantasy as "any departure from consensus reality" (Hume 1984: 21) thus highlights the historical contingency of its definition, for as Hume points out, "'consensus' immediately refers us both to the world of the author and that of the audience" (1984: 23). It is thus necessary to resist the tendency to categorize as fantastic those things that a reader today is likely to find implausible and to try instead to identify those things that a medieval reader might have thought improbable. It is also worth remembering that very many modern readers believe in the existence of the supernatural in some form or other. The fact that the sagas of Icelanders report on magic curses, hauntings by the undead, prophecies, and miracles attributed to the Christian God in exactly the same way as they report disputes between chieftains, killings, and legal proceedings at the Althing might be taken as prima facie evidence that the former were felt to be as plausible as the latter.[17]

Another problematic term here is "supernatural." It presupposes a distinction between "natural" and "supernatural" that may be anachronistic insofar as it depends on an understanding of the "laws of nature" that is distinctively modern. The supernatural became prominent as a category against which to define the natural in the thirteenth century, when sagas of Icelanders began to be written (Bartlett 2008), but the modern use of "supernatural" obscures a distinction that was made by scholastic theologians. Robert Bartlett (2008: 18–19) notes, for example, that Gervase of Tilbury, writing in 1215, was careful to distinguish the miraculous, which was supernatural and caused by God, from the marvelous, which was beyond human understanding but nevertheless "natural." Bartlett further notes (2008: 20, 23) that for many thirteenth-century writers, demons and magic were natural, not supernatural, marvels and that the canonization process in this period took pains to distinguish the magical (natural) from the miraculous (supernatural). In recent work on Old Norse–Icelandic literature some scholars have preferred the term "paranormal" to "supernatural" (Ármann Jakobsson 2013 and Mayburd 2017). Ármann Jakobsson favors "paranormal" because it "has its roots in human experience rather than in nature" (2013: 199n2). "Paranormal" may, however, imply that there is something unlikely about such phenomena, insofar as they are not "normal," whereas for a believer in their reality they may be as normal as anything else that they encounter. "Superhuman" is another possibility, but there are many purely natural phenomena that are superhuman in the sense of being more powerful in some ways than a human (volcanoes, elephants, or stars, for instance), and on the other hand some manifestations of the supernatural/paranormal could be considered subhuman rather than superhuman. None of these terms is unproblematic, therefore. In what follows I use "supernatural" in a way that encompasses both the supernatural and the marvelous as thirteenth-century theologians defined them.

Eyrbyggja saga is particularly rich in episodes involving different forms of the supernatural. In chapter 61 of the saga, it is said of Þrándr Ingjaldsson that "[Hann] var kallaðr eigi einhamr, meðan hann var heiðinn, en þá tók af flestum trollskap, er skírðir váru" ("When he was a heathen he was known as a shape-shifter, but most people gave up magic when they were baptized"). The boundary between human and animal (crossed in shape-shifting) here becomes associated with that between nature and the supernatural. Baptism brings an end to such boundary crossing, as the conversion to Christianity is seen as an essential stage on the way to the foundation of a stable Icelandic nation.

In the same saga, a remarkable series of hauntings at Fróðá are eventually ended when the twin forms of human social regulation, the law and the Christian religion, are deployed against the nonhuman (or no longer human) supernatural. The undead Þóroddr and his men are prosecuted, and a priest says mass and hears confessions. Order is reestablished through a combination of law and Christianity.[18]

In the Fróðá episode and in many other saga hauntings, the distinctive quality of Norse revenants is what William Sayers calls their "intense corporality" (1996: 244). The supernatural can be manifested in very solidly physical form, and this is especially true of the kind of undead or revenant being called a *draugr* in Old Norse. This physicality troubles and problematizes a simple opposition between the natural and the supernatural. Nor is this the only distinction undermined by the revenants of the sagas. Sayers writes of their "crossing of the boundary back into life" (1996: 243):

> Ignoring the boundary between death and life as set in natural law, *draugr* predation on the community also ignores the laws of property and social hierarchy and violates the norms of reciprocity by being one-sided and wholly destructive. (Sayers 1996: 258)

Nevertheless, Sayers argues that the ghosts at Fróðá are open to legal arguments because of "their nostalgia for communal life" (1996: 249; see also Martin 2005).

The most frequently occurring supernatural beings in sagas of Icelanders besides ghosts are two kinds of female spirit. *Dísir* (singular *dís*) are divine beings who appear more often in mythological texts than in the sagas (but see below on Þiðranda þáttr). The "fetch" (*fylgja*, plural *fylgjur*) appears in two forms: as an animal consistently associated with an individual as their familiar spirit but visible only as death approaches for the saga character (except in this last respect, this kind of fetch is very like the daemon of Philip Pullman's fiction); or as a female guardian spirit, whose departure portends death. One's destiny is also often revealed in dreams in the sagas. There are on average three or four dreams per saga. Rather than provide insights into a character's subconscious, as readers schooled in psychoanalytic theory might expect, saga dreams are typically prophetic and thus associated with the supernatural in its broadest sense.[19]

Magic appears in many of the sagas of Icelanders.[20] It takes a variety of forms, including prophecy, cursing, and manipulation of people's health or the natural environment (especially the weather). Magic provides women with an agency that they otherwise lack and a form of powerful knowledge that in some ways parallels knowledge of the law among men; the number of male sorcerers in the sagas of Icelanders (29) is roughly the same as the number of female witches (33), but the women tend to be treated in more detail (Mitchell 2011: 191). Memorable witches who use magic for evil purposes include, among others, the aged Þuríðr in *Grettis saga*; Þórveig in *Kormáks saga* (who curses Kormákr so that he will never enjoy his beloved Steingerðr); and Queen Gunnhildr of Norway, who appears in several sagas and features prominently in both *Egils saga* and the early chapters of *Njáls saga*, where she too links magic and sexuality when she curses Hrútr with an inability to consummate his marriage with Hallgerðr. The most prominent male figure to employ magic is perhaps Egill Skallagrímsson in *Egils saga*. He ritually curses King Eiríkr and Queen Gunnhildr (ch. 57) and also uses his knowledge of runes to cure a victim of an incompetently carved healing spell (ch. 72).

The sagas of Icelanders are set in the period leading up to, and just after, the conversion to Christianity, and magic can often be associated with paganism. Stephen Mitchell refers to its appearance in the genre as "a form of pagan resistance to the inevitability of Christianity" (2011: 92). It would, however, be unwise to draw too sharp a distinction between pagan magic and Christian miracles. As Mitchell says, both are exemplary of a "magical world view" according to which the supernatural can be harnessed to effect changes in the world (2011: 42).

Alongside pagan magic the sagas of Icelanders also feature several Christian miracles. We noted an example of miraculous male lactation in *Flóamanna saga* in the previous chapter. The account of Iceland's conversion in *Njáls saga* includes a contest between the missionary Þangbrandr and a pagan *berserkr* in which the former's ability to create fire miraculously demonstrates the truth of his creed (ch. 103). Later in the saga, the blind Ámundi miraculously receives the gift of sight for just long enough to kill the slayer of his father (ch. 106).

Many more instances of magic and the miraculous appear in sagas of Icelanders, but we will end this chapter with another narrative of the conversion period to set beside the account of Þangbrandr in *Njáls saga*. *Þiðranda þáttr ok Þórhalls* (*The Tale of Thidrandi and Thorhall*) is one of several *þættir* concerned with the conversion period.[21] A seer called Þórhall spámaðr (seer or prophet) warns his friend Hallr of Síða not to allow anyone to go outside one night. Hall's eighteen-year-old son does, however, go out to answer knocking at the door, thinking that it is shameful to ignore visitors. He sees nine women dressed in black with drawn swords and another nine in white riding from the south on white horses. He is attacked by the black-clad women and later dies of his wounds. Þorkell declares that the women must be the family's fetches (*fylgjur*) and that the events indicate there will soon be a change of religion on the island "ok mun því næst koma siðr betri hingat til landz" (ch. 3; "and that better traditions will then come to Iceland").[22] The black-clad women were *dísir* seeking recompense for the imminent loss of the family to the Christian faith. The narrator endorses Þorkell's view. At the end of the þáttr, Þorkell has a vision of the hills opening and living creatures great and small preparing to move at the coming of Christianity.

Some topics discussed in this chapter have received considerable attention from critics (feud, women, the supernatural/paranormal), but others much less (notably the environment and human-animal relations, though this is changing). This chapter has brought these topics together to show how they relate to issues of identity that are at the heart of the sagas of Icelanders genre. We will go on in the next chapter to see how these issues play their part in individual saga narratives.

4

READING SELECTED SAGAS

Having discussed *Hrafnkels saga* in the course of the previous chapter, we will now look in turn at some more of the most acclaimed and most frequently read sagas of Icelanders. We will see how the source traditions discussed in chapter 2 and the material explored in chapter 3 are combined in individual sagas. To convey how themes are employed to literary effect, I will follow the plot of each text quite closely, rather than separate out each thematic strand. We begin not with a saga proper but with *Auðunar þáttr vestfirzka*, the best known of the *Íslendinga þættir*, short stories or tales of Icelanders.

Auðunar þáttr vestfirzka

Up to about a hundred *þættir* survive, with the exact number depending on what one counts as a þáttr (see Rowe 2017: 152), but they are not usually preserved independently in medieval manuscripts. Instead, they are integrated into larger works, above all in compilations of kings' sagas. The primary meaning of Old Norse *þáttr* is "thread." The word was used figuratively to refer to parts of a larger whole, such as a family, and then to mean "part of a text" or "part of a manuscript." It is now used in a more technical sense to mean a short prose narrative. The dividing line between a long þáttr and a short saga is a blurred one, and the two terms are used interchangeably of a few texts, such as *Ǫlkofra saga/þáttr*. A þáttr is defined not only by length, however: the tales tend to treat a common stock of themes in similar ways. A large subgroup, to which *Auðunar þáttr* belongs, contains stories of Icelanders' experiences at foreign royal courts. Other types of þáttr include: tales of the conversion period, usually set in Norway but occasionally in Iceland (e.g., the tale of Þiðrandi discussed at the end of the previous chapter); skáld *þættir*, recounting anecdotes involving poets; dream *þættir*; and legendary *þættir*, short stories resembling the *fornaldarsögur*. Stylistically, the *þættir* share the characteristics of "saga style": a neutral, apparently objective, narrative voice, straightforward syntax (joining clauses by coordination or parataxis), and verbal tense shifts. Humor is prevalent in the *þættir*, and it tends to be of a lighter hue than the often grim humor of the longer sagas; *þættir* often end happily. Dialogue—often very lively—features more prominently than in the sagas, too. Many *þættir* are set slightly later than the *Íslendingasögur* (e.g., during the reign of Haraldr harðrádi of Norway, that is, 1045–1066).[1]

"The Tale of Audun from the West Fjords" (CS I: 369–74) is a charming and perfectly constructed short story. It is extant in three main manuscripts, each a kings' saga compilation: Morkinskinna, Flateyjarbók, and Hulda. The Morkinskinna manuscript dates from the last quarter of the thirteenth century but derives from a text probably written in the 1220s, the same decade to which scholars ascribe the original composition of *Auðunar þáttr* (which does not necessarily mean that it was first written down in the original Morkinskinna manuscript). Flateyjarbók is a massive late-fourteenth-century manuscript. The Hulda manuscript is also from the last quarter of the fourteenth century. Another twelve surviving manuscripts derive from these three versions. The three main texts agree on the basic story, but each includes unique material. The Flateyjarbók version is slightly longer than that in Morkinskinna and includes more scene-setting detail in the first part of the tale; the Hulda version expands considerably on the Morkinskinna text, with some differences of detail. The discussion here follows the Morkinskinna text, which is preferred by most editors and most English translators of the þáttr, including Anthony Maxwell for his CS translation. However, Hermann Pálsson (1971: 121–28) chose to translate the Flateyjarbók text, and Miller, the critic who has written at greatest length on the tale, prefers the Flateyjarbók version, claiming that it "makes better sense and is smarter than the other versions on issues that figure at the intellectual core of the story" (Miller 2008: 4).[2]

The story begins by introducing a man called Auðunn, whose family come from the West Fjords of Iceland. He is said to have little money but sets aside most of what he does have to provide three years' food and lodging for his mother while he makes a journey abroad. After a visit to Norway, Auðunn travels to Greenland, spends a winter there and buys a bear, presumably a polar bear, though we are never told that it is white. The bear is described as "gersimi mikla, ok gaf þar fyrir alla eigu sína" (ch. 1; "a great treasure for which he traded everything that he owned"). From Greenland, Auðunn sails back to Norway, intending to travel onward to present the bear as a gift to King Sveinn of Denmark. The text does not explain why Auðunn wishes to make this—for him—extravagant gift to Sveinn in particular. King Haraldr of Norway learns of Auðunn's arrival with a great bear, however, and summons Auðunn. A terse, rather tense, conversation follows in which Auðunn declines to sell (or give) the bear to Haraldr, even at twice the price Auðunn paid for it. Haraldr is taken aback when Auðunn tells him he intends to present the gift to Sveinn of Denmark: "Hvárt er, at þú ert maðr svá óvitr, at þú hefir eigi heyrt ófrið þann, er í milli er landa þessa, eða ætlar þú giptu þína svá mikla, at þú munir þar komask með gersimar, er aðrir fá eigi komizk klaklaust, þó at nauðsyn eigi til?" (ch. 1; "Are you so ignorant that you have not heard about the enmity between our countries, or do you reckon your luck so great that you can go with treasures where others cannot travel safely [. . .]?"). Luck is a key motif in the story, and when Auðunn stubbornly refuses to do anything other than he originally intended, Haraldr allows him free passage, provided he returns and tells Haraldr how Sveinn rewards him: "Kann at vera, at þú sér gæfumaðr" (ch. 1; "It may well be that you are a fortunate man").

By the time that Auðunn arrives in Denmark, he has spent all his money and is reduced to begging for food for himself and his bear. A steward of the king, Áki, takes advantage of Auðunn's vulnerable position by forcing him to give up a half share in the bear in return for food. They then go to King Sveinn, who is not impressed when he learns of Áki's behavior:

Ok þótti þér þat til liggja, þar sem ek settak þik mikinn mann, at hepta þat eða tálma, er maðr gerðisk til at færa mér gersimi ok gaf

fyrir alla eign, ok sá þat Haraldr konungr at ráði at láta hann fara í
friði, ok er hann várr óvinr? (ch. 1)

Did you think it appropriate, given the fact that I have made you
a powerful man, to impede and hinder a man from bringing me a
treasure he has given all his possessions to buy, when King Harald
thought it advisable to give him safe conduct, even though he is our
enemy?

Sveinn exiles Áki and accepts the bear as if Auðunn alone had given it to
him. Auðunn then stays with the king for some time but later risks royal
displeasure by asking to leave: the king is, however, pleased to hear that
Auðunn wishes to go on pilgrimage to Rome, for which he is given much
silver by the king, who asks to see him on his return.

The text shows little interest in the journey to Rome, Auðunn's time
there, or his return journey, except that it tells us that on the way back he
became very ill and lost a lot of weight. He has used up all the money, is
reduced to begging again, and "Hann er þá kollóttr ok heldr ósælligr" (ch.
2; "He grew bald and was quite miserable"). When he arrives back at the
Danish court at Easter, he does not dare present himself in public but loi-
ters in a church waiting for the king to pass by, made all the more reluctant
to appear by the king's men being drunk. When he does come before the
king, the courtiers laugh at Auðunn, though the king remarks that "betr
hefir hann sét fyrir sinni sál heldr en ér" (ch. 2; "he has better provided for
his soul than you have").

King Sveinn invites Auðunn to stay with him permanently, but
Auðunn says that he intends to go back to Iceland, as the money he left
for his mother will now have run out. Again, the king is obliged to see the
justice of Auðunn's intentions. He gives Auðunn a series of treasures as
repayment for the bear: a ship, a pouch of silver, and an arm ring. Auðunn
returns via Norway, where he again meets King Haraldr and provides him
with his promised report. Haraldr is eventually obliged to recognize that
Sveinn rewarded Auðunn more generously than he would himself have
done. Auðunn passes to Haraldr the arm-ring Sveinn had given him, in
recognition of Haraldr's nobility: "þú áttir kost at taka hvártvegja frá mér,
dýrit ok svá líf mitt, en þú lézt mik fara þangat í friði" (ch. 4; "you had the
power to deprive me of both the bear and my life, yet you let me travel in

peace"). On his return to Iceland, it is said that Auðunn was considered "inn mesti gæfumaðr" ("an exceedingly fortunate man"). The tale ends by asserting that "Frá þessum manni, Auðuni, var kominn Þorsteinn Gyðu-son" ("Thorstein Gyduson is descended from this man Audun"), a remark seemingly intended to endorse the tale's historicity.

Indeed, although the rags-to-riches theme of the tale is redolent of fairy tale, it is quite securely situated in history. We know from other sources that Þorsteinn Gyðuson died circa 1190 and the two kings who feature in the story, Haraldr harðráði (r. 1046–1066) and Sveinn Úlfsson (r. 1047–1074), were indeed at war during the third quarter of the eleventh century. The giving of a polar bear as a gift to a Scandinavian ruler by an Icelander is also attested in other sources, though there is no reference elsewhere to confirm Auðunn's historical existence.

The tale is open to a straightforward moral reading. It exemplifies the view that generosity will be rewarded, just as Áki's meanness is punished, that gift-giving is an effective means of establishing reciprocal bonds, and that although one may be "lucky," good fortune and good character are closely related. Auðunn does, in a sense, make his own luck.

Both times that Auðunn comes to Denmark (with the bear and after his pilgrimage), his behavior has impoverished him. Such behavior is apparently imprudent but turns out to be wiser than it seems and works to his benefit. Auðunn's paying for the bear with everything he had is referred to several times in the tale. Giving all one has for a great treasure inevitably recalls Christ's parables in Matthew 13:44–46, but there is nothing in the tale to suggest a full-scale religious allegory, and one should be wary of pursuing the echo too far. It is, admittedly, true that although nothing is said about Auðunn's religious activities in Rome, the holy city appears right at the center of the text. Miller points out that the name of the city occurs after seventy-three lines of the text in Flateyjarbók, with seventy-six lines to come (2008: 50). In extending from Greenland to Rome, the tale stretches from the westernmost limit of Christendom to its center. Moreover, there is a sense in which Auðunn undergoes a kind of figurative resurrection when he returns to Denmark after his pilgrimage—at Easter. But tempting though it may be to build upon such details, it is hard to see how they might add up to a consistent Christian message.

The moral seems to be a more general one that there are times when the wisest course of action is that which appears to be imprudent; the truly wise (or truly lucky) person will recognize such occasions and act appropriately. As Miller points out, Auðunn "becomes prudent once he has something to lose" (2008: 77). He knows when to stop pushing his luck and relying on his audacity.

Although it is perhaps less obvious on a first reading, the story also resonates with the characteristic themes of the sagas of Icelanders that we looked at in chapter 3, including issues of national, gender, and species identity. In terms of Icelandic national self-understanding in relation to peculiarly Icelandic legal structures, there is a legal basis to the central focus on gift-exchange. Miller shows that "the [Icelandic] law backs the deep cultural commitment to reciprocating a gift, especially when the gift reaches amounts of non-trivial value" (2008: 102). The tale is more profoundly invested in issues of national identity through its presentation of relations between an Icelander and foreign royalty. *Auðunar þáttr* belongs to a major category of *þættir* often known as *útanferðar þættir*, tales of journeys abroad. Around thirty to forty such tales tell of the journey of an Icelander to a foreign court, usually that of Norway. Common themes explored in these *þættir* include friendship, hospitality, reconciliation, and religion: one can see that *Auðunar þáttr* is not uncharacteristic of the concerns of the genre. But an underlying theme of these tales is the relationship between Norway and Iceland. The plots revolve around the encounter between a foreign king and an Icelander of (necessarily) lower social status, but the Icelander often appears to be treating the king as a near equal; the Icelander's qualities are recognized at the foreign court and he is rewarded by the king, returning to Iceland with his status enhanced. The tales make a not particularly subtle point about the worth of Icelanders compared to Norwegian kings.

If gender appears not to be an issue in this tale, it may be because the reader too readily associates gender only with women. Auðunn's mother is the only female mentioned in the text, and she never appears or speaks, serving mainly as evidence of Auðunn's praiseworthy filial affections. Yet in its focus on homosocial bonds between men that are established and maintained through gift-giving, the tale relies on shared understandings and constructions of masculinity. Edward Fichtner (1979) has read the tale as an account of an initiation into adulthood and into the adult custom of gift-giving. In this sense, the tale is about becoming a man, about the modes of behavior deemed appropriate for men in the world, and about the rewards that come from conforming with these expectations.

In the context of examples of hair loss provoking ridicule found in Old Icelandic literature, Auðunn's hair loss can be read as emasculating (see Phelpstead 2013: 8). As the king points out, however, the blessings obtained by Auðunn from his pilgrimage more than compensate for his baldness and the negative meaning it might normally carry.

An ecocritical reading of *Auðunar þáttr* would focus on the bear. It is taken from its natural habitat and treated as an object to be exchanged between humans, a "great treasure" (*gersimi mikil*). This term, *gersimi*, paradoxically indicates the value placed on the bear at the same time as it aligns the creature with inanimate objects rather than living human beings, and so devalues it. The word *gersimi* is also used in the tale of the ring given by Sveinn to Auðunn and then by him to Haraldr, and of the sword and cloak given Auðunn by Haraldr. The fact that the bear is valuable because of its rarity outside Greenland leads Miller to connect it to the dangers polar bears face today because of global warming: "The plot of the tale actually depends on polar bears being scarce in the medieval Scandinavian world, though their scarcity there arises for rather different reasons than it does in ours" (2008: 1). Unlike inanimate treasures, however, the bear needs to eat to live, and it seems to be perceived to be a more valuable gift alive than dead. When Auðunn's money runs out, he is forced to beg for food for both himself and the bear, recognizing their common creaturely and dependent nature.

Short though it is, *Auðunar þáttr* is a wonderfully rich text. It is a beautifully constructed and entertaining short story open to a variety of readings, depending on one's critical perspective. Small details—Auðunn's post-pilgrimage baldness, the bear's need to eat to stay alive—turn out to carry significant meaning. This touching tale is doing important ideological work: it engages with questions of national, gendered, and species identity and interrogates "the intersection of the moral and the economic" (Miller 2008: 1) at the same time as (and indeed because) it so effectively entertains.

The Poets' Sagas (*Skáldasögur*)

Half a dozen of the sagas of Icelanders form a subgroup known as the *skáldasögur*, or poets' sagas. Unlike sagas focusing on the history of a family or locality, these narratives are more tightly focused on the life of a single individual. The saga about medieval Iceland's greatest poet, *Egils saga Skallagrímssonar*, is much longer and richer than the other poets' sagas and is discussed separately below. In this section we concentrate on the other *skáldasögur*: *Kormáks saga, Hallfreðar saga vandræðaskálds, Bjarnar saga Hítdœlakappa, Fóstbrœðra saga*, and especially *Gunnlaugs saga ormstungu*.[3]

Characters in many sagas of Icelanders speak verse on occasion, but poetic composition is a more central aspect of the main characters in the poets' sagas. Most of these figures serve as court poets abroad, mainly in Norway, but also in Sweden, Denmark, Orkney, Ireland, and England (on the role of court poet in the skald sagas, see Whaley 2001). The primary duty of such court poets was to compose verse in praise of the ruler, memorializing his deeds and commemorating his death. The nature of this role can be better understood using the concept of a heroic age or heroic society and in light of the anthropological categories of shame and guilt cultures. The nature of heroic society was articulated most influentially in H. M. Chadwick's book *The Heroic Age* (1912), though it had been in use before that and had notably been invoked by the great scholar of medieval literature, W. P. Ker, who argued in his *Epic and Romance*, first published in 1896, that "the heroic age of the ancient Germans may be said to culminate, and end, in Iceland in the thirteenth century" (1957: 57). Chadwick argued that societies produce "heroic" literature when they reach a particular stage of development (the "heroic age"). Different societies have attained this level of development at different periods of history, but when they have done so they have produced similar kinds of verbal art. The heroic age proper of the Germanic-speaking peoples was the post–Roman Age of Migrations in the fourth to sixth centuries, but similar social conditions pertained in the later Viking Age of the ninth to eleventh centuries when skalds in the poets' sagas performed at court. Personal allegiances are central to such societies. Because there is competition between potential leaders, praise poetry celebrating great leaders and heroes becomes a characteristic literary form.

In a classic account of heroic poetry, C. M. Bowra links the nature of heroic society to the kind of verbal art it values:

> The conception of the hero and of heroic prowess is widely spread, and despite its different settings and manifestations shows the same main characteristics. [. . .] An age which believes in the pursuit of honour will naturally wish to express its admiration in a poetry of action and adventure, of bold endeavours and noble examples. (Bowra 1952: 2–3)

In anthropological terms, heroic society is a shame culture, one in which one's reputation defines who one is and one's identity is simply what one appears to other people to be. In such a culture, honor is the highest virtue and shame the worst that can befall someone. In a guilt culture, on the other hand, the enjoyment of one's clear conscience is the highest good and what one thinks of oneself is more important than one's public reputation. In medieval Scandinavia and Iceland, the transition from a shame to a guilt culture was (partly) effected by the conversion to Christianity, but the process was a gradual one, taking place over several centuries.[4]

A culture that values honor and reputation above all else tends also to value poetry that makes known and spreads abroad the heroic deeds of a warrior or leader. The role of poetry in such a culture is, however, two-sided. The obverse of the poet's duty to praise is his ability to blame and to destroy a reputation. The nickname of the central character of *Gunnlaugs saga* recognizes this power: *ormstunga* means "serpent-tongue." So alongside praise poetry we find insulting verse. In Iceland, such verse could be associated with the concept of *níð*, and libelous verse was forbidden by Icelandic law.

Poetry in praise of rulers is not, in fact, prominent in the poets' sagas, though they do include examples of it and describe occasions on which it was composed or recited. The limited overlap between verse in these sagas and verse by the same poets that is preserved in kings' sagas suggests that medieval writers were aware of generic differences between these kinds of saga (cf. the discussion of genre in ch. 1 above). The view of praise poetry sketched above nevertheless proves illuminating of a much more prominent concern of the poets in these sagas: love poetry. One can see love poetry as a specialized form of praise poetry. Moreover, just as the praise of heroic deeds contrasts with verse insult, including accusations of cowardice, so a woman's reputation can be compromised by inappropriate verse (hence, presumably, the ban in Icelandic law on all love poetry: see ch. 3 above). In the poets' sagas, we see praise and blame attached to different objects: the poet composes verses celebrating the woman he loves and insulting his male rival.

Four of the poets' sagas (*Kormáks saga, Gunnlaugs saga, Bjarnar saga,* and *Hallfreðar saga*) center on a love triangle in which the eponymous poet has the opportunity to marry the woman he loves but for some reason (not always made clear) he fails to do so, though he continues to love her. The plots of *Gunnlaugs saga* and *Bjarnar saga* are even more similar. In both texts two poets meet at a foreign court, one already betrothed to a woman back in Iceland; the poets fall out and the other man then returns to Iceland and marries the woman to whom his rival was betrothed. Kormákr, Hallfreðr, and Gunnlaugr (as well as Egill in *Egils saga*) conform to a stereotypical image of a skáld that reflects characteristics of the pagan god Óðinn: they are temperamentally difficult and striking, but not conventionally attractive, in appearance. In *Bjarnar saga* it is not Bjǫrn but his rival Þórðr Kolbeinsson who conforms to the type. Although these are sagas of Icelanders, much of their action takes place abroad.

Kormákr Ǫgmundarson is known from other sources to have been a court poet in Norway, but *Kormáks saga* ignores this to concentrate on his fateful love for Steingerðr.[5] *Kormáks saga* is usually considered one of the earliest of the sagas of Icelanders. The verse preserved in the saga is of high quality and individual episodes are memorable and effective, but there are problems with the structure of the saga, and the relationship between the verse and the prose is sometimes awkward. Sixty-four of the eighty-five verses in the saga are attributed to Kormákr, and nearly all of them refer to Steingerðr, sometimes rather incongruously. Though the love between Kormákr and Steingerðr is mutual, Kormákr fails to attend his wedding; he continues to love Steingerðr, but she marries first Bersi and then Þorvaldr. Magic and the supernatural feature prominently in the saga. One explanation for Kormákr's failure to marry Steingerðr is that he has been cursed by a witch whose son he had killed (ch. 5), and the saga ends when Kormákr is killed by a giant in Scotland (ch. 27).

Whereas Kormákr's love for Steingerðr dominates his saga, in *Hallfreðar saga* the eponymous poet's love for Kolfinna is but one strand in the narrative. When his beloved marries another man, Hallfreðr goes abroad and much of the saga is devoted to his adventures in the service of King Óláfr Tryggvason of Norway. Óláfr was acknowledged in Iceland as the Norwegian king who promoted the island's conversion to Christianity, and some of the most compelling moments in this saga chart Hallfreðr's less than wholehearted change of faith at the king's urging. Only at the end of the saga, with his rejection of his personal spirit or fetch, does Hallfreðr fully embrace his new faith, and at that point the text takes on a quasi-hagiographical hue, with the "miraculous" retrieval of his body thanks to a dream, the making of church vessels from gifts he received from Óláfr, and Hallfreðr's burial on the holy island of Iona. This saga survives in two versions: an abbreviated version in Möðruvallabók and a fuller text split up and incorporated into the so-called *Greatest Saga of King Óláfr Tryggvason (Óláfs saga Tryggvasonar en mesta)*. A mixed text drawing on both of these is preserved in Flateyjarbók. The close, though complicated, relationship between Hallfreðr and King Óláfr in the saga seems to have drawn it into the orbit of kings' saga texts.

Whereas in *Kormáks saga* the love triangle narrative focuses on Kormákr's love for Steingerðr, in *Bjarnar saga* the emphasis is much more on the rivalry between the two men who love Oddný eykyndill ("island-candle"): Bjǫrn Arngeirsson and Þórðr Kolbeinsson. As we saw in chapter 3, Bjǫrn insults Þórðr by carving an image of them both in a compromising position; Jenny Jochens (1999b and 2001: 328–31) has analyzed the relationship between the two men in terms of Eve Kosofsky Sedgwick's concept of the homosocial and how it relates to the homosexual, even suggesting that the conflict between the two men could have been precipitated by an unwanted advance made by Þórðr toward Bjǫrn (of which there is, however, no overt record in the saga). The supernatural appears in this text when Bjǫrn kills a flying dragon in England (ch. 5).

A likely early date for *Bjarnar saga* may account for some weaknesses in style and structure (although often dated to ca. 1215–1230, some would put it later: CS ascribes it to the late thirteenth century). The text is poorly preserved: the best surviving manuscript is from as late as the seventeenth century (a copy of a fourteenth-century manuscript of which a fragment survives) and even that text is missing the start of the saga, which modern editions supply from a version of the saga about King Óláfr Haraldsson in Bæjarbók (MS AM 73 fol.).

At the heart of *Fóstbrœðra saga* there is a relationship between two men not of rivalry, as in other poets' sagas, but of sworn brotherhood. Þorgeirr Hávarson and Þormóðr Kolbrúnarskáld swear to avenge each other if either is killed. The saga tells first of their joint adventures, then of Þorgeirr's experiences and death back in Iceland. Þormóðr then takes vengeance for Þorgeirr in Greenland as promised. Þormóðr earns his nickname, Kolbrúnarskáld, after composing a love poem to Þorbjǫrg Kolbrún, but whereas other *skáldasögur* heroes are models of fidelity in love, Þormóðr later adapts his poem for another woman, called Þórdís. When Þorbjǫrg discovers this, she makes Þormóðr's eyes ache until he confesses. He later becomes a court poet to King Óláfr Haraldsson and dies with his lord at the Battle of Stiklarstaðir.

Having briefly sketched ways in which issues of gender, sexuality, religion, and the supernatural arise in four of the poets' sagas, in the rest of this section we will focus in more detail on one specific text, *Gunnlaugs saga ormstungu*.[6] This is probably the most widely read and studied of the *skáldasögur* (in the English-speaking world, at least) and, as Bjørn Bandlien notes, "Of all the sagas of Icelanders, it is perhaps this one that has had most appeal for a modern audience" because of its romantic subject matter (2005: 272). Its relatively small cast and clear plot add to its attraction for the modern reader. The saga is usually thought to be relatively late, perhaps dating from the last decades of the thirteenth century (a claim in one manuscript that the saga is by Ari Þorgilsson is clearly wrong). The saga must have been written after *Bjarnar saga* and *Hallfreðar saga*, which appear to have influenced it, and after *Eyrbyggja saga* and *Laxdœla saga*, which are mentioned in the text.

Gunnlaugs saga begins by introducing the family of the woman with whom Gunnlaugr will fall in love. Þorsteinn is the son of the famous poet

Egill Skallagrímsson (the subject of *Egils saga*). He has a dream that is interpreted for him by a visiting Norwegian, Bergfinnr: a swan becomes the subject of a fight between an eagle and a hawk. Bergfinnr believes that the birds are people's fetches and that the swan represents the beautiful baby girl to whom Þorsteinn's wife is about to give birth: the eagle and hawk represent two men who will fight over her and both die.

Although Þorsteinn disbelieves the interpretation, it may account for his commanding his wife that if she gives birth to a girl rather than a boy while he is away, the baby must be left out to die. The narrator, in an aside typical of this saga's explanations of the alterity of the past, notes that in the heathen period poor people sometimes had children exposed if they could not afford to provide for them, though "it was always considered a bad thing to do" (ch. 3; "ok þótti þó illa gǫrt ávallt"). Þorsteinn's plan accords with the likelihood that such infanticide would more often have been committed against girls than boys (cf. Clover 1990). When a girl is born, however, Þorsteinn's wife has the child taken to safety with her sister-in-law. Six years later, Þorsteinn is introduced to a beautiful girl at his sister's farm and discovers that it is his own daughter, Helga. He is pleased to have been thwarted in his attempt to kill the girl and bestows on her the nickname "in fagra," the fair or the beautiful. She now goes to live with her parents.

The poet Gunnlaugr is introduced with a description that mixes positive and negative attributes: among the latter is an ugly nose and an impetuous and stubborn nature. He is "skáld mikit ok heldr níðskár ok kallaðr Gunnlaugr ormstunga" (ch. 4; "a gifted poet, albeit a somewhat abusive one, and was called Gunnlaug Serpent-tongue"). At the age of twelve, Gunnlaugr comes into conflict with his father over his wish to travel abroad. He goes to stay for a year with Þorsteinn and learns the law from him (an example of the oral transmission of legal knowledge—and so power—in this period). Gunnlaugr and Helga, whose golden hair is so long it completely covers her body, fall in love and Gunnlaugr tricks Þorsteinn into teaching him how to betroth himself to Helga: this is taken to be a joke at the time, though one feels Gunnlaugr may have meant more by it.

Hrafn Ǫnundarson, a good poet and the final member of the love triangle, is introduced in chapter 5. At this point, too, we are told that "þessu nær urðu þau tíðendi, er bezt hafa orðit hér á Íslandi, at landit varð allt kristit, ok allt folk hafnaði fornum átrúnaði" (ch. 5; "it was about this time that the best thing ever to have happened in Iceland occurred: the whole country became Christian and the entire population abandoned the old faith"). Gunnlaugr is now eighteen and his father at last allows him to go abroad. However, when he turns down the offer of horses from Þorsteinn, Helga's father, on the grounds that he is going abroad, but asks to marry Helga, Þorsteinn responds:

> Vita skyldir þú fyrst, hvat þú vildir. Ertu eigi ráðinn til útanferðar ok lætr þó, sem þú skylir kvángast? Er þat ekki jafnræði með ykkr Helgu, meðan þú ert svá óráðinn. (ch. 5)
>
> You should have worked out what you wanted in the first place. [. . .] Haven't you decided to go abroad? And yet you're carrying on as if you want to get married. It wouldn't be suitable for you and Helga to marry while you are so undecided.

The next day, Gunnlaugr enlists his father's help in arranging the marriage. Þorsteinn agrees that Helga will wait for three years while Gunnlaugr is abroad but not be formally betrothed to him. She is not consulted about the arrangement, which is made between the two fathers.

Gunnlaugr's confidence and impetuosity get him into trouble in Norway; its ruler, Earl Eríkr of Hlaðir, predicts that the eighteen-year-old will not live another eighteen years after Gunnlaugr's "serpent-tongue" is unleashed on one of his men. Gunnlaugr flees to England, where his praise poem makes a much better impression on King Aðalráðr (Æthelræd), who rewards him with a fur-lined scarlet cloak. The narrator here interjects another of his historical explanations, saying that at that time the same language was in use in England as in Denmark and Norway but that after England's conquest by William the Bastard (better known today as the Conqueror) everyone there speaks French (ch. 7). Neither statement is historically accurate, but the attempted explanation—and the implicit recognition of the unlikelihood of foreign rulers understanding skaldic verse addressed to them—is another instance of the narrator's sensitivity to the alterity of the past. From England Gunnlaugr travels to Dublin, where the inexperienced King Siggtryggr has to be advised by his treasurer not to give Gunnlaugr an inappropriately generous gift in exchange for the first praise poem anyone has addressed to him (ch. 8). After winning further recognition at the court of the earls of Orkney, Gunnlaugr travels to Sweden.

At the royal court in Uppsala, Gunnlaugr meets Hrafn. They become good friends but quarrel over the presentation of their praise poems to the Swedish king, and as Hrafn leaves Sweden he tells Gunnnlaugr that their friendship is at an end (ch. 9). On his return to Iceland, Hrafn sets about courting Helga, and when Gunnlaugr fails to return within the three-year period he had promised, a marriage between Hrafn and Helga is arranged. Gunnlaugr, meanwhile, leaves Sweden for England again before returning to Norway, from where he catches the last ship of the season back to Iceland. The poet Hallfreðr vandræðaskáld is onboard the ship and tells Gunnlaugr of the planned marriage of Helga and Hrafn. Gunnlaugr returns to his father's farm on the very night of the wedding, but an injury leaves him unable to go there to prevent it. The narrator reports of the wedding at Borg, "Er þat flestra manna sǫgn, at brúðrin væri heldr dǫpr" (ch. 11; "Most people say that the bride was rather gloomy").

A little after the wedding, Hrafn has a dream that he reports to Helga in verse. Helga realizes that Gunnlaugr must have returned and her marriage then falls apart. When Helga and Gunnlaugr meet at another marriage feast, it is clear that she still loves him: "eigi leyna augu, ef ann kona manni" (ch. 11; "if a woman loves a man, her eyes won't hide it"). Gunnlaugr's status has been enhanced by his time at royal courts abroad, and so has his appearance: he is wearing fine clothes given him by King Siggtryggr of Dublin. In private conversation, Gunnlaugr declares his continuing love for Helga in verse (including the stanza given as an example of dróttkvætt in ch. 2 above). He also gives Helga the scarlet cloak that King Æthelræd had given him. After this meeting, Helga rejects her husband, Hrafn (ch. 11).

Gunnlaugr challenges Hrafn to a duel at the Althing, something the narrator notes was legal "in those days." The fight ends inconsequentially and the next day the Althing passes a law to prevent the repetition of such incidents, so the duel is said to have been the last in Iceland. Hrafn suggests that the two rivals go abroad so that they can fight, and Gunnlaugr accepts. When they eventually meet in Sweden, Gunnlaugr cuts off Hrafn's leg and he has to balance on a tree stump (ch. 12). He says that he could continue if he were able to drink some water. Gunnlaugr offers to fetch some if Hrafn will promise not to trick him, but Hrafn breaks his promise and attacks Gunnlaugr as he offers his helmet full of water. Gunnlaugr accuses Hrafn of having behaved in an "unmanly way" ("ódrengiliga"); Hrafn agrees: "En þat gekk mér til þess, at ek ann þér eigi faðmlagsins Helgu innar fǫgru." (ch. 12; "I did it because I would not have you receive the embrace of Helga the Fair"). Gunnlaugr then kills Hrafn but later dies from his own wounds.

In a final chapter, the fathers of both Gunnlaugr and Hrafn have dreams in which their sons' deaths are revealed. Helga is married off again to a man called Þorkell but "she did not really love him" (ch. 13). The saga ends with a poignant scene in which the dying Helga asks for the cloak Gunnlaugr gave her and dies staring at it.

Most of the characters in *Gunnlaugs saga* are known from other sources, but Helga is known only from two references in *Egils saga* (chs. 79 and 87). These references seem to indicate the existence of oral traditions about the rivalry of Gunnlaugr and Hrafn in the period when that saga was written (ca. 1220–1230). The saga's apparent plausibility as a historical account is enhanced by the references to the legal history of dueling and to the exposure of infants and its explanation of how Gunnlaugr was understood in England. We know the legal and linguistic history to be inaccurate, but the attempts at explanation demonstrate a sensitivity to the difference of past from present and a desire to explain how the one has created the other.

The writer was probably working with verses already in existence. The skaldic verse contained in the poets' sagas is by far the most important source material for their writers. The court poems in praise of rulers are the most likely to be authentic. It is much harder to date the other verse in these sagas, including the love poetry. Kari Ellen Gade (2001) argues on linguistic grounds that much of the verse attributed to Kormákr and Hallfreðr may date to the right period, the late tenth to the early eleventh century, but this need not mean it is correctly attributed to those poets. The verse ascribed to Bjǫrn and Gunnlaugr seems mostly to be later in date, but earlier than the saga-prose, so the saga writers could have thought it was authentic.

The prominence of overseas adventures in the poets' sagas makes for comparison with those *þættir* that recount the experiences of Icelanders abroad (the *útanferðar þættir* cf. Lindow 2001). As in those *þættir*, one can detect an ambivalent view of the Norwegian monarchy and its relation to Iceland. The kings recognize and reward Icelanders for their poetic and other skills, but, on the other hand, they are sometimes perceived as a potential threat to Icelandic independence. King Óláfr Tryggvason becomes the central figure here, esteemed for his role in the conversion of Iceland but with an awareness that his interest in the island and its affairs prefigured a thirteenth-century power play that resulted in Iceland submitting to Norwegian rule.

The poets' sagas both reflect and perpetuate certain possible ways of being a man: as poet, warrior, lover, husband, ruler. The rivalries between lovers bring men into relation with each other, as well as with the woman they love, who in turn finds herself "between men," both in the sense of between rivals and, often, as an object exchanged between father and future husband. Although love rivalry is much less prominent in the longest of the sagas about an Icelandic poet, *Egils saga*, many other themes in these shorter poets' sagas resonate in that text, to which we will now turn.

Egils saga Skallagrímssonar

The tenth-century Viking-poet Egill Skallgrímsson is the first Icelandic skald known to have produced praise poems for a king. Yet Bruce Lincoln writes that the saga about him is "an openly anti-monarchic text and a great champion of Icelandic independence" (2014: 44). *Egils saga* is generally agreed to have been written circa 1230.[7] The oldest manuscript fragment probably dates from the mid-thirteenth century and is the earliest evidence for the existence of the text, but the complete saga is preserved in three redactions from the fourteenth century onward. The fullest and earliest of these is in the compilation of sagas of Icelanders known as Möðruvallabók, but modern editions supplement this text from other manuscripts.[8]

Egils saga is not as exclusively focused on the career of the central figure as other sagas of skalds, does not make nearly so much of the theme of love rivalry, and is on a much more ambitious scale. Egill is the central figure from chapter 31 to chapter 86 of the saga; the first thirty chapters recount deeds of his grandfather, Kveld-Úlfr, and father, Skalla-Grímr, and a final chapter after Egill's death (87) provides information about his notable descendants.

The saga begins by introducing the shape-shifter Kveld-Úlfr and his two sons, the handsome Þórólfr and the dark and ugly Grímr. The opening chapters are set in the period when Haraldr hárfagri was uniting the kingdom of Norway under his rule; Kveld-Úlfr refuses to be drawn into the conflict between his local king and Haraldr. The rewards and perils of proximity to kings is a prominent theme throughout much of the rest of the saga. Chapter 4 tells of the discovery of Iceland, a new land that attracts many of those unable or unwilling to endure Haraldr's rule in Norway. Although Kveld-Úlfr foresees that his family will not benefit from connections with Haraldr, his son Þórólfr joins the king and fights with him at the decisive Battle of Hafrsfjǫrðr (ch. 9). Afterward, Þórólfr creates enemies for himself in a dispute over property with the sons of Hildiríðr, who succeed in slandering him to the king; Þórólfr is trapped in a house that is set on fire, breaks out, and receives a fatal final blow from the king himself (ch. 22). Þórólfr's brother Grímr—known on account of premature hair loss as Skalla-Grímr, "Bald-Grim"—seeks compensation from King Haraldr but refuses to serve the king in his brother's place. Skalla-Grímr and his father set off for Iceland. Kveld-Úlfr dies and his body is cast overboard; Skalla-Grímr then settles in Iceland, where his father's body comes ashore (ch. 28).

Egill Skallagrímsson is introduced, with his brother Þórólfr, in chapter 31. Like his namesake uncle, Þórólfr is fair-haired, good-looking, and much loved; Egill is ugly, eloquent, physically strong, dark-haired, and difficult to deal with. He is also presented as a precocious poet; the saga quotes two verses he is said to have composed at the age of three. An episode follows describing the elopement of Bjǫrn Brynjólfsson with Þóra, the sister of Skalla-Grímr's foster-brother. Þórólfr Skallagrímsson helps reconcile his father with Bjǫrn and journeys with the latter to Norway to make peace with Þóra's brother. While in Norway Þórólfr repeats his namesake uncle's mistake and becomes fatefully involved with the Norwegian royal family, befriending and going raiding with King Haraldr's favorite son, Eiríkr blóðøx (Bloodaxe). After returning to Iceland, Þórólfr brings Ásgerðr, the daughter of Bjǫrn and Þóra, to Norway. He also brings his brother Egill, who was a troublesome youth: as a seven-year-old he kills a playmate (ch. 40), and at the age of twelve he comes into conflict with his father. Þórólfr and Egill stay with the chieftain Þórir, whose son, Arinbjǫrn, befriends Egill. Þórólfr marries Ásgerðr. Egill meets King Eiríkr at a feast and gets very drunk; Queen Gunnhildr and the host Bárðr try to poison Egill, but he uses runes to destroy the drinking horn and slays Bárðr. Arinbjǫrn persuades his father to reconcile Egill with the king, and Þórir pays compensation. Egill then goes raiding in the Baltic.

Egill and Þórólfr next sail to England, then under the rule of King Aðalsteinn (Æthelstan). The brothers are prime-signed while there—a preliminary to baptism allowing those accepting it to mix with Christians—and fight for Aðalsteinn against Óláfr of Scotland in a battle at Vínheiðr (chs. 52–54). This battle is generally identified with the one known from Anglo-Saxon sources as the Battle of Brunanburh, which took place in 937. Þórólfr is killed in the battle, but the victorious Aðalsteinn compensates Egill for the death of his brother and Egill composes a poem in the king's praise.

In chapter 56, Egill marries his brother's widow, Ásgerðr; his unhappiness before doing so and sudden change of mood when the marriage takes place may suggest a previously hidden desire for his brother's wife. If so, there is a hint here of the typical *skáldasögur* theme of rivalry between men over a woman. When Ásgerðr's father dies, Egill becomes involved in a dispute over the inheritance, which is seized by her brother-in-law, Berg-Ǫnundr, supported by King Eiríkr and Queen Gunnhildr. As a result, Egill is exiled from Norway. Before returning to Iceland, however, he kills Berg-Ǫnundr and sets up a *níðstǫng*, "scorn-pole," cursing the king and queen to drive them from the land.

Egill's curse takes effect when Eiríkr is driven out of his kingdom by Hákon, the foster-son of Aðalsteinn of England. Eiríkr takes refuge in England and is given control of Northumbria by King Aðalsteinn. Gunnhildr casts a spell to deprive Egill of peace until she sees him again. He goes abroad for the third time but is shipwrecked off the Northumbrian coast and seeks out his friend Arinbjǫrn, who is in Eiríkr's company (ch. 59). They go to the king to plead for Egill's life. Egill is given a night's reprieve, during which he composes a poem in praise of his erstwhile enemy, Eiríkr: this is known as *Hǫfuðlausn*, "head-ransom." Eiríkr is sufficiently impressed by Egill's performance of his praise poem that he allows Egill to go free (chs. 60–61). After further adventures abroad, Egill returns to Iceland. When Eiríkr Bloodaxe is killed, Arinbjǫrn returns to Norway and Egill makes a final foreign trip to visit his long-standing and loyal friend (ch. 67). The prominence of this friendship in the saga faintly echoes the male-male bond between the sworn brothers of *Fóstbrœðra saga*.

Egill's skill with runes is again demonstrated in chapter 72, when he realizes that runes carved to cure a farmer's daughter are in fact making her worse. He destroys the runes and carves new ones that effect a cure.

In the final chapters of the saga, we see a different Egill at home in Iceland in old age, preoccupied above all with his poetry, though still able to stand up for his family when required (as in chs. 80–82). When his son Bǫðvarr is drowned, Egill locks himself in his bed closet and refuses to eat or drink until tricked into taking sustenance by his daughter Þorgerðr (ch. 78). She persuades him to make a memorial poem, *Sonatorrek* ("Loss of Sons": the earlier death of his son Gunnarr is awkwardly mentioned for the first time at this point). This long chapter (78) also includes a poem, *Arinbjarnarkviða*, in praise of Egill's friend Arinbjǫrn.

In old age, Egill befriends a young poet, Einarr Helgason, and after the death of his wife goes to live with his daughter Þórdís and her husband. A memorable picture of the elderly Egill is painted in chapter 85, where he is mocked by women for his decrepitude and laments in verse the ravages of old age in strikingly gendered terms (see pp. 72–73 above). Like his father before him, he is unwilling for his heirs to benefit from his treasure, and the last thing he does before his death is to hide the two chests of silver he acquired on his foreign travels.

The saga ends with Egill's son-in-law converting to Christianity and having a church built, to which Þórdís has Egill's bones moved. They are said to have been later dug up and found to be larger than any other man's. Chapter 87 provides a brief account of Egill's notable descendants.

As can be seen from this summary, much of *Egils saga* takes place outside Iceland, where the experience of Egill and other members of his family with kings justifies Lincoln's description of the saga as "anti-monarchic."

As Gabriel Turville-Petre writes, "It is widely agreed that Egill [. . .] was the most successful of the scalds or Norse poets" (1976: 15).[9] *Egils saga* refers to six major poems by its eponymous poet, and texts of three of them are preserved in connection with the saga. Of these, only one (*Arin-bjarnarkviða*) is preserved with the saga in Möðruvallabók (at the end of the saga, rather than at the point the poem is mentioned in ch. 78; this poem is not preserved in the other main manuscripts). Modern editions normally supply the texts of the other two poems at the appropriate points in the text from the other redactions: *Hǫfuðlausn* in ch. 60 and *Sonatorrek* (preserved only in Ketilsbók) in ch. 78, where Möðruvallabók gives just the first stanza. All that remains of the other three lengthy poems are the first stanza of two shield poems (chs. 80 and 81) and a stanza and refrain from a poem in praise of King Aðalsteinn/Æthelstan of England. The saga is also a rich source of individual verses, mostly attributed to Egill. Most of the verse in the saga is generally accepted as authentic and an important source for the saga prose, though some of it is almost certainly not by Egill (including, for example, the poetry allegedly composed at the age of three).

Learned physiognomic literature influences the characterizations of two branches of Egill's family: he and his father are dark-haired, ugly, and prematurely bald, whereas Egill's brother and uncle, both called Þórólfr, are light-haired and handsome. Poetic gifts and longevity are limited to the ugly side of the family, perhaps reflecting the influence of medieval theories of the humor of melancholy, as well as the stereotypically "Odinic" aspects of the poets in other *skáldasögur*. The saga-author must also have known a variety of other sources, including historical materials on the kings of Norway and the poets' sagas of Kormákr and Hallfreðr. There are close parallels with passages in *Heimskringla*, the history of the kings of Norway traditionally attributed to Snorri Sturluson, and several scholars since the early nineteenth century have attributed the authorship of *Egils saga* to Snorri: he was a descendant of Skalla-Grímr and owned estates formerly belonging to his ancestor's family; his well-documented interests in Norwegian history and Icelandic poetry would also have made Egill an attractive subject for him. Some stylistic analysis has supported the claim of common authorship for *Heimskringla* and *Egils saga*.[10]

Egill's character is a compelling but highly contradictory one. At times he behaves as a cruel, coarse, and avaricious Viking, yet he is also an eloquent poet of paternal grief, a loyal and appreciative friend, and, in his own way, even a religious man. Assuming that *Sonatorrek* is authentic, it provides an almost uniquely personal insight into the relationship between a Norse-speaking pagan and his god, Óðinn.

The Vínland Sagas: *Eiríks saga rauða* (*Eirik the Red's Saga*)

Two sagas that focus on the settlement of Greenland, the discovery of North America, and encounters there with the indigenous population are known as the Vínland sagas.[11] Although most of the events they recount take place outside Iceland, they concern characters of Icelandic origin and the narratives begin and end in Iceland, so these two sagas are conventionally counted among the sagas of Icelanders. Vínland (Anglicized to Vinland by omitting the accent) was the name given by the Norse-speakers to part of the land that they found west of Greenland (the other parts being called Helluland and Markland).[12] *Grœnlendinga saga* (*The Saga of the Greenlanders*) was perhaps composed circa 1200; it is incorporated in separate sections in the late-fourteenth-century Flateyjarbók manuscript. *Eiríks saga rauða* (*Eirik the Red's Saga*) has been variously dated to the early or later thirteenth century. The main surviving versions are in the fourteenth-century Hauksbók (followed in many editions and translations) and the early-fifteenth-century Skálholtsbók (which is the version translated in CS). Many scholars have seen *Eiríks saga* as a more tightly structured adaptation of *Grœnlendinga saga*, but Ólafur Halldórsson's argument that similarities between the two texts could arise from independent reliance on oral traditions has been influential in recent decades (Ólafur Halldórsson 1985, followed in Gísli Sigurðsson and Kunz 2008: xvii, for example). Although shorter, *Grœnlendinga saga* recounts six voyages to Vínland, as against the three in *Eiríks saga*. In *Grœnlendinga saga*,

Bjarni Herjólfsson glimpses Vínland before Leifr Eiríksson's "discovery" of the land; *Eiríks saga* consistently favors Leifr and so makes no mention of Bjarni's preempting him. Freydís Eiríksdóttir, whom we memorably met in chapter 1 above, is portrayed more positively in *Eiríks saga* than in *Grænlendinga saga*.

Knowledge of Vínland in medieval Iceland and Scandinavia is confirmed by Adam of Bremen writing in the 1060s, Ari Þorgilsson in early-twelfth-century Iceland, the probably mid-thirteenth-century anonymous Norwegian *Historia Norwegie*, and the so-called *Geographical Treatise* from twelfth- or thirteenth-century Iceland. Trips to Markland for timber continued until at least 1347, when the Icelandic Annals record such a trip for the last time. While these texts indicate that Norse-speakers discovered territory west of Greenland and encountered there a people whom they named Skrælings, several details appear purely fictional to the modern reader. *Historia Norwegie* describes the Skrælings as "manikins" (Latin *homunciones*; Kunin and Phelpstead 2001: 3), and the *Geographical Treatise* claims that land reaches across the north from north Norway across to Greenland and that some people think Vínland is connected to Africa (Kålund 1908: 12).

Besides references in medieval texts, a range of other evidence has been employed in modern discussions of the Vínland experience. A map discovered by an American bookseller in 1953 became known as the Vínland Map. It appears to be a medieval map that shows Vínland as an island west of Greenland and claims were made for a dating circa 1440. If authentic, this would be the earliest representation of the New World. In fact, the map almost certainly dates from after 1920 and is merely the most famous of several American Viking hoaxes.[13]

Genuine archaeological evidence to support the accounts in the Vínland sagas was discovered during excavations conducted by Helge and Anne Stine Ingstad at L'Anse aux Meadows, Newfoundland, between 1961 and 1968. Their finds included eight house sites, boathouses, cooking pits, a charcoal kiln, bog-iron (unknown to indigenous North Americans at this time), and a cloak pin of a type connected with Sogn, Norway. Most of the material is typically Norse. The site seems to have been used for just a few years circa 1000. Too far north for vines to grow, L'Anse aux Meadows is unlikely to be Vínland itself but rather a base for explorations further south.

Although archaeology confirmed a historical basis to the Vínland sagas, they cannot be regarded as entirely reliable historical sources. Their genealogies and interest in place-names and topography suggest a narrator intent on presenting what (was believed to have) happened. But, in addition to marvelous material that is implausible to modern readers, one can also detect ideological bias behind the apparently objective narratives. *Eiríks saga*, for example, gives Þorfinnr Karlsefni greater prominence than he has in *Grænlendinga saga*. He happens to have been an ancestor of Haukr Erlendsson, in whose manuscript, Hauksbók, *Eiríks saga* is preserved. As we will see in the discussion that follows, *Eiríks saga* is also shaped by a strongly vested interest in the struggle between paganism and Christianity.

Eiríks saga begins with early settlers of Iceland who will be the ancestors of Guðríðr, who will marry one of Eiríkr rauði's sons. With the introduction of Auðr djúpúðga, the matriarchal settler who also appears in *Laxdœla saga* and other sagas (ch. 1), the writer's interest in religious history is immediately apparent. Auðr is a Christian who is said to pray in Iceland on a hill called Krosshólar, where she has crosses set up. Eiríkr rauði comes with his father to Iceland because of his involvement in killings in their native Norway, but he is then outlawed from Iceland because he kills there, too. He goes in search of a previously spotted new land and becomes its first settler, giving it the name Greenland "því at hann kvað men þat mjǫk mundu fýsa þangat, ef landit héti vel" (ch. 2; "as he said people would be attracted to go there if it had a favorable name"). Among those attracted to the island is Guðríðr's father, Þorbjǫrn, whose poor financial situation leads him to take his family there.

Natural environment and the supernatural are linked when there is a very poor season (or great famine: *hallæri mikit*) in Greenland (ch. 4) and this leads the islanders to consult a prophetess (*spákona*), Þorbjǫrg, who is known as *lítil-vǫlva* ("little sibyl"). The account of the ritual she performs in order to learn the future is full of vivid detail, but whether it preserves genuine information about pre-Christian practices or is a colorful imaginative construction of the saga-writer remains uncertain. Although reluctant on account of her Christian faith, Guðríðr is pressed into assisting Þorbjǫrg as she is the only person present who knows the required chant. Þorbjǫrg foresees not only an end to the period of adversity but also an illustrious future for Guðríðr's descendants, over whom a "bright ray will shine" (ch. 4; "skína bjartar geislar"). This foreshadows the genealogy at the end of the saga, which celebrates the line of Icelandic bishops who traced their ancestry back to Guðríðr.

The religious theme continues when, on a trip to Norway, Eiríkr rauði's son Leifr is asked by King Óláfr Tryggvason to bring about the conversion of Greenland to Christianity (ch. 5). Earlier texts (including, for example, *Historia Norwegie*) ascribed Greenland's conversion to the Icelanders. In promoting the idea that it was instigated by the Norwegian king, *Eiríks saga* seems here to be influenced by the life of Óláfr by the Icelandic monk Gunnlaugr Leifsson, composed in Latin circa 1200 but surviving now only in fragments translated into Old Icelandic and incorporated in other texts. Óláfr was never officially declared a saint (unlike his namesake and successor, Óláfr Haraldsson), but Gunnlaugr's life of the king was hagiographic in approach and ascribed the conversion of much of the north to Óláfr's initiative.

On his way back to Greenland to fulfil Óláfr's commission, Leifr is blown off course and discovers a new land to the west of Greenland. It is described in idealized terms that recall the descriptions of an Icelandic golden age discussed in chapter 3 above: "Váru þar hveitiakrar sjálfsánir ok vínviðr vaxinn. Þar váru þau tré, er mǫsurr heita" (ch. 5; "Fields of self-sown wheat and vines were growing there; also there were trees known as maple"). When Leifr returns to Greenland, he preaches the new faith and informs the islanders of the interest taken in them by Norway's king by passing on messages from Óláfr. His father, Eiríkr rauði, is reluctant to convert, but Eiríkr's wife, Þjóðhildr, is eager to do so and has a church built. She also refuses to sleep with Eiríkr any more, much to his chagrin. Whether this is because they now follow different religions or because she espouses chastity after her conversion is not entirely clear. Her behavior does, however, suggest an agency and independence on her part that resonates with the other portraits of confidently strong-willed women in this saga.

When Þorsteinn Eiríksson marries Guðríðr Þorbjarnardóttir, the two families on which the saga has focused are brought together (ch. 6). A sickness strikes the area where they live; ghosts of those killed by disease are seen by a farmer's wife and, after he has succumbed to the disease himself, Þorsteinn Eiríksson returns from the dead to inform his wife that burial practices must now be brought into conformity with the church's requirements. When her father also dies, the widowed Guðríðr goes to live with her father-in-law Eiríkr.

Guðríðr does not, however, remain a widow for long. A man called Þorfinnr Karlsefni comes to Greenland, spends Yule with Eiríkr, and marries Guðríðr (ch. 7). They set out for Vínland with others, including Eiríkr's illegitimate daughter, Freydís, and a disagreeable man called Þórhallr veiðimaðr (the hunter). They endure a harsh winter that leads to a shortage of food because they were ill-prepared. Þórhallr is discovered lying on his back, staring, and mumbling; soon after, a whale is caught, but its meat makes everyone ill. Þorhallr claims that the whale was a reward from the god Thor for the poem he composed in his honor, thus explaining his earlier mumbling. The others then refuse to eat more of the whale and throw it back into the sea. Although the narrative seems to accept that honoring the pagan god did indeed cause the appearance of the whale, the greater power of the Christian God is apparent when the weather improves after the company reject the whale meat (ch. 8). Þórhallr himself comes to an appropriate end when his ship is separated from the others and blown to Ireland, where he is enslaved and later dies (ch. 9). The saga's interest in the conflict between paganism and Christianity is at its most obviously partisan in these episodes.

Karlsefni's company proceeds to a place known as Hóp (meaning, "Tidal Pool"): "Þeir fundu þar á landi sjálfsána hveitiakra [...] en vínvið [...] Hverr lœkr var þar fullr af fiskum" (ch. 10; "There they found fields of self-sown wheat [...] and vines [...] Every stream was teeming with fish"). This description echoes that when Leifr first sees Vínland (ch. 5). The expedition then encounters and trades with Skrælings, until the latter are frightened by a bull. The Skrælings return to attack and the pregnant Freydís confronts both the Skrælings and her companions' cowardice. Karlsefni's company realizes that despite the richness of the land, the constant threat of attack from the indigenous population means that they must leave Vínland.

Another unfamiliar threat emerges when Þorvaldr Eiríksson is killed by a uniped (ch. 12), a one-footed imaginary being often associated with Africa in the Middle Ages (following Isidore of Seville's *Etymologies*). This suggests that the *Geographical Treatise* was not alone in imagining a land link between North America and Africa (in *Grœnlendinga saga*, Þorvaldr is more realistically shot not by a uniped but by Skrælings). Tensions now also emerge among the settlers: "Gengu menn þá mjǫk í sveitir, ok varð þeim til um konur, ok vildu þeir, er ókvæntir váru, sœkja til í hendr þeim, sem kvæntir váru" (ch. 12; "Many quarrels arose, as the men who had no wives sought to take those of the married men"). After capturing two native boys who are later taught the Norse language, the company returns to Greenland. Bjarni Grimólfsson and half his men enter waters infested by timber-eating worms, and although they manage to protect one ship with tar, it will accommodate only half the men. Bjarni swaps places with one of those whom the casting of lots consigned to death and is presumed lost. The final chapter of the saga tells of the journey of Karlsefni and Guðríðr to Iceland, where their descendants include three Icelandic bishops.[14]

This discussion of *Eiríks saga* reveals the ways in which it draws on various kinds of source material to present the past in a way that celebrates ancestors of three Icelandic bishops as key players in the clash of Christianity and paganism in Greenland and Vínland. The grounding of the Vínland sagas in history, corroborated to some extent by archaeological finds in Newfoundland, depends upon the passing on of oral traditions from the early eleventh century to the thirteenth century, when the sagas were written down. The saga authors also drew on written sources including other sagas and more learned traditions (for the uniped, for example).

Eiríks saga celebrates the roles of King Óláfr Tryggvason and Leifr Eiríksson in conversion, contrasting them with figures who resist the new faith (Eiríkr and Þorhallr). Identity is also defined by difference from the Skrælings. The reliance of the adventurers and settlers on their natural environment becomes apparent during food shortages in both Greenland and Vínland and is reflected too in the idealized descriptions of both lands. The marvelous, superhuman, or supernatural also figures prominently, from the uniped and the Sea of Worms to the provision that Thor and the Christian God make for their followers. Sexual desire causes conflict among the would-be settlers, and when the men fail to live up to ideals of gendered behavior during the Skræling attack, Freydís emphasizes her womanhood by confronting the attackers bare-breasted. The saga features several strong female characters besides Freydís, from the matriarchal Auðr, through the "little sibyl," to Guðríðr, ancestor of bishops. The genealogy that ends the saga connects the distant to the much more recent past, underlining the relevance of the story to a thirteenth-century sense of Icelandic identity.

Outlaw Sagas: *Gísla saga* and *Grettis saga*

A group of three sagas focus on the lives of men who become outlaws: *Gísla saga Súrssonar*, *Grettis saga Ásmundarsonar*, and *Harðar saga Grímkelssonar* (also known as *Harðar saga ok Holmverja*).[15] These sagas portray life on the margins, literally outside the law, and explore the character and psychology of men who manage to survive for an unusually long time in this state. According to *Gísla saga* (ch. 22), Gísli Súrsson was the second-longest surviving outlaw in Icelandic history, after Grettir Ásmundarson, the hero of *Grettis saga*. The terminology of outlawry in Old Norse employs natural imagery to convey a sense of outlaws as beyond human society: words for outlaw include *vargr* (literally "wolf"), *skógarmaðr* ("forest man"), and *urðarmaðr* ("man of the wilds"). The term for full outlawry, *skóggangr*, literally means "going into the forest."

Fate (or luck) plays an unusually prominent role in both *Gísla saga* and *Grettis saga* (the two outlaw sagas on which we will concentrate in this section). Other themes also connect the outlaw sagas (Clunies Ross 2010a: 134): the central characters are difficult when young, have poor relationships with their fathers (though Grettir and Gísli are both very close to their mother), and compose occasional verse.

Gísla saga is generally dated to the first third of the thirteenth century, or to 1230–1250, but Andersson describes this as "even more insecure than most datings" (2006: 77). The saga survives in two more or less complete versions of different lengths; there are also fragments of a third. The two full versions differ considerably, especially in the first part of the saga, set in Norway. The longer version is nearly a quarter as long again as the shorter version of the saga on which most critical attention has been focused.[16] Of all sagas of Icelanders, *Gísla saga* makes most striking use of eddaic motifs (Clark 2012: 89). It is also an especially interesting saga from the point of view of gender and sexuality; as Judith Jesch writes, "*Gísla saga* explores the tensions of married life and personal relationships in early Iceland in a way that no other saga does" (1991: 193).[17]

Gísla saga opens in Norway and introduces several features that will re-appear later in the saga. A berserkr called Bjǫrn inn blakki (the pale) kills an uncle of the saga's eponymous hero in a duel, and Gísli's namesake, an-other uncle, takes vengeance using a sword called Grá-síðr ("Gray-side"). This sword, later made into a spear, plays a fateful role at several points in the saga. Sexual themes are also introduced when Gísli's widowed sister-in-law, Ingibjǫrg, suggests to Gísli that she may always have preferred him to her late husband: "Eigi var ek af því Ara gift, at ek vilda þik eigi heldr átt hafa" (ch. 1; "I did not marry Ari [Gísli's brother] because I preferred him to you"). Gísli marries her after killing the berserkr. He refuses to return Gray-side to its owner, which leads to his death.

Þorbjǫrn inherits the farm and among his sons is the Gísli who gives his name to the saga. In the second duel of the saga, Gísli stands in for a man called Kolbjǫrn in a contest with a man called Skeggi. Thinking that both Kolbjǫrn and Gísli are too cowardly to fight, Skeggi has an insulting carving made of them both. But Gísli does turn up and cuts off Skeggi's leg.

Þorbjǫrn, Gísli, and his brother Þorkell survive an attempt by Skeggi's men to burn them in their home by dowsing the flames with whey, from which Þorbjǫrn acquires the nickname *súrr* ("whey"): Gísli's patronymic Súrsson comes from that nickname. The family flee Norway for Iceland. There Gísli marries a woman called Auðr, whose brother is Vésteinn, and a man called Þorgrímr marries Gísli's sister Þórdís (ch. 5). The brothers Gísli and Þorkell, together with their brother-in-law Þorgrímr and Gísli's brother-in-law Vésteinn, take part in a vividly described ritual of swearing blood-brotherhood, promising to take vengeance for one another, but the arrangement falls apart when Þorgrímr refuses to bind himself to Vésteinn, and Gísli then declines to forge ties with Þorgrímr. This episode sets up the central conflict of the saga: Gísli will later be outlawed for killing one brother-in-law to avenge the other.

After returning to Iceland from abroad, Þorkell overhears his wife, Ásgerðr, ask Gísli's wife, Auðr, to cut a shirt for her husband (i.e., Þorkell himself). In replying that Ásgerðr would not be asking someone else to do it if the shirt were for Vésteinn (Auðr's brother), Auðr implies knowledge of an adulterous love affair. Ásgerðr in turn refers to Auðr seeing a lot of Þorgrímr before she married Gísli, but Auðr says that she has never been unfaithful to her husband. This declaration prefigures the deep loyalty that she will show him later in the saga. Having learned of his wife's infidelity, Þorgrímr at first refuses to have Ásgerðr in bed with him, but when she threatens to divorce him and take back her bride-price and dowry, he reconsiders and they are reconciled. When Auðr tells her husband, Gísli, of the conversation, he declares that "þat mun fram koma, sem auðit verðr" (ch. 9; "whatever is meant to happen will happen").

Though his belief in fate lasts throughout his life, the saga notes that Gísli has stopped sacrificing to the pagan gods since spending time in (Christian) Denmark (ch. 10). The saga presents him as a "noble heathen," close to Christianity but living before Iceland's conversion.[18] He is contrasted with a character called Þorgrímr nef (nose), who is "seiðskratti, sem mestr mátti verða" (ch. 11; "the worst kind of sorcerer imaginable"). Gísli's brother has had Þorgrímr forge the fragments of the sword Grayside into a spearhead. Despite Gísli's attempt to warn him away, Vésteinn comes to stay with Gísli after returning to Iceland and is killed in bed by a man with a spear (ch. 13). Gísli then reveals to his wife that dreams he had had before the killing revealed who the killer is—the jealous Þorgrímr reveals in a verse in the next chapter that he was responsible. Gísli fulfils his oath to Vésteinn by taking the spear Gray-side, which had been left behind after the killing, and going to his brother-in-law's farm. In an extraordinary scene, he goes to the bed closet where Þórdís and Þorgrímr are asleep and accidentally touches his sister's breast. Waking and thinking this is her husband, she asks Þorgrímr why his hand is so cold. Þorgrímr asks if she wants him to "turn toward her" (i.e., be intimate) but falls asleep again when she does not reply. Gísli then warms his hand and again wakes Þorgrímr, who thinks his wife is seeking his attention, but Gísli pulls away the bed clothes and spears Þorgrímr to death, an act of penetration obviously sexualized by the context (ch. 16).

Þorgrímr's brother Borkr and his cousin Eyjólfr seek Þorgrímr's slayer. Borkr pays the sorcerer Þorgrímr nef to cast a spell ensuring that Þorgrímr's killer cannot be assisted by others, occasioning strong condemnation of magic by the narrator (ch. 18). Borkr marries his brother's widow, Gísli's sister Þórdís. She interprets a verse Gísli has spoken to mean that he killed her previous husband and she informs Borkr of this, implicitly inciting him to kill her own brother: "Eru opt kǫld kvenna ráð" (ch. 19; "Women's counsel is often cold"), as Borkr says.

The complex web of familial conflict and loyalty in the saga is reminiscent of, and indebted to, heroic poetry preserved in the *Poetic Edda*. Gísli himself recognizes this when he laments that his sister is not like the legendary Guðrún Gjúkadóttir whose loyalty was to her blood relatives and who killed her husband to avenge her brothers (ch. 19, verse 12).

Borkr takes Gísli to court for the killing of Þorgrímr and Gísli is declared an outlaw and remains one until his death (ch. 21). The rest of the saga tells of his efforts to avoid being caught, involving disguises and tricks that show great resourcefulness, but "þó varð hann eigi gæfu-maðr" (ch. 27; "luck was not with him"). He has already had prophetic dreams, but now these become a much more prominent part of the narrative; in particular he now frequently dreams of two women, one in black and one in white. The good, white woman promises Gísli he will go to a luxurious and beautiful hall after his death (ch. 30). The dreams lead Gísli to fear the dark, something he shares with the other great saga outlaw, Grettir Ásmundarson (ch. 33; see below).

Eyjólfr offers Auðr money to betray her husband, the first of two such attempts he makes, but she remains loyal (ch. 23). When he tries again, Auðr asks to see the three hundred silver pieces he has offered her (ch. 31). When she starts to count them in her lap, her foster-daughter rushes to tell Gísli he is being betrayed, but his faith in his wife does not waver (ch. 32). Auðr puts the money in a purse and hits Eyjolfr with it, drawing blood and shaming him: "Skaltu þat muna, vesall maðr, meðan þú lifir at kona hefir barit þik" (ch. 32; "Remember for as long as you live, wretch, that a woman has struck you"). Eyjólfr's order to his men ("Hafið hendr á hundinum ok drepi, þó at blauðr sé"; "Seize the cur and kill it, though it be a bitch") confirms his cowardice and unmanliness: the men refuse to harm Auðr.

When Eyjólfr and his men finally catch up with Gísli, the two men taunt each other with accusations of cowardice and unmanliness (ch. 34). Eyjólfr indeed prefers to order others to do the fighting, even though Auðr is fighting with a club on her husband's side. Against overwhelming numbers, Gísli puts up heroic resistance but is finally killed, for despite his strength and accomplishments he lacked luck (ch. 36).

When Eyjólfr reports to Bǫrkr that their enemy has been killed, Bǫrkr's wife (Gísli's sister) wounds Eyjólfr and declares herself divorced from Bǫrkr, even though she had instigated action against Gísli by revealing his confession to the killing of Þorgrímr. In the final chapter of the saga, we are told that Auðr and Vésteinn's widow, Gunnhildr, left Iceland together for Denmark, became Christians there, and went to Rome on pilgrimage, never to return.

Gísla saga powerfully explores the conflicting demands of family, marriage, and friendship in the working out of a feud. Men are heroes and cowards, exemplifying masculine ideals or falling short of them; women incite men to violence, but Auðr exemplifies faithful devotion to her husband. The white and black women of Gísli's dreams embody a moral or even spiritual dimension that also finds expression in Gísli's abandoning of the pagan gods and his wife's death as a pilgrim in Rome. Gísli is portrayed as an unlucky victim of fate, but, though he cannot avoid final defeat, he resists heroically for as long as he can.

Grettir Ásmundarson, the hero of the other outlaw saga that we will consider here, probably lived from a little before 1000 until about 1031. *Grettis saga Ásmundarsonar*, the saga about him, is usually thought to be among the last of the sagas of Icelanders to be written and is generally dated to the early fourteenth century, circa 1310–1320 (though Heslop 2006: 75–78 favors a late-fourteenth or early-fifteenth-century date).

Grettis saga is widely regarded as one of the four greatest sagas of Ice-

landers, along with *Egils saga, Laxdœla saga,* and *Njáls saga.* The prominence of supernatural creatures in the narrative (ghosts, trolls, berserkers)
and its use of folklore motifs set it apart somewhat from other sagas of Icelanders, and it shares many elements with the legendary sagas, or *fornaldarsögur.* In other ways, however, *Grettis saga* is a typical *Íslendingasaga*:
feud, the law, and outlawry are central to its narrative. As in texts such as
Eiríks saga rauða and *Gunnlaugs saga*, we see the importance of sea-voy-
ages across the North Atlantic, with Grettir's ancestors leaving Norway
to raid in the British Isles and then settle in Iceland, and Grettir himself
making fateful journeys to Norway before returning to live the life of an
outlaw in Iceland. The love-triangle theme explored in the poets' sagas re-
appears in the final section of *Grettis saga*, too, and Grettir's sexual activities and explicit poems invite comparison with the exploration of sexual
themes in other sagas of Icelanders.

Grettis saga has a clear structure, though like all the longer sagas it has
an episodic construction. Chapters 1 to 13 are a kind of prologue: they deal
with Grettir's ancestors, especially his great-grandfather, Ǫnundr tréfótr
(Wooden-leg). Chapters 14–82 comprise a biography of Grettir from
boyhood to his death as an outlaw. This section divides into two parts:
the period before Grettir is outlawed (chs. 14–46) and the nineteen years
he survived as an outlaw (chs. 47–82). Chapters 83–93 form an epilogue
focusing on Grettir's Norwegian half-brother, Þorsteinn drómundr (the
Galleon): it tells of his vengeance for Grettir in Byzantium, his love affair
there with a married woman called Spes, and then their life in Norway
and their pilgrimage to Rome as penance for their adultery.

Grettis saga contains more than seventy verses, most attributed to Grettir. Several of his verses are unusually sexually explicit and a strong thread
of verbal skill and humor runs through the saga: jokes, verbal jousting,
sarcasm, and the telling use of proverbs and aphorisms.

Just as fate dominates *Gísla saga*, so characters refer to Grettir as
ógæfumaðr—a man of ill luck. His half-brother Þorsteinn, on the other
hand, is a lucky man. Grettir's luck notably fails him in his encounters
with sorcery and the supernatural. He fights three kinds of supernatural
opponent: berserkrs (in Norway), revenants (including the most famous
ghost in all the sagas, Glámr), and trolls.

In addition to folklore motifs, the text also has connections with foreign literatures. Perhaps most obviously, the final section of the saga, *Spesar þáttr*, contains motifs from the legend of Tristan and Isolde and is deeply influenced by romance. The troll-slayings in Bárðardalr (chs. 64–66), on the other hand, have been compared to Beowulf's fights against Grendel and Grendel's mother in the Anglo-Saxon heroic poem *Beowulf*. In both cases there are two separate fights, the first inside a building against a monster of one sex and the second against a monster of the other sex in a cave under or behind water. In both texts, the first monster escapes having lost an arm, and companions desert the hero when blood comes to the surface in the second fight. The nature of the connection between the two texts (if any) remains elusive.[19]

Grettis saga begins by introducing Ǫnundr. References in this opening chapter to his family's connection with King St Óláfr become significant later in the saga when Óláfr rejects Grettir despite their being related. Haraldr hárfagri is fighting his way to power in Norway and Ǫnundr joins Harald's opponents (ch. 2); they fight at the Battle of Hafrsfjǫrðr, the battle that is conventionally regarded as the moment Haraldr secured his right to the whole Norwegian kingdom: "Koma hér ok flestar sǫgur við, því at frá þeim er jafnan flest sagt, er sagan er helzt frá gǫr" (ch. 2; "Most sagas refer to it, because it is such matters that sagas usually relate"). In the battle Ǫnundr's leg is cut off; its prosthetic replacement gives him the nickname "Wooden-leg." For his opposition to Haraldr, Ǫnundr is exiled from Norway and travels to the Hebrides and then Ireland, stating, "Eigi nenna at gerask konungsþræll ok biðja þess, er hann átti áðr sjálfr" (ch. 3; "He had no intention of becoming the king's slave, he said, and begging for what he had previously owned himself"). Once he learns that his lands in Norway have been confiscated by Haraldr, Ǫnundr goes to Iceland but finds the best land has already been taken while he was in the British Isles and on Viking raids. He settles at the appropriately named Cold Back Mountain (Kaldbakr).

The saga now switches attention to Ǫnundr's son, Ásmundr, the future father of Grettir (ch. 13). In Norway, Ásmundr marries Rannveig and has a son, Þorsteinn drómundr (nicknamed "galleon" because he moves slowly), who will eventually take vengeance for his half-brother Grettir in the last part of the saga. Rannveig dies, Þorsteinn is left in Norway, and Ásmundr returns to Iceland, where he marries his second wife, Ásdís. Their son Grettir is described as handsome, red-haired, and freckled (ch. 14). He is a problem child, as illustrated in the way he undertakes tasks that he is given. When told to look after geese, he kills the goslings and breaks the wings of the geese; when asked to rub his father's back by the fire, he scratches it with a wool-comb; and when asked to look after the horses, he indulges in a sadistic act of cruelty by flaying the horse Kengála.

When he is fourteen, Grettir takes part in a ball game with other children; he ends up in a fight but comes off worse, remarking, "Þræll einn þegar hefnisk, en argr aldri" (ch. 15; "Only a slave takes vengeance at once, and a coward never"). During a quarrel over a food bag on a journey to the Althing, Grettir is taunted with the ball game incident and kills Skeggi, though in self-defence against an axe attack; he announces the killing in a cryptic verse, is sentenced to lesser outlawry, and sails for Norway (ch. 17).

Even on the sea journey, Grettir affronts and annoys people with his laziness and his insulting verses; the crew euphemistically accuse him of preferring to stroke the belly of the captain's wife than share in the work, though he later proves very helpful and wins their respect. This is the first hint of Grettir's sexual exploits: the woman is indeed said to sew his shirt sleeves for him, a sure sign of affection in the sagas.

In Norway, Grettir experiences his first encounter with the supernatural when he stays with Þorfinnr son of Kárr (ch. 18). The undead Kárr walks abroad, but Grettir is determined to dig into his grave mound; he takes the treasure from it, fights Kárr, decapitates him, and places his head against his buttocks. Þorfinnr is grateful for the treasure but denies Grettir a kind of sword known as a *sax* that he has set his heart on. While Þorfinnr is away, Grettir saves his wife and household from a group of berserk troublemakers (chs. 19–20) and is rewarded with the *sax* by Þorfinnr.

After returning to Iceland from his Norwegian exile (chs. 17–24), Grettir decides to do something about having been humiliated in the ball game when he was fourteen years old and fights with Auðunn (ch. 28). An opportunity for Grettir to test his strength comes at the haunted farm of Þórhallr Grímsson (ch. 32). Few want to work at Þórhallr's haunted farm, but a herdsman called Glámr agrees to look after his sheep. Glámr is said to be big, strong, and of a strange appearance; he declares that he is not afraid of ghosts. Glámr comes from Sweden, the last part of Scandinavia to convert to Christianity, and he refuses to enter a church or to fast on Christmas Eve. He is killed in a snowstorm that night by some kind of being that is never seen again; Glámr's body cannot be buried in church and will not lie quietly: he takes to riding on the roof of the house.

Þórhallr hires a new farmhand, Þorgautr, but he too goes missing at Christmas Eve and is found the next day with all his bones broken—by Glámr, it appears. A cowherd is then killed, followed by all the livestock. Þórhallr leaves the farm, but Glámr then attacks other farms in the same valley. Þórhallr returns to his farm in the spring, but Glámr kills his daughter there.

Grettir hears of the killings and, sensing a challenge, offers to stay there with Þórhallr. Glámr enters the hall of the farmhouse and grasps at Grettir. They fight inside the house until they crash outside and Grettir falls on top of Glámr: the moonlight shines in the revenant's eyes and Glámr curses Grettir so that he will never become any stronger, will fall into outlawry and killings, will be plagued with bad luck, and "Þá legg ek þat á við þik, at þessi augu sé þér jafnan fyrir sjónum, sem eg ber eftir, ok mun þér þá erfitt þykja einum að vera, ok þat mun þér til dauða draga" (ch. 35; "This curse I lay on you: my eyes will always be before your sight, and will make you find it difficult to be alone. And this will lead to your death").

Grettir beheads Glámr and places his head by his buttocks—as with Kárr earlier in the saga—and the body is then burned and the ashes scattered to prevent further hauntings. The power of Glámr's curse survives him, however. Grettir

var orðinn maðr svá myrkfælinn at hann þorði hvergi at fara einn saman, þegar myrkva tók. [...] ok þat er haft síðan fyrir orðtæki, at þeim ljái Glámr augna eða gefi glámsýni, er mjǫg sýnisk annan veg en er. (ch. 35)

had grown so afraid of the dark that he did not dare to go anywhere alone after nightfall. [...] It has since become a saying about people who suffer hallucinations that Glam lends them his eyes or they see things with Glam's eyes.

The fight with Glámr and the ghost's curse mark a turning point in the saga: from this point on, Grettir's luck is all against him.

Grettir learns that his distant relative St Óláfr has become king in Norway and he decides to go there to try to become his retainer (ch. 37). When he arrives on this second visit to Norway, an event takes place that shapes the whole of the rest of his life. Grettir swims ashore at Staðr to get fire, but he surprises the people at the farmhouse and is attacked (without provocation)—in the melee the house catches fire (ch. 38). Grettir swims away but it turns out that the farm and all the people in it have been burned to ashes. The killings are entirely accidental, and Grettir is the innocent party, having been attacked, but when the Icelandic father of those killed, Þórir of Garðr, learns of their death (ch. 46), he has Grettir outlawed in his absence. This is the full outlawry that Grettir endures for the rest of his life and that makes him unable to settle anywhere in Iceland.

Meanwhile, back in Norway, Grettir offers to undergo ordeal by fire to prove to King Óláfr that he was innocent of the killings, but he loses his temper with a boy who insults him on the way to the ordeal and the boy is killed. Óláfr cancels the ordeal and declares that Grettir is a man of great misfortune: "Ef nǫkkurum manni hefir verit fyrirmælt, þá mun þér hóti helzt" (ch. 39; "If any man has ever been accursed, it must surely be you"). Even when Grettir explains to the king how they are related, he cannot secure a place as the king's retainer (there is a contrast with the *þættir* of Icelanders abroad).

Grettir returns to Iceland to discover that he is an outlaw and that both his father and his brother Atli are dead. He has to visit his mother in secret, but on the second occasion he does so he is able to report that he has killed Þorbjǫrn øxnamegin ("Oxen-Might") and his son in vengeance for the killing of Grettir's brother Atli. An interesting statement is made about the spear thrown by Grettir in this encounter:

Spjótit þat sem Grettir hafði týnt, fannsk eigi fyrr en í þeira manna minnum, er nú lifa; þat spjót fannsk á ofanverðum dǫgum Sturlu lǫgmanns Þórðarsonar ok í þeiri mýri, er Þorbjǫrn fell, og heitir þar nú Spjótsmýrr; ok hafa menn þat til merkja at Þorbjǫrn hafi þar drepinn verit, þótt í sumum stǫðum segi, að hann hafi á Miðfitjum drepinn verit. (ch. 49)

The spear that Grettir had lost was not found for a long time, until the days that people still alive today can remember. It was found toward the end of Sturla Thordarson the Lawspeaker's life, in the marshland where Thorbjorn was killed, which is now known as Spotsmyri (Spear-Mire.) This is taken as proof that Thorbjorn was killed there, although some accounts say that he was killed in Midfitjar.

This allusion to the lawspeaker and author provides a reference for dating the saga (assuming it is not a later interpolation): Sturla died in 1284. The reference to variant traditions and the place-name etymology help to construct the text as history.

Grettir continues to travel around Iceland in secret, stealing what he needs when he cannot get it any other way and performing a number of feats of strength. A couple of incidents occur in which Grettir takes in a fellow outlaw who attempts to kill him for the reward placed on his head (twice the amount normally offered, later raised to three times the amount, chs. 51, 59). Grettir eventually learns his lesson but finds it impossible to be alone.

Grettir kills a troll woman and a troll who have been haunting Sandhaugar at Christmas (chs. 64–66). Afterward, he is advised to hide on the island of Drangey and his brother Illugi accompanies him because of his fear of the dark; their mother, Ásdís, has bad dreams and warns him to beware of witchcraft.

While on the island, the brothers' slave, Þorbjǫrn glaumr, allows the fire to go out and Grettir swims ashore to retrieve fire from a farm on the mainland. When he is discovered there by the farmer's daughter and maidservant, the maid makes fun of his small penis and suffers for it in a way that shows she was wrong to think that its surprising size indicated anything about his virility (see further Phelpstead 2007: 428–30).

One of the owners of the island of Drangey, Þorbjǫrn Ǫngull ("hook"), tries unsuccessfully to evict Grettir. He then enlists the help of his foster-mother, Þuríðr, an old woman skilled in magic:

En þó at kristni væri á landinu, þá váru þó margir gneistar heiðninnar eftir. Það hafði verit lǫg hér á landi, at eigi var bannat at blóta á laun eða fremja aðra forneskju, en varðaði fjǫrbaugssǫk, ef opinbert yrði. (ch. 78)

Yet although Christianity had been adopted in Iceland, many vestiges of heathendom remained. It had been the law in Iceland that sacrifices and other black magic were not forbidden if they were practiced in private but were punishable by lesser outlawry if they were done publicly.

Þuríðr has her son ferry her out to the island and puts a curse on Grettir (ch. 78). She then puts a spell on a large piece of driftwood. Grettir twice rejects the wood, sensing its cursed quality, but is injured trying to chop it when his slave brings it home. The wound becomes infected and spreads. Þorbjǫrn then attacks the island again, taking advantage of Grettir's incapacity to shamefully kill him and execute his brother Illugi when the latter refuses to forgo vengeance. The saga encapsulates Grettir's misfortune in the remark, "Sá hann flest fyrir þó að hann gæti eigi að gert" (ch. 82; "He could foresee most events, but could do nothing about them").

The interlacing of key themes gives this main part of the saga a strong sense of coherence, though on the surface it may seem a highly episodic narrative. Glámr's curse leads Grettir to risk his life by taking in other outlaws for company and being unable to survive alone; Grettir's bad luck, to which King Óláfr refers, dogs him throughout this part of the saga, in which he spends nineteen years as an outlaw and is finally killed for a crime he did not commit; the supernatural continually impinges on Grettir's life, in the form of the demonic boy at the Norwegian court, the trolls Grettir kills at Sandhaugar, and the witch's spell that renders him unable to defeat Þorbjǫrn Ǫngull. We see too the importance of the law and the use made of it by Þórir of Garðr to prevent Grettir's outlawry from being lifted. Shame and honor are prominent motives for the behavior of numerous characters in this part of the saga. The historicity of the saga is constructed by allusions to other texts, by the incorporation of verses attributed to the characters, and (in the account of the rediscovery of Grettir's spear) by explicit allusion to events within living memory. And, characteristically, although the text might be seen as fundamentally tragic, it is shot through with moments of dark but very funny comedy.

Grettis saga features few prominent female characters. There is, of course, the witch Þuríðr, but there is nothing admirable about her. A more positive portrait of a female character in *Grettir's saga* is that of the hero's mother, Ásdís. After the deaths of her sons, Grettir and Illugi, she summons men to help and protect her (ch. 83). She is so well-liked that everyone supports her, even those who had been Grettir's enemies. She shows her mettle when Þorbjǫrn Ǫngull arrives with Grettir's head and exchanges verse with her. Her emotional control and fearlessness in this horrific situation earns her further praise:

> Þá mæltu margir, at eigi væri undarligt, þó at hún ætti hrausta sonu, svá hraust sem hún var, þvílík skapraun sem henni var gǫr. (ch. 83)
>
> Many people said it was not surprising that she had such brave sons, considering how brave she was herself, after all she had suffered.

Things turn out badly for Þorbjǫrn Ǫngull because his use of sorcery puts him beyond the pale, and, far from winning the reward for killing Grettir, he is lucky to escape from the Althing alive. Some argued there that witchcraft should be punished by death rather than the outlawry that is agreed.

Grettir's Norwegian half-brother, Þorsteinn drómundr, hears the news of Grettir's slaying and Þorbjǫrn Ǫngull's presence in Norway. Þorbjǫrn flees the country to enter military service in Constantinople, but Þorsteinn pursues him and when Þorbjǫrn's identity is revealed by his possessing the *sax* he has won from Grettir, Þorsteinn seizes the sword and takes vengeance.

People are surprised that Þorsteinn has traveled so far to take vengeance for Grettir, and this unusual dedication to revenge is commented on several times in the remainder of the saga. Þorsteinn is imprisoned in Constantinople. From this point on, the influence of medieval romance on the text is pronounced, and the change of tone is indicated by the courtly musical skill with which Þorsteinn passes his time in prison. A rich and noble woman, Spes (Latin for "hope"), hears the singing and is so impressed she pays the ransom to release Þorsteinn. We are told that there is little love in Spes's marriage to her husband, Sigurðr, and this sets up the story of adulterous love that follows.

Þorsteinn and Spes are three times surprised by Sigurðr and three times deceive him. Spes then agrees to swear an oath to clear her name,

acting on advice from Þorsteinn's friend Haraldr Sigurðarson, the future
king Haraldr harðráði of Norway. At this point the story follows closely
the legends of Tristan and Isolde, who deceive Isolde's husband, King
Mark of Cornwall, in precisely the way that Spes deceives Sigurðr, swearing an oath that is literally true but contriving an incident involving her
lover in disguise that enables the oath to be made in good faith.

On the way to swear her oath, Spes is helped across a dirty ditch by a
beggar who manages to drop her and then slide his hand along her leg in
the ensuing struggle; despite doing such a bad job, Spes rewards him with
a gold coin. The man is, of course, Þorsteinn in disguise, and the incident
enables Spes to declare:

> En fyrir þat vil ek sverja, at engum manni hefi ek gull gefit ok af
> engum manni hefi ek saurgazk líkamlega, utan af bónda mínum og
> þeim vándum stafkarli, er tók sinni saurugri hendi á lær mér, er ek
> var borin yfir díkit í dag. (ch. 89)
>
> I swear that I have not given any man gold and been defiled by
> him apart from my husband and that wicked beggar who put his
> muddy hand on my thigh when he carried me over the ditch today.

The narrative of romantic love—and indeed the love triangle—in *Grettis saga* invites comparison, of course, with the love triangles in poets' sagas. Within *Grettis saga*, the love story also develops in a new direction
a theme running through the saga: that of sexual relations between men
and women. So, far from being a complete departure from the rest of the
saga, *Spesar þáttr* thus continues a long-running theme, though its more
courtly treatment of that theme is quite different in tone from earlier in
the saga.

Having cheated to clear her name, Spes is able to divorce Sigurðr, who
is forced to leave the country, and Spes and Þorsteinn are then able to
marry. The saga does not end with a happy-ever-after marriage, though.
After two years, Þorsteinn and Spes leave Constantinople to go to Norway. When they grow old there, they decide to seek forgiveness for their
sins and resolve to go on pilgrimage to Rome to seek absolution there.
They are given a light penance and end their lives as hermits in separate
stone cells. So, both *Gísla saga* and *Grettis saga* end with penitents in

Rome. These two sagas about marginal figures excluded from human society find resolution at the very center of Christendom.

Laxdœla saga

Laxdœla saga is renowned for its focus on female experience. It features a wider range of female characters than any other saga of Icelanders, from a sex slave who turns out to be a princess to a matriarchal early settler, and from a woman who marries four times to a devout nun (actually the same woman: after outlasting four husbands, Guðrún Ósvífrsdóttir becomes an anchorite and nun in old age). The interest in female experience ensures that the issue of whether women are consulted about and consent to their marriage is a recurring concern of the narrative. At the heart of the saga is a tragic love triangle involving Guðrún and two foster-brothers, Kjartan Ólafsson and Bolli Þorleiksson. This triangle is reminiscent of the poets' sagas and of the heroic poetry of the *Poetic Edda*: in that collection, another Guðrún finds herself married to the wrong one of two men. The interest in women's experience and female perspectives is so strong that scholars have persistently raised the possibility that the saga may have been written by a woman, though it is impossible to know one way or the other.[20]

Besides connections with poets' sagas and eddic poetry, *Laxdœla saga* shares several characters with other sagas: key figures appear also in *Egils saga*, *Eyrbyggja saga*, *Gísla saga*, and *Njáls saga*. The influence of romance is more obvious in *Laxdœla saga* than any other saga of Icelanders. This is a saga of superlatives, of beautiful women, handsome heroic men, and gorgeous clothes.

In this book, I have preferred "sagas of Icelanders" to the alternative English term "family sagas," but *Laxdœla saga* truly is a narrative of a family. Hundreds of individuals are named in the saga, but nearly all the major characters are either descendants of Ketill flatnefr ("flat-nose") or related to his descendants by marriage. Genealogy is as strong an interest of the writer as in any saga of Icelanders, and although the information about ancestors supplied when a major character is introduced can overwhelm modern readers, those family relationships are essential to understanding the complex feuds in the saga.

In the opening chapters of *Laxdœla saga*, Ketill, a chieftain in Norway at the time that Haraldr hárfagri is consolidating a united kingdom, consults his family as to whether they should fight Haraldr or escape abroad. When his son Bjǫrn says, "Ek vil gera at dœmum gǫfugra manna ok flýja land þetta" (ch. 2; "I want to follow the example of other worthy men and flee this country"), he implicitly claims that the ancestors of the Icelanders were "worthy." The family decides to leave. Ketill's sons have heard there is good land available in Iceland, with plenty of beached whales and excellent fishing all year. Ketill, however, goes west to the British Isles instead of to Iceland: "Í þá veiðistǫð kem ek aldregi á gamals aldri" (ch. 2; "I do not intend to spend my old age in that fishing camp"). He travels to Scotland with his daughter Unnr (*in djúpúðga*, the Deep-minded; as we have seen, she is known in other texts as Auðr). He dies there and Unnr's son is also killed. Unnr reveals "what an outstanding woman" she is by escaping with her followers to Orkney and then to the Faroes, arranging marriages on her way. She is a matriarchal figure and the first of the remarkable women featured in this saga.

Unnr eventually joins her brothers in Iceland, takes land there, and distributes it among her followers. In her old age, she exhorts her favorite grandchild, Óláfr feilan, to marry and she nominates him as her heir. She hands over her farm to him on his wedding day and dies that night. She is given a ship burial in a mound, indicating that in this saga, unlike in *Landnámabók* and *Gísla saga*, she is not a Christian (ch. 7). When Óláfr feilan's brother-in-law, Dala-Kollr, dies, his youngest son, Hǫskuldr, inherits from him and becomes a major figure in the first part of the saga. Hǫskuldr's mother, Þorgerðr, goes to Norway, where she remarries, having the freedom to do so as a widow, although it later turns out that Hǫskuldr takes a different view of her capacity to act independently of a male guardian.

Þorgerðr has a son, Hrútr (Hǫskuldr's half-brother), and returns with him to Iceland when her new husband dies. Hǫskuldr marries a woman called Jórunn Bjarnardóttir. Hǫskuldr makes a trip to Norway for building timber (Iceland became deforested soon after the settlement and apart from driftwood all timber for construction had to be imported). While there, he buys a slave woman; he is told by her seller that she has *ljóðr mikill* ("a major flaw")—she cannot speak. However, he not only buys her but sleeps with her the same evening (ch. 12). The Norwegian king Hákon recognizes Hǫskuldr's worth but cannot persuade him to stay in Norway. There is some friction with Jórunn when Hǫskuldr returns home with his new slave, whose bed he abandons to rejoin his wife. The slave gives birth to an exceptional and precocious baby boy called Óláfr. Hǫskuldr one day discovers her talking with her baby and realizes that she had only been pretending to be unable to speak. The slave now reveals that she is Melkorka, daughter of an Irish king called Mýrkjartan. Hǫskuldr establishes her and her son on a separate farm. A man called Þórðr goddi fosters Óláfr in return for help from Hǫskuldr. Óláfr is handsome and dresses well, earning the nickname *pái*, "peacock," from his father (ch. 16).

Hǫskuldr deals with hauntings by Killer-Hrappr, who had asked to be buried upright in his kitchen doorway and whose ghost has been killing servants (ch. 17). Hǫskuldr disinters the body and has it buried further away. The hauntings decrease, but Þorsteinn surtr is drowned on his way to live at Hrappr's old farm and the sighting of a large seal is seen as a portent of his death (ch. 18).

The saga's description of Hrútr's visit to Norway agrees with the account in *Njáls saga* of his relationship to Queen Gunnhildr. *Laxdœla saga*, however, is not as revealing about their closeness and does not portray her as a witch.[21] Gunnhildr's recognition of Hrútr's worth is another example of Icelanders' recognition abroad as an indicator of status. When Hrútr returns to Iceland, he argues with his half-brother, Hǫskuldr, over the share of their mother's property that Hrútr is owed. Hǫskuldr claims that because their mother remarried without his consent (as her male guardian after her husband's death), Hrútr, the product of that second marriage, has no right to inherit. Thanks largely to the peacemaking of Hǫskuldr's wife, Jórunn, an agreement is reached between the brothers.

Melkorka now marries Þorbjǫrn skrjúpr ("pock-marked"), partly to spite Hǫskuldr and partly to give her son Óláfr the resources to travel abroad and find his royal Irish grandfather. She has taught him to speak Irish fluently in preparation, and when they meet, Mýrkjartan tells Óláfr that "no one speaks better Irish" (ch. 21). The impression Óláfr makes in Ireland, with his grandfather wanting to make him his heir, and in Norway, which he visits before and after going to Ireland, offers yet more evidence of an Icelander's merit being recognized abroad. When he returns to Iceland, his father proposes that he should marry Þorgerðr, daughter of the poet Egill Skallagrímsson. When this is put to Egill at the Althing, he says that Þorgerðr must be consulted. She is at first opposed to the idea but is won over when Óláfr woos her for himself dressed in the fine clothing he was given while abroad (ch. 23). The newly married couple live at Killer-Hrappr's old farm and Óláfr has to deal with hauntings by the still undead man, eventually burning Hrappr's body and having the ashes dumped at sea (ch. 24).

The next chapters tell of tension between Hǫskuldr's son Þorleikr and Hrútr. A resolution appears to be reached when Hrútr offers to foster Þorleikr's son Bolli, who becomes close to Óláfr's own son, Kjartan (chs. 25–28). This arrangement, however, sows seeds that will bear fruit in the climactic tragedy at the heart of the saga.

The topos of the Icelander receiving recognition abroad is taken to an extreme level when Óláfr pái goes to Norway for timber and Earl Hákon says he is honored to have his wood cut down by Óláfr. A troublemaker called Geirmundr comes back to Iceland with Óláfr and seeks to marry Óláfr's daughter, Þuríðr: this is effected after Geirmundr pays Óláfr's wife, Þorgerðr, to support his marriage to their daughter (ch. 29). The subsequent marriage is, however, a cold one, and it ends when Geirmundr drowns with their daughter on a journey abroad. Þorgerðr had previously taken Geirmundr's sword Leg-biter (*Fótbítr*), which he then cursed with words that foreshadow Kjartan's death later in the saga: "þetta sverð verði þeim manni at bana í yðvarri ætt, er mest er skaði at, ok óskapligast komi við" (ch. 30; "it will be the death of that man in your family who will most be missed and least deserve it").

Another descendant of Ketill flatnefr is now introduced: Guðrún Ósvífsdóttir is said to be "kvenna vænst, er upp óxu á Íslandi, bæði at ásjánu ok vitsmunum" (ch. 32; "the most beautiful woman ever to have grown up in Iceland, and no less clever than she was good-looking"). Dreams she has are interpreted as being about the four husbands she will have and their fates (as well as the conversion to Christianity). The interpreter, Gestr, also foresees that one day Bolli will kill his foster-brother Kjartan and so bring about his own end. Intertwined with the introduction of Guðrún, her first meeting with Kjartan and Bolli, and her first marriage is the story of the failed marriage between Þórðr Ingunnarson and Breeches-Auðr (discussed in chapter 3 above). Having divorced their respective partners for cross-dressing, Þórðr and Guðrún marry. Auðr later takes revenge by attacking Þórðr in bed, in a scene reminiscent of the bed-closet attacks in *Gísla saga*. Þórðr then becomes involved in a case against a family of sorcerers of Hebridean origin and is drowned in a blizzard that they have summoned (ch. 35). The family later cause the death of one of Hrútr's sons and are all hunted down and killed. Guðrún is grief-stricken at the death of her second husband and names him after the son whom she later bears: this Þórðr is fostered by Guðrún's kinsman, Snorri goði (also one of the main characters in *Eyrbyggja saga*).

Kjartan and Bolli now prepare to sail abroad. Guðrún is displeased when Kjartan tells her of his plans and wants him to take her with him, but he does not regard this as possible. In Norway, Kjartan meets King Óláfr Tryggvason; the king predicts he will become a Christian. After observing a Christmas church service at which the king speaks, Kjartan, Bolli, and other Icelanders in Norway are indeed baptized. When Kjartan decides not to go back to Iceland as a missionary, the king sends instead the priest Þangbrandr, who returns to Norway after mixed results in Iceland. When the king sends additional missionaries the next summer, Bolli also returns to Iceland, telling Kjartan, "Hǫfum þat fyrir satt, at þú munir fátt þat, er á Íslandi er til skemmtanar þá er þú sitr á tali við Ingibjǫrgu konungssystur" (ch. 41; "I also take for granted that you remember little that might entertain you in Iceland when you're conversing with the king's sister Ingibjǫrg").

Óláfr's emissaries persuade the Althing to convert to Christianity. Bolli visits Guðrún and tells her of Kjartan's relations with Ingibjǫrg; she refuses to marry Bolli, but with her father's support he eventually persuades her, though Guðrún shows little affection for Bolli after their marriage (ch. 43).

Before Kjartan sets out from Norway the following summer, Ingibjǫrg gives him a fine headdress as a wedding present for Guðrún. The saga is notably reticent about the exact nature of Kjartan's relationship with the Norwegian princess. When he learns of Guðrún's marriage, Kjartan shows no sign of his feelings. When he and his father go to a feast at Ósvífr's, he makes a point by dressing in the fine clothes and armor with which he has been rewarded in Norway. Although Kjartan and Bolli meet with a kiss, Kjartan refuses gifts that Bolli offers. However, he soon arranges to marry a woman called Hrefna and their marriage is described as "one of great affection" (ch. 45; "Tókusk góðar ástir með þeim Kjartani ok Hrefnu"). Tensions—all the more powerful because so much goes unsaid—surface at a feast at which Kjartan promotes Hrefna to the seat of honor formerly occupied by Guðrún. His sword and Hrefna's headdress are stolen, and Guðrún is fairly open about having stolen the latter.

Kjartan becomes a spectacle visited by people from near and far as the first person in newly converted Iceland to fast by abstaining from meat during Lent (ch. 45).[22] Events in the saga are now routinely related to the passage of the liturgical year; it is after Christmas that hostility comes to a climax when Guðrún incites her brothers to attack Kjartan by insulting their manliness and claiming that they would have made good daughters for a farmer. She also threatens Bolli with divorce if he does not go with them. Just as her namesake in the *Poetic Edda* incited her brothers to kill Sigurðr, Guðrún goads her husband into killing the man she was to marry. Kjartan is outnumbered when attacked. Bolli stands by, watching until taunted by his foster-brother, but Kjartan will not fight the man he grew up with: "Víst ætlar þú nú frændi, níðingsverk að gera, en miklu þykki mér betra að þiggja banaorð af þér, frændi, en veita þér þat" (ch. 49; "An evil deed this is, that you're about to do, kinsman, but I'd rather receive my death at your hands than cause yours"). He casts his weapons aside and accepts death in a martyr-like way. Having struck the fatal blow, Bolli holds Kjartan in his arms as he dies and regrets the deed immediately. Guðrún, however, is very pleased at the news, chillingly remarking that "ek tel þat þó síðast, er mér þykkir mest vert, at Hrefna mun eigi ganga hlæjandi at sænginni í kveld" (ch. 49; "most important, to my mind, is the thought that Hrefna won't go to bed with a smile on her face this evening"). Hrefna in fact soon dies of a broken heart.

Óláfr pái prosecutes the killers, obtaining the outlawing of Guðrún's brothers but insisting (because of family ties) that Bolli be fined rather than outlawed. Óláfr dies soon afterward, but his remaining sons hate

Bolli and it is clear that the feud will be reignited. Óláfr's widow, Þorgerðr, is instrumental in stirring up hostility again. She incites her sons to kill first a man who witnessed the killing and has been mocking the way Kjartan died and then Bolli. Like Guðrún, she achieves her purposes by casting aspersions on their manliness, saying that their grandfather Egill Skallagrímsson would have acted differently and that she thinks that "yðr til þess betr fellda, at þér værið dœtur fǫður yðvars ok værið giftar" (ch. 53; "you would have made your father better daughters to be married off, than sons"). When they go to kill Bolli, Þorgerðr accompanies them because she thinks that they will need further urging; she continues to incite them until they kill Bolli.

After Bolli's death, Guðrún gives birth to another son who is named Bolli after his late father. Twelve years later, she enlists the support of her relative Snorri goði in taking vengeance for her husband's death. She also incites her sons by showing them Bolli's bloodstained clothes (ch. 60), which she has clearly kept carefully all this time (cf. Hildigunnr in *Njáls saga*, as discussed in chapter 3 above).

As the feud continues, there are some notable supernatural occurrences: Þorgils sees his fetch and, more unusually, his cloak speaks a verse at the Althing prophesying its owner's death (ch. 67). There is also some typically grim saga humor when a man called Þorgils is killed counting out a compensation payment and his head counts "eleven" as it flies off his body (ch. 67).

Snorri goði arranges another marriage for Guðrún, to which she and her sons consent; she and her new husband, Þorkell Eyjólfsson, are said to love each other very much (ch. 69). Her sons Bolli and Þorleikr are bored sitting at home "sem konum" (ch. 70; "like the women do") and Þorleikr spends some time in the service of King Óláfr Haraldsson in Norway. When he returns, the brothers plan to attack the Óláfssons but Snorri goði says that their father Bolli's killing has been avenged sufficiently and instead mediates a settlement and compensation (ch. 71). The brothers achieve more honor abroad, with Bolli Bollason venturing as far as service in Constantinople. He later returns to Iceland with such fine clothes from the Byzantine emperor that he becomes known as Bolli inn prúði, Bolli the Elegant (ch. 77).

After prophetic dreams and portents, Guðrún's husband Þorkell is drowned, after which she sees ghosts. She is stricken by his death and "Guðrún gerðisk trúkona mikil. Hon nam fyrst kvenna saltara á Íslandi. Hon var lǫngum um nætr at kirkju á bœnum sínum" (ch. 76; "Guðrún became very religious. She was the first Icelandic woman to learn the Psalter, and spent long periods in the church praying at night"). Later we are told, "Hon var fyrst nunna á Íslandi ok einsetukona" (ch. 78; "She was the first woman in Iceland to become a nun and an anchoress").

In Guðrún's old age, she has a conversation with her son Bolli in which he asks her which man she most loved. She evades the question by describing each of her husbands, but when pressed admits that "Þeim var ek verst, er ek unni mest" (ch. 78; "To him was I worst whom I loved most" [my trans.]). Bolli seems to know what she means, but the text does not explicitly state that she was referring to Kjartan, and other readings are possible, even that as a nun she might now be thinking of Christ as the bride of her soul, against whom she had previously sinned. She dies old and blind, and the saga ends by telling of the death of her son Gellir in Denmark. *Laxdœla saga* is preserved with a þáttr (which unusually is preserved only with the saga, not integrated into kings' saga manuscripts), *Bolla þáttr*.[23] This short tale tells of events when Bolli visits the north of Iceland, from which he wins further renown.

Njáls saga

Njáls saga (also called *Brennu-Njáls saga*: "the saga of Burnt-Njáll") is the longest, richest, and most celebrated of the sagas of Icelanders. It is set in the period between the mid-tenth and early eleventh centuries and tells mainly of events in the south of Iceland, though characters in the saga journey to mainland Scandinavia, to the British Isles, and as far afield as Rome and Constantinople. The saga was written between circa 1275 and circa 1290. Detailed legal passages in the saga show influence from the *Járnsíða* law code introduced to Iceland from Norway in 1271, and the oldest manuscript fragments date from circa 1300. The anonymous author was well acquainted with earlier sagas and with a range of other texts, including the Bible, saints' lives, and romances. More manuscripts survive of *Njáls saga* than of any other Icelandic saga: about twenty from the medieval period and a large number of later paper manuscripts.[24] Despite its length and complexity, *Njáls saga* is remarkably tightly constructed. There are many parallels and echoes between different parts of the saga, and key events are foreshadowed earlier in the narrative.

Njáls saga begins with seventeen chapters that function as a prologue to the rest of the narrative. Among other things, these chapters introduce issues of gender and sexuality that are explored with skill and subtlety through the saga as a whole.[25] After being betrothed to Unnr, the daughter of Mǫrðr gígja, Hrútr Herjólfsson travels to Norway, where he conducts an affair with Gunnhildr, the king's mother. When Hrútr decides to return to Iceland, Gunnhildr accuses him of failing to reveal his engagement to an Icelandic woman and curses him: "Þú megir engri munúð fram koma við konu þá, er þú ætlar þér á Íslandi, en fremja skalt þú mega vilja þinn við aðrar konur" (ch. 6; "You will not have any sexual pleasure with the woman you plan to marry in Iceland, though you'll be able to enjoy yourself with other women"). On his return, Hrútr marries Unnr but she later obtains a divorce on the grounds that he has been unable to consummate the marriage. In an awkward conversation with her father, she reveals her husband's problem:

Þegar hann kemr við mik, þá er hǫrund hans svá mikit, at hann má ekki eptirlæti hafa við mik, en þó hǫfum vit bæði breytni til þess á alla vega, at vit mættim njótask, en þat verðr ekki. En þó áðr vit skilim, sýnir hann þat af sér, at hann er í œði sínu rétt sem aðrir menn. (ch. 4)

When he approaches me his penis is so big that he is unable to have any gratification from me, and although we have both tried every way to enjoy each other, it doesn't work. Yet before we part he shows that he is as normal in nature as other men. (my trans.; Unnr uses a euphemism for penis: *hǫrund* literally means "human flesh" or "skin.")

Unnr obtains a divorce, but her father proves unable to recover her dowry from Hrútr.

Hrútr's beautiful niece, Hallgerðr—whom Hrútr earlier foresaw would be the cause of much trouble when he asked how thief's eyes had come into the family (ch. 1)—marries twice, the first time without and the second with her consent. Each marriage ends with the killing of her husband by her foster-father, Þjóstólfr, after Hallgerðr has been slapped by her husband. After the second such killing, Hallgerðr sends Þjóstólfr to Hrútr, who realizes her intention and kills him (ch. 17).

The next part of the saga (chapters 18–81) centers on Gunnarr Hámundarson of Hlíðarendi, a handsome and heroic close friend of the eponymous Njáll Þorgeirsson of Bergþórshváll. The divorced Unnr asks Gunnarr, a relative, to recover her dowry from Hrútr. Gunnarr accomplishes this by challenging Hrútr to a duel—the very tactic Hrútr himself had used to avoid meeting Mǫrðr's claim for the dowry. Gunnarr subsequently encounters Hallgerðr at an assembly meeting and later becomes her third husband, at the same time as Þráinn Sigfússon marries her daughter Þorgerðr.

Soon after this, Hallgerðr and Njáll's wife, Bergþóra, argue about the seating arrangements at a feast. This disagreement, and the perceived slight to honor associated with it, sets in motion a feud in the course of which they orchestrate a series of tit-for-tat killings that take place while Gunnarr and Njáll are away at the Althing each summer. The two friends, however, refuse to be drawn into their wives' conflict and pay each other compensation for the killings in an attempt to prevent the feud's escalation.

One hard winter, Hallgerðr obtains food stolen from a local farmer, Otkell, who earlier refused to sell to Gunnarr. Hallgerðr thus confirms Hrútr's perception about her thief's eyes much earlier in the saga. When Gunnarr discovers the theft, he slaps Hallgerðr, a blow that she promises to remember and repay and that echoes the slaps from her two previous husbands that led to their deaths. Despite Gunnarr's desire to pay compensation to Otkell for the theft, he refuses to be reconciled and the conflict comes to an end only when Gunnarr kills Otkell and his friend Skammkell (whose ill advice has fanned the conflict). Njáll, an outstanding lawyer, manages to arrange a settlement, but being gifted with prophetic foresight he warns Gunnarr never to kill twice in one family and to keep to all settlements that he makes (ch. 55). Violence that breaks out during a horsefight leads to an attack on Gunnarr, but he kills fourteen of his attackers. While Njáll advises Gunnarr in the legal case that follows, his opponents employ the services of Unnr's son Mǫrðr Valgarðsson, and he advises that they arrange an attack in such a way that Gunnarr will kill Þorgeirr Otkelsson and so kill twice in one family (in this way, Njáll's warning will become a self-fulfilling prophecy). This is eventually achieved and Gunnarr is sentenced to lesser outlawry of three years' exile. He sets out to his ship but falls from his horse and comments on the beauty of his farm. He decides to return home, thus becoming a full outlaw who may be killed with impunity. This part of the saga comes to a climax when Gunnarr is attacked in his home and makes an heroic stand alone against his opponents. When his bowstring breaks, he asks Hallgerðr for a strand of her hair with which to repair his weapon, and she chooses this moment to remember the slap he gave her, refuse his request, and so seal his fate. Gunnarr's son Hǫgni and Njáll's son Skarpheðinn take vengeance against Gunnarr's attackers, but the case is eventually settled.

The next part of the saga (chs. 82–132) begins with Þráinn Sigufússon traveling abroad, followed by Njáll's sons Grímr and Helgi, who befriend Kári Sǫlmundarson in Orkney. In Norway, Þráinn helps a killer called Hrappr to escape from Earl Hákon. His fellow Icelanders Grímr and Helgi Njálsson suffer for this before escaping with Kári. On returning to Iceland, Grímr and Helgi seek compensation from Þráinn, but when he refuses and insults them, they kill him. Njáll then offers to foster Þráinn's son, Hǫskuldr, whom he foresees will be a good man (ch. 94). When Hǫskuldr is grown up, Njáll arranges for him to marry a woman called Hildigunnr; she agrees only on the condition that a chieftainship (goðorð) be found for Hǫskuldr, ensuring her the social status she desires. Njáll brings this about by deliberately giving legal advice that wrecks lawsuits; he is then able to propose the creation of a Fifth Court to resolve such issues in the future and additional associated chieftaincies, one of which is awarded to Hǫskuldr (ch. 97). Njáll's fostering of Hǫskuldr Þráinsson, though it was intended as a peacemaking gesture, does not prevent Þráinn's brother-in-law, Lýtingr, from killing Njáll's illegitimate son (also called Hǫskuldr) in vengeance for Þráinn's death.

The conversion of Iceland to Christianity (including Þangbrandr's mission) constitutes an important turning point in the narrative (chs. 100–105). The conversion's impact is illustrated soon afterward when

Hǫskuldr Njálsson's blind son Ámundi is miraculously granted sight just long enough to enable him to kill his father's murderer, Lýtingr (ch. 106).

Hǫskuldr Þráinsson becomes a popular chieftain, and men desert Mǫrðr Valgarðsson in his favor, leading Mǫrðr's father to advise Mǫrðr to sow enmity between Njáll's foster-son, Hǫskuldr, and his actual sons. This leads eventually to Hǫskuldr's death at the hands of his foster-brothers; in refusing to fight and dying with the words, "Guð hjálpi mér, en fyrirgefi yðr" (ch. 111; "May God help me and forgive you!"), Hǫskuldr becomes a martyr figure who embodies the change from a heroic to a Christian ethos.

Hǫskuldr's widow, Hildigunnr, remains, however, firmly committed to the pursuit of vengeance and takes upon herself the role of whetter, inciting her uncle Flosi to avenge Hǫskuldr by confronting Flosi with her husband's bloodstained cloak. Flosi prefers to make a settlement, but this is wrecked at the last moment by the exchange of insults between Flosi and Skarpheðinn Njálsson involving accusations of sexual misbehavior. Flosi gathers a large company of men and attacks Njáll's home, Bergþórshváll. A series of dramatic and memorable incidents leads to the climax of the saga, in which Njáll, Bergþóra, their sons, and their young grandson are burned to death inside their home. Njáll rejects the burners' offer to come out unharmed: "Eigi vil ek út ganga, því at ek em maðr gamall ok lítt til búinn að hefna sona minna, en ek vil eigi lifa við skǫmm" (ch. 129; "I will not leave, for I'm an old man and hardly fit to avenge my sons, and I do not want to live in shame"). When his wife, Berþóra, is also offered free passage, she too declines: "Ek var ung gefin Njáli, ok hefi eg því heitið honum, at eitt skyldi ganga yfir okkr bæði" (ch. 129; "I was young when given to Njal, and I promised him that we should both share the same fate"). Even more movingly, their grandson, Þórðr, insists on dying with them.

Only Þórðr's father, Kári, escapes from the burning house, and the rest of *Njáls saga* (chapters 133–59) charts Kári's revenge. Of the bereaved, only he and Þorgeirr skorargeirr refuse to be party to a legal settlement (chronicled in great detail in the saga) with those responsible for the burning. After killing five of the burners, Þorgeirr makes a settlement with Flosi, leaving Kári to continue his pursuit of vengeance. Kári is assisted for a while by Bjǫrn of Mǫrk, a character who introduces considerable comic relief into the grim narrative of revenge killings. Toward the end of the saga, many burners are killed in the Battle of Clontarf (1014 C.E.), in which Christians under King Brjánn of Ireland engage with and (though only with the loss of the king) defeat pagan forces under Sigtrggr of Dublin (ch. 157). Brjánn's death (on Good Friday) is accompanied by miracles: his blood heals a boy whose arm had been cut off, and his own decapitated head miraculously attaches to his body, confirming Brjánn's saint-like status. A series of portents around the Norse world accompany the battle, including a grisly vision of women weaving with men's entrails and reciting a poem in eddic meter, *Darraðarljóð* (ch. 157).[26] In the conclusion of the saga, both Flosi and Kári journey to Rome and receive papal absolution for their sins. By chance Kári is shipwrecked near Flosi's farm in Iceland and the two men are finally reconciled, with Kári marrying Flosi's niece and Hǫskuldr's widow, Hildigunnr.

Andersson has called *Njáls saga* "the best and bleakest of the sagas" (2006: 208). Although there are many moments of comedy, some of it very grim, *Njáls saga* is a profoundly tragic account of the way in which the desire to preserve honor drives a process of blood feud that brings both good and bad men to their deaths despite all that well-meaning people do to try to avert further bloodshed. The saga implicitly lays much of the blame for continuing violence on women: Hallgerðr and Bergþóra mastermind a series of killings in defiance of their husbands, Hildigunnr goads Flosi into action against Hǫskuldr's killers, and the Battle of Clontarf is instigated by Queen Kormlǫð. Women also use expectations of male behavior to further their aims and "lace their goading throughout the saga with accusations of effeminacy against the men" (O'Donoghue 1992: 91).

As we saw in chapter 2, Njáll famously remarks that "with law our land shall rise, but it will perish with lawlessness" (ch. 70). Yet for all the emphasis on legal process in the saga, it is remarkable that the law so frequently fails. Andersson pertinently writes of the "author's ongoing preoccupation with the theme of the law's inadequacy to deal with civil mischief" (2006: 200). Feuds are ended not merely by legal decision but by self-sacrifice, as when Hallr of Síða renounces his right to compensation for the death of his son in a fight that breaks out at the Althing after the

Burning (ch. 145), or when vengeance has been taken so far that the momentum of the blood feud finally dissipates.

Njáls saga features a rich cast of highly individualized characters: the heroic Gunnarr, who is mystified by his own distaste at killing; the wise and peace-loving Njáll, whose wisdom, foresight, and legal expertise cannot prevent the deaths of almost all of those closest to him; the scheming Mǫrðr Valgarðsson; the ugly and sarcastic Skarpheðinn; the proud and indomitable Hallgerðr—the list could go on. Unforgettable incidents abound, too: Hildigunnr's inciting of Flosi to vengeance by shaking the dried blood from her murdered husband's cloak over him; the deeply poignant scene in which Bergþóra says she will die with Njáll, and their young grandson insists on being allowed to die with them both; Þorgrímr's answer when asked if Gunnarr is at home: "Vitið þér þat, en hit vissa ek, at atgeirr hans var heima" (ch. 77; "Find that out for yourselves, but I've found out one thing—that his halberd's at home"), after which he falls down dead from the wound he has just received; Kári's beheading of Gunnarr Lambason in front of the earl of Orkney—again the list could be greatly extended. In Njáls saga, an extraordinary richness of character and incident is woven into a cohesive whole of exceptional power.

We have thus far primarily been concerned with the sagas of Icelanders as texts in which medieval Icelanders engaged with issues of identity. However, as I indicated at the start of this book's preface, the identities of readers today inform their encounter with the texts. The next chapter examines the effect of beliefs about identity on the history of the translation of the sagas into English.

5

THE SAGAS IN ENGLISH

The postmedieval reception of Old Norse–Icelandic literature in the English-speaking world has often been stimulated or sustained by beliefs about identity. In Britain, scholarly and more popular interest in Viking and medieval Scandinavia was inspired from the eighteenth century onward by perceptions of the genetic, cultural, and linguistic contributions made by Viking settlers there in the ninth to eleventh centuries. Similarly, for Protestant Americans of northern European descent, the Norse discovery and temporary settlement of North America provided a congenial alternative to the dominant narrative of the discovery of America by the Mediterranean Catholic, Christopher Columbus.[1] This chapter will show how issues of identity inform the history of the translation of sagas of Icelanders into English.

Scholarly enthusiasm for Old Norse language and literature in Britain began in the seventeenth century. Early interest focused on Norse poetry rather than on the prose (or prosimetric) sagas: George Hickes's landmark *Thesaurus Linguarum Septentrionalium* of 1703–1705 included an account of the Norse language and a version of "The Waking of Angatýr," the first complete translation of an Old Icelandic poem into English. Later in the eighteenth century, Bishop Thomas Percy published Icelandic texts and English translations in his *Five Pieces of Runic Poetry* (1763; see Clunies Ross 2001 and 1998). Percy was also responsible for *Northern Antiquities* (1770), an adapted translation of Paul-Henri Mallet's *Introduction à l'histoire de Dannemarc*. As mediated by Percy, Mallet's historical work was a standard source of information on Viking and medieval Scandinavia well into the Victorian period, with revised versions of the translation appearing in 1809 and 1847.

The translation of saga prose into English began with extracts concerning incidents in British or Irish history, passages that were clearly felt to be of particular interest to an English-language readership. The earliest translations of such passages from the sagas of Icelanders appeared in 1788: a single chapter from *Eyrbyggja saga* and a more extensive selection from *Laxdœla saga* translated by Grímur Jónsson Thorkelin (Kennedy 2007: 56). In 1814, Sir Walter Scott published a summary or abstract of *Eyrbyggja saga*, the earliest more or less complete retelling of a saga of Icelanders in English. Scott had a deep and enduring interest in Old Norse–Icelandic literature (as reflected in several of his novels, above all in *The Pirate* [1822]), and he kept abreast of international scholarship by acquiring an impressive collection of books on the subject. He writes, "Of the various records of Icelandic history and literature, there is none more interesting than the Eyrbyggja-Saga" (Percy 1847: 517). His retelling became more widely known when reprinted in Blackwood's revision of Percy's *Northern Antiquities* (Percy 1847: 517–40).

The earliest British enthusiasts for Old Norse–Icelandic literature depended heavily on foreign scholarship, including the pioneering printed editions of medieval texts produced in Sweden and Denmark in the seventeenth and eighteenth centuries (Wawn 2005: 322–25). Access to this material was facilitated by the editors' provision of translations and editorial material in Latin, the international scholarly language of the time. Scott relied on the Latin version of *Eyrbyggja saga* included in Grímur Jónsson Thorkelin's 1787 Copenhagen edition of the saga to produce his abstract. Scott's retelling of *Eyrbyggja saga* betrays the influence of this intermediary version in its excessively Latinate diction: Snorri goði is referred to as a "pontiff" and Þorbjǫrn digri's nickname ("the fat") is rendered as "the Corpulent." Nevertheless, Scott's retelling, with occasional historical digressions for the reader's benefit, is a readable account of the saga, if one marred by what D'Arcy and Wolf call "many careless and crass errors" (1987: 34). In maintaining that it "must simply remain an interesting literary curiosity" (1987: 38), they underplay its influential role in the reception of medieval Icelandic literature in the English-speaking world:

the abstract's reprint in Blackwood's revision of Percy's *Northern Antiquities* gave it a wide readership. Lord Dufferin's retelling of the saga in his highly entertaining travel book of 1857, *Letters from High Latitudes*, seems, for example, to be following Scott, as indicated by his reference to Snorri goði as a "Pagan Pontiff" (Dufferin 1989: 97).

The first complete Icelandic saga to be published in English translation (rather than summary) was George Stephens's version of *Friðþjófs saga hins frækna*. This is not a saga of Icelanders but a romantic *fornaldarsaga*, or saga of the legendary past, that was extraordinarily popular throughout the nineteenth century, often in the form of a verse paraphrase by the Swedish bishop Esaias Tegnér, also several times translated into English (see Wawn 2000, chs. 5, 8). *Friðþjófs saga* is now a little-read text, but it appealed to Victorian sentimentality and was central to the canon of medieval Icelandic literature as received in Victorian Britain. It is partly set in Orkney, so, like other sagas popular in the nineteenth century, it has an obvious interest for British readers.

Ever since partial translations of *Eiríks saga rauða* and *Grœnlendinga saga* appeared in English in Joshua Toulmin Smith's *The Discovery of America by the Northmen in the Tenth Century* in 1839, there has been a sustained Anglophone interest in the two Vínland sagas and their accounts of the Viking discovery of North America (Kennedy 2007: 56–60). Translations of these sagas (made mainly from Carl Rafn's Danish translations) appeared in North Ludlow Beamish's identically titled *The Discovery of America by the Northmen in the Tenth Century* in 1841, and in the many decades since numerous further versions have appeared, making them the most frequently translated of all the sagas of Icelanders. Most of the early versions of the Vínland sagas were, like Beamish's, made from intermediate translations in other languages (Kennedy 2007: 60).

Apart from the two Vínland sagas, the first of the sagas of Icelanders to appear complete in English was the greatest of them, *Brennu-Njáls saga*. George Webbe Dasent (1817–1896) worked on his translation while a diplomat in Sweden in 1843, but it was not published until 1861, when he had become professor of English language and literature at King's College, London. It was immediately and lastingly popular: Wawn (2000: 142) notes that it achieved prepublication sales of a thousand copies, and it had wide circulation well into the twentieth century, thanks to reprints in the Everyman Classics series in 1911 and 1957. Indeed, it had the field to itself until a second English translation of *Njáls saga* by Carl F. Bayerschmidt and Lee M. Hollander was published in 1955. Dasent's *Burnt Njal* achieved an idiomatic English style, largely free of archaism, without sacrificing accuracy, except where Victorian sensibilities called for greater reticence than had been displayed by the Icelandic saga-author, as in the description of Hrútr Herjólfsson's marital problems (see Wawn 2000: 147–48, 155). The virtues of Dasent's style are evident in this passage from the first main climax of the saga, the attack on Gunnarr of Hlíðarendi:

> Gunnar made a stout and bold defence, and now wounds other eight men with such sore wounds that many lay at death's door. Gunnar keeps them all off until he fell worn out with toil. Then they wounded him with many and great wounds, but still he got away out of their hands, and held his own against them a while longer, but at last it came about that they slew him. (Dasent 1861: I, 246)

In a 1957 reprint of Dasent's version, Gabriel Turville-Petre praised the translation's style: "Dasent is one of the few who has succeeded in conveying the rhythm of Icelandic prose, and no translator so nearly gives the reader the impression he would gain by reading the Icelandic text" (Turville-Petre 1957: x). In the extract just quoted, Dasent confines himself to vocabulary of Germanic origin with the exceptions only of "defence" and "toil," but does so without resorting to archaism or obviously artificial word choices. The parataxis of the original is followed ("and," "but"), but the word order is idiomatic English, save for the inversion of "other eight," which literally follows the Icelandic *aðra átta*. The vacillation of tenses in the original is preserved, with present tenses used to translate *særir* (wounds) and *verr* (keeps), but otherwise this is a natural English style that does not draw attention to itself.

The original, two-volume, publication of *Burnt Njal* included a vast array of editorial material—a wide-ranging introduction of more than two hundred pages, notes, maps, a nearly seventy-page appendix, and an exceptionally detailed index—but almost all of this was omitted in later reprintings. Dasent also produced a version of *Gísla saga* (1866) and contributed translations of kings' sagas to the Rolls Series, but none of these later translations matched the achievement or acquired the popularity of his version of *Njáls saga*.

Among the readers inspired by Dasent's work was the phenomenally prolific polymath Sabine Baring-Gould (1834–1924). Inspired by his reading of sagas to visit Iceland in 1862, he published a book about his trip the following year: *Iceland: Its Scenes and Sagas*. The book includes several extensive paraphrases of saga narratives by the author. Baring-Gould writes, "My specimens of the Sagas have been selected with a view towards illustrating the voyages, quarrels, litigations, and superstitions of the ancient Icelanders" (Baring-Gould 2007: xli). He claims that the sagas are "downright history," and although he recognizes that not all sagas are of equal authority, "there is no difficulty whatever in distinguishing fact from fiction in these works of a bygone age" (Baring-Gould 2007: xliii). He retells much of *Grettis saga*, clearly a favorite of his, across four different chapters of the book and also includes extensive accounts of parts of *Egils saga*, *Vatnsdœla saga*, *Bandamanna saga*, *Flóamanna saga*, and a version of the king's saga about Óláfr Tryggvason. These retellings have been revealed recently to be mere hints of Baring-Gould's translational activity: manuscripts discovered by Andrew Wawn in Devon Record Office reveal that Baring-Gould was in fact the most prolific of all Victorian saga translators. Thirty-six notebooks comprising an estimated half a million words contain translations of seventeen sagas and short stories, "work of remarkable linguistic scrupulousness and intellectual ambition" (Wawn 2007a: 219; see also Wawn 2007b). Motivated in part by ludicrously fanciful ideas about his own Nordic ancestry, Baring-Gould taught himself to read Old Icelandic and between the 1860s and 1890s produced what Wawn calls "by far the most substantial body of saga translation undertaken by any old northernist in Victorian Britain" (2007a: 228). Had this work been published, it would have given Victorian readers a much more extensive and much better informed appreciation of Iceland's literary heritage.

A watershed in the history of the translation of sagas into English came in 1869 with the first of a series of translations produced by another great Victorian polymath, William Morris (1834–1896), in collaboration with the British-resident Icelandic scholar Eiríkr Magnússon (1833–1913).

Morris has justly been called "late Victorian Britain's most celebrated Ice-
landophile" (Wawn 2000: 34). He began to learn to read Icelandic after
meeting Eiríkr Magnússon in 1868.[2] The many saga translations that they
produced exerted a seminal influence on Victorian and later enthusiasm
for Old Icelandic literature: a recent commentator claims that "probably
no serious saga translator since 1869 has been totally uninfluenced" by
their work (Kennedy 2007: 54). Such influence has, however, often taken
the form of a sometimes forcefully expressed reaction against the idiosyn-
cratic stylistic approach that Morris and Magnússon took.

In just a few years, the two men made English versions of a remarkable number of Icelandic sagas: most were translated between 1868 and
the early 1870s, though some were published only twenty years later as
part of a handsome six-volume collection, *The Saga Library*, of which volumes I–II comprised sagas of Icelanders (*Hávarðar saga Ísfirðings, Bandamanna saga, Hœnsa-Þóris saga, Eyrbyggja saga, Heiðarvíga saga*) and III–VI
the kings' saga collection *Heimskringla*. Their other translations of sagas
of Icelanders included *Grettis saga* (1869) and versions of *Gunnlaugs saga*
and *Víglundar saga* included in *Three Northern Love Stories* (1875). Later
posthumously published translations include forty chapters of *Egils saga*
(Morris 1936) and *The Story of Kormak the Son of Ogmund* (Morris 1970);
further unpublished translations and fragments remain in manuscript.
The prominence of sagas of Icelanders in their work is noteworthy in the
context of Victorian saga translation. Apart from the Vínland sagas and
Dasent's versions of *Njáls saga* and *Gísla saga,* only one other example
of the genre had previously appeared complete in English: Sir Edmund
Head's 1866 translation of *Víga-Glúms saga.* Head was, like Morris, a pupil
of Eiríkr Magnússon, but he adopted a very different, plain style for saga
translation (see Kennedy 2007: 74–75). Morris and Eiríkr Magnússon's
interest in the sagas of Icelanders can thus be seen as inaugurating a shift
of attention away from kings' sagas and legendary sagas toward what has
become in the twentieth and twenty-first centuries the most widely read
and admired Icelandic saga genre.

The highly distinctive style that Morris and Eiríkr Magnússon adopt
for their translations from Old Icelandic has evoked strongly critical reactions from many readers ever since the earliest reviews, though there have

also been a few more positive responses. This passage from the opening chapter of their version of *Eyrbyggja saga* (*The Story of the Ere-Dwellers*) illustrates their approach:

> Now the bonders bemoaned them of that to the king, and prayed him deliver them from that un-peace. Then Harald the king took such rede that he caused dight an army for West-over-the-sea, and said that Ketil Flatneb should be captain of that host. Ketil begged off therefrom, but the king said he must needs go; and when Ketil saw that the king would have his will, he betook himself to the faring, and had with him his wife and those of his children who were at home. But when Ketil came West-over-sea, some deal of fighting had he and his, and ever got the victory. (Morris and Magnússon 1891–1905: II, 4)

"Bonders" here transliterates rather than translates Norse *bœndr*—roughly, "farmers," but quite often used by early translators as a technical term. "Un-peace," where "hostility" or "conflict" might be more natural, likewise reflects the Norse *ófriði*, which consists of a negative prefix *ó-* and *friði* ("peace"). "Rede" is an archaic English word chosen for its etymological relationship to Norse *ráð*; "West-over-sea" makes a place-name of the Norse *vestr um haf*. Flatneb selects archaic or dialectal "neb" (rather than "nose") for its closeness to Norse *nefr*; "faring" is related to the Norse verb *fara* used in the passage.

A famous attack on Morris's approach came from a rival partnership between an English scholar and English-domiciled Icelander, F. York Powell and Gudbrand (Guðbrandur) Vigfusson. In the introduction to their *Corpvs Poeticvm Boreale*, they lament,

> There is one grave error into which too many English translations of old Northern and Icelandic writings have fallen, to wit, the affectation of archaism and the abuse of archaic, Scottish, pseudo-Middle-English words. This abominable fault makes a Saga [. . .] sound unreal, unfamiliar, false. (Gudbrand Vigfusson and York Powell, 1883: I, cxv; Eiríkr Magnússon responded in Morris and Eiríkr Magnússon 1891–1905: VI, vii–viii)

In 1937, Dorothy Hoare argued that "in the ingenious search for the words which come nearest to the actual form of the Icelandic, the life and nearness, the directness [of the original] has vanished" (52). The effect is, she claims, "entirely different" from that obtained by reading the Icelandic for oneself. While the approach of Morris and Eiríkr Magnússon certainly emphasizes the alterity of the medieval text by using archaic vocabulary and morphological forms, their preference for linguistic forms that English shares (or shared) with Icelandic focuses attention on historical connections between the English and Icelandic languages.

John Kennedy (2007: 29–36) draws an apposite distinction between archaism and "Icelandicized" translation, arguing that although they are often accused of archaism, the translations of Morris and Eiríkr Magnússon employ nonstandard English that is chosen because of its closeness to Old Norse–Icelandic, rather than simply its age. The result is, ironically, that the saga translations of Morris and Eiríkr Magnússon can best be enjoyed by those readers whose knowledge of Old Icelandic enables them to appreciate the linguistic connections to which the translators draw attention by their stylistic choices (Swannell 1961: 377; see also Felce 2016): readers with little need for a translation in the first place. There is, nevertheless, a vigor to the translations of Morris and his collaborator that even readers innocent of Icelandic may savor.

Eiríkr Magnússon is thought to have provided the first English translations of three more sagas of Icelanders that were included in John Coles's 1882 account of *Summer Travelling in Iceland*: *Bandamanna saga*, *Hrafnkels saga Freysgoða*, and *Þórðar saga hreðu*.[3] At the end of the nineteenth century, W. G. Collingwood (1854–1932) emerged as a major figure in British medieval Icelandic studies, traveling to Iceland in 1897 and publishing a translation of *Kormáks saga* with Jón Stefansson in 1902. Collingwood's saga studies are informed by his interest in the Norse cultural inheritance of the Lake District area of northern England, and he is one of the most prominent examples of the importance of regional, rather than simply national, identity as a stimulus to interest in Old Norse literature (see Townend 2009).

Victorian saga scholarship was far from a purely masculine endeavor and, appropriately enough given the text's particular interest in female characters and possible female authorship, the first English translation of *Laxdœla saga* was by a woman, Muriel Press (1899). Her version appeared with minimal apparatus, though a brief editorial note acknowledged the contribution of "a competent Icelander"; the translation was republished with new editorial material by Everyman Classics in 1964. A considerably less successful version of the same saga was published by Robert Proctor in 1903: in contrast to Press's straightforward and plain style, Proctor was one of the few to try to emulate Morris and Eiríkr Magnússon's approach. However, he added a further barrier between the reader and the original: Magnus Magnusson and Hermann Pálsson, later translators of *Laxdœla saga*, describe Proctor's version as "incredibly inaccurate" (quoted in Kennedy 2007: 103).

Many previously untranslated texts appeared in English for the first time in *Origines Islandicae* by Gudbrand Vigfusson and F. York Powell (1905). This massive two-volume collection of material dealing with the settlement and early history of Iceland included full or partial translations of many sagas of Icelanders (in addition to other kinds of text), usually alongside the Icelandic original. The translations eschew archaism (except that "thou" forms are used in direct speech), but the value of the work was undermined by inaccuracies, an unattractive layout, and some questionable editorial policies (Kennedy 2007: 98–100).

One of the few translators besides Proctor to follow the example set by William Morris and Eiríkr Magnússon was E. R. Eddison, now better known as an early fantasy novelist than as a saga translator. He claimed that his 1930 translation of *Egils saga* was the first published in English, arguing that the version published by his predecessor W. C. Green in 1893 did not merit the description: "His version [. . .] in its flaccid paraphrasing, its lack of all sense of style, its Latinized constructions, and (a comparatively venial offence) its foolish and unavowed expurgation, conveys no single note or touch of the masterpiece with which he was dealing" (Eddison 1930: xiii). Eddison's preface notes that several episodes in the saga take place in England "and this in itself may be thought to give this saga a special interest to English readers" (1930: xii). He goes so far as to claim that no Englishman can read the saga carefully "without becoming aware that this is not a foreign book but curiously his own, curiously

English": character traits and outlooks that have come to be considered English "have come down to us through the Norse strain in our own ancestry" (1930: xii).

In an extensive "Terminal Essay" on his translation principles, Eddison argues that "for an Englishman to render the sagas into his own language is to labour under no alien sky and dig no inhospitable soil" (1930: 229). In support of this claim, he provides a very long note listing English words "substantially the same" as their Old Norse equivalents. He also offers a stout defense of archaism. The following passage provides an example of his approach; Egill has arrived in York, then ruled by his enemy Eiríkr blóðøx, and his friend Arinbjǫrn has made Egill compose a praise poem to the king in the hope of saving his life:

> Then saith the King, "Exceeding great masterfulness layest thou on this, Arinbjorn, to give Egil aid. Loth must I be to do thee scathe, if it must come to this, if thou wilt rather lay down thy life than he were slain. Yet enough and to spare be my causes against Egil, whatsoever I may let do unto him."
>
> And when the king had spoken these words, then went Egil before him and began his song, and quoth it high, and had a hearing forthwith:

> West over sea
> bear I with me
> God's wish-strand's spray;
> Such is my way,
> Launch'd I mine oak
> When the ice broke;
> Loaded I her
> With praise-plunder. (1930: 141)

The syntax here carefully shadows the Norse original in a way that is certainly defamiliarizing; some readers will find it awkwardly off-putting. The "Icelandicizing" approach of translators like Eddison arguably works best when translating skaldic verse, a highly wrought and stylized medium. In the translation here of the opening verse of Egill's *Hǫfuðlausn*, Eddison preserves the end rhyme of the original, and the phrases "wish-strand's spray" and "praise-plunder" are suited to a poetic context.[4]

By the middle of the twentieth century, more than half of the sagas of Icelanders had been published in English, and a handful had appeared in three or more different translations (*Bandamanna saga, Gunnlaugs saga, Hrafnkels saga, Laxdœla saga*, and the Vínland sagas; see Kennedy 2007: 135). In the second half of the century, the approach taken by Morris, Eiríkr Magnússon, and E. R. Eddison was abandoned in favor of more idiomatically modern English syntax and vocabulary. The predilection for sagas of Icelanders over other genres also became more marked, with nearly 50 percent of all translations from Old Norse–Icelandic between 1950 and 2000 being devoted to the sagas of Icelanders (Kennedy 2007: 155).

One of the most important contributors to Norse-Icelandic literary studies around the middle of the twentieth century was the Welsh scholar, novelist, and short story writer Gwyn Jones, who published numerous saga translations over several decades from the mid-1930s. These translations have perhaps not been held in such high regard as the translation of the medieval Welsh *Mabinogion* on which he collaborated with Thomas Jones, and although almost all of them were republished at least once, only the handy collection of shorter sagas, *Eirik the Red and Other Sagas* (1961), remains in print, as an Oxford World's Classic. Gwyn Jones's skill as a creative writer is evident in his translations, which have been neatly characterized by John Kennedy as "lively, modern, and entertaining, and sometimes more colourful than a literal reading of the Icelandic texts would justify" (2007: 130).

Another scholar with a sure sense of English style, the Icelander Hermann Pálsson, who was based at the University of Edinburgh for much of his life, has been called "clearly the dominant figure in translating Old Icelandic literature into English during the second half of the twentieth century" (Kennedy 2007: 157). Sometimes alone but often in collaboration with Magnus Magnusson, Paul Edwards, or Denton Fox, Hermann Pálsson published translations of many sagas over a period of more than forty years, from the publication of *Njáls saga* in 1960 onward. Many of these translations were of sagas of Icelanders, though they also included kings' sagas, legendary sagas, and romances. Most of the translations appeared in the Penguin Classics series, and Hermann Pálsson's approach to translation fitted well with the aims and intended readership of that series. He and his collaborators aimed above all for accessibility and readability, even at the cost of downplaying the alterity of the medieval texts. These are saga translations for readers of novels, assimilating the text as far as possible to that genre's appearance and conventions.[5] The following passage from *Egils saga* can be compared with the version by E. R. Eddison given above:

> "You're being very impertinent, Arinbjorn," said the King, "over the help you're giving Egil. I'd be very reluctant to cause you any injury, should things come to that, and should you choose to sacrifice your own life rather than see him killed. But whatever I decide to have done to him, I've plenty to charge him with."
>
> When the King said this, Egil stepped forward to face him, began to declaim his poem, and was given an immediate hearing:

By sun and moon
I journeyed west,
My sea-borne tune
From Odin's breast,
My song-ship packed
With poet's art:
It's word-keel cracked
The frozen heart.

Unlike translations that emphasize the linguistic proximity of English and Icelandic, this version happily employs vocabulary of Latin or Romance origin: impertinent, reluctant, sacrifice, declaim. The prose reads easily, with no sense of the "foreignness" of the text, but the verse is too obviously contrived to produce rhymes and introduces imagery of sun, moon, and singing that are not in the original.

In contrast to Hermann Pálsson's readable accessibility, some of his contemporaries produced translations that convey a sense of the alterity of the originals by translating very literally, preserving stylistic features such as the vacillation of tenses that most translators into English have tended to smooth over by putting the narrative entirely into the past tense. The Canadian George Johnston published a translation of *Gisla saga* in 1963 (since reprinted with translations by Anthony Faulkes in *Three Icelandic Outlaw Sagas*, 2001). Johnston explains that he originally intended to make a version that would be "as readable as a novel," but that he rewrote it following the Icelandic more closely to produce a version

> livelier, subtler and more readable, slightly outlandish in tone, the style directly geared to the telling of the tale. [...] It seemed to me that the "otherness" of the Icelandic was best preserved by letting its word-order and idiom, especially in the shifting of tenses, play their part in the English too. (Johnston 1963: xi)

The need to convey a sense of the alterity of the original texts is expressed even more forcefully in translations of *Gunnlaugs saga ormstungu* and *Hávarðar saga Ísfirðings* produced by two anthropologists, E. Paul and Dorothy Durrenberger. In their introduction to *Hávarðar saga*, they explain their determination "neither to convert it into a novel nor to make it seem romantically archaic," and they are explicit that "Sagas are not novels" (1996: 38, 40). A paragraph from chapter 3 of the saga illustrates how they convey a sense of the alterity of the text, but without recourse to archaic vocabulary:

> It was one day that Ólafur goes to his sheep house because the weather was hard in the winter, and people much needed to take care of their sheep. The weather had been hard during the night. And when he intended to go home he sees that a man walks to the house. Brandur the strong has come there. Ólafur received him well. Brandur took his greeting well. Ólafur asked why he came so late. (1996: 50)

The Durrenbergers preserve the vacillating tenses of the original (goes, intended, sees, walks, has come, received, etc.). Unidiomatic phrasing also follows the Norse text closely ("It was one day that," "took his greeting"). No attempt is made to smooth over the simple structure of the short sentences and paratactically linked clauses. The retention of the accent on

Ólafur's name and of the nominative ending -ur in both names (oddly, in *modern* Icelandic spelling rather than using the Old Norse forms Óláfr and Brandr) also emphasizes the "foreignness" of the text.

It is impossible to refer here to all the many English translations of sagas of Icelanders that are of interest. One final landmark publication must, however, be mentioned: the complete translation of all sagas of Icelanders produced by a team of Icelandic and native English-speaking scholars under the editorship of Viðar Hreinsson and published by Leifur Eiríksson Publishing in 1997 (CS). The five volumes include forty sagas and forty-nine tales of Icelanders (*þættir*). Translations by thirty native English speakers were revised in light of comments from eleven Icelanders. The style adopted across the collection deliberately steers a middle course between misrepresentative accessibility and overly literal translation: the language is clear, readable, and modern. Tense vacillation is not preserved. To reflect the remarkable consistency with which the corpus presents details of life in saga Iceland, all the translators translated certain technical and other terms in the same way, though more variety of approach is evident in how they faced the challenge of translating skaldic verse. The original five-volume edition was very expensive, but selected sagas from the collection are readily affordable in a series of paperback reprints: ten sagas and seven tales appeared in *The Sagas of Icelanders: A Selection* (2000), and many individual sagas have now been reprinted in Penguin Classics, superseding the contributions to that series involving Hermann Pálsson in the twentieth century. These Penguin Classic incarnations of the translations come with helpful and up-to-date introductory and explanatory materials, making them ideal for readers new to the sagas.

As we have seen in this chapter, the history of the translation of sagas of Icelanders into English begins with texts that relate to the history of English-speaking countries in North America and the British and Irish Isles. From the eighteenth century through to the mid-twentieth, many translators claimed some kind of special affinity between medieval Iceland and modern English-speaking peoples. A genre that I have argued is profoundly concerned with questions of Icelandic identity was thus enlisted in support of beliefs about British and American identity. In recent decades, a more global perspective has prevailed. The inclusion of such a large number of saga translations in the Penguin Classics series from the early 1960s onward made a point about the value and importance of the sagas in world literature by including them alongside "classics" translated from many other languages or written originally in English. The production at the end of the last century of a complete set of translations of the corpus into English can likewise be seen as making use of the world's most widely understood language to enable as many readers as possible to enjoy this fascinating group of texts. Alongside this global perspective, however, we can also detect a determination to celebrate the Icelandic provenance of these remarkable works. The *Complete Sagas of Icelanders* (not *Complete Family Sagas*, as the project could equally have been called, given that both terms are used interchangeably in English) involved a team of Icelanders working with the English-speaking translators and the volumes were published in Reykjavík (though many of the translations have since been reprinted elsewhere). The collection begins with no fewer than three forewords by, respectively, the then president of Iceland, then Icelandic minister of education, science, and culture, and a former director of the Manuscript Institute of Iceland. Each of them balances national and international perspectives in claiming worldwide relevance for these Icelandic narratives.

Every age needs its own translations of the sagas, finds what it wants in them, and to an extent makes them in its own image. The fact that all the sagas of Icelanders are now available in English, many of them in several different versions, certainly does not mean that the process of translation has come to an end.

CONCLUSION

Identity and Alterity

Much literary and cultural theory of recent decades has been concerned with aspects of identity, whether in terms of nation (postcolonial theory), gender and sexuality (feminist and queer theory), or the relations between humans and their environment, including other animals (ecocriticism and animal studies). In offering a new perspective on the sagas of Icelanders in this book, I have been inspired by this theoretical work to present the sagas as narrative explorations of identity. They reflect, but also help to construct, medieval Icelandic beliefs about the past and about how the present came to be. The narratives also illuminate beliefs about how humans relate to animals, to their physical environment, and to the supernatural. Some saga characters exemplify ideals to which men and women could aspire. But in also describing characters who fail or deliberately refuse to meet society's expectations, the sagas also offered opportunities for readers to imagine different possibilities and alternative identities.

Identity is defined in relation to alterity or otherness. The past is other, and its difference from the present can enable one to see how much of what is taken for granted in the present could be different. The past also shapes the present, so to understand one's present identity one needs to know where one has come from. As presented in this book, the sagas of Icelanders are narratives of the past in which Icelandic writers of the thirteenth and fourteenth centuries explored their identities. But these texts are now themselves part of the past, and the unfamiliar perspectives on such things as gender, sexuality, human-animal relations, and the super-natural that we find in the sagas confront us with the contingency of our own beliefs.

As I noted in the preface, one of the ways the study of medieval literature productively denaturalizes our commonsense beliefs is through making us aware of the contingency of many of our ideas about what a literary text is. In chapter 2, we saw that the sagas of Icelanders drew on oral traditions of various kinds. Some material preserved in the sagas, including some of the skaldic verse, existed in some form before the sagas were written down. Writers were influenced by textual models available to them in hagiography, other Christian literary forms, and romance. The nature of a manuscript culture means that as soon as a saga was copied, it began to change, whether the copier intended the changes or not. That instability of the text continues in printed editions and translations, each shaped in part by the beliefs of its editor or translator. A saga's identity is more unstable than we might expect.

In chapter 3, I argued that Icelandic national identity, a sense of difference from inhabitants of other polities, resided especially in the law, a central concern of the sagas of Icelanders as they tell of feuds and their resolution. We also saw how the sagas give expression to ideals of gendered identity and sexual behavior—even as they offer opportunities to resist those ideals by reading against the grain. The difference between humans and (other) animals was seen to be blurred in narratives of human-animal interaction. The apparent acceptance of the reality of the supernatural in the sagas challenges modern readers with a naturalist or materialist worldview to reflect on the historical contingency of beliefs that they may take for granted.

Chapter 4 looked in turn at some of the most read and most widely acclaimed of the sagas of Icelanders. The readings of each saga sought to show how the texts molded traditions of the kind described in chapter 2 and employed the themes examined in chapter 3. We followed the narrative of each saga closely so as to see how themes were employed to literary effect.

In chapter 5, we saw that ideologies of national identity stimulated translation of the sagas into English and how beliefs about the affinity of the Norse and English languages and their speakers influenced the stylistic choices made by some translators. We also saw a variety of different approaches to the alterity of these texts, with some translators intent on preserving that sense of otherness and others determined to make the texts as accessible to modern readers as possible.

The account of the sagas of Icelanders presented in this book has been inspired by a belief that encountering the otherness of the sagas can lead to an enhanced understanding not only of the past and the texts it produced but also of our own identities in the present.

Glossary

Althing (Alþingi): The Icelandic national assembly, which met for two
weeks each June and had both a legislative and a judicial function.

Berserkr (pl. berserkir): A Scandinavian warrior believed to possess
superhuman strength when fighting in a frenzy. Anglicized as
"berserk" or "berserker."

Dróttkvætt: "Court meter." The complex metrical form employed in the
vast majority of surviving skaldic verse.

Edda: The early thirteenth-century Prose Edda by Snorri Sturluson is
a handbook for poets. It includes accounts of Norse mythology,
poetic diction, metaphorical expressions known as kennings, and a
praise poem illustrating 102 skaldic verse forms. The name Edda (of
uncertain origin and meaning) was later applied also to an anthology
of mythological and heroic poetry in MS GKS 2365 4to (known as
Codex Regius, from the 1270s): this collection is usually referred to
as the Poetic Edda. Though later in date than Snorri's Edda, the Poetic
Edda includes texts of poems that he used as sources and must have
known from an earlier manuscript and/or oral tradition. The poems
in GKS 2365 4to and others in similar style preserved elsewhere are
known as "eddic" or "eddaic" verse (as distinct from skaldic poetry).

Fornaldarsögur: "Sagas of antiquity," but more often known in English as
legendary sagas. These sagas are set in the period before Iceland was
settled and recount events in mainland Scandinavia. As their usual
English name suggests, their subject matter is frequently marvelous.

Goði (pl. goðar): A chieftain in the Icelandic Free State. In the pre-Christian period, the *goðar* exercised priestly functions as well as political leadership and so in some English saga translations the term is rendered "priest."

Grágás: The collection of laws from the Free State period.

Hungrvaka: A history of the first native bishops of Iceland up to the late twelfth century.

Íslenzk fornrit: "Old Icelandic Texts." The name of the series of standard scholarly editions of medieval Icelandic literature published by Hið íslenzka fornritafélag (Old Icelandic Text Society) in Iceland.

Íslendingabók: A history of Iceland from its settlement to 1120 written by Ari Þorgilsson. The text is the oldest surviving prose narrative in Old Norse.

Íslendingasögur: The modern Icelandic term for the sagas of Icelanders (also known in English as family sagas).

Járnsíða: Law code given to Iceland by the Norwegian king Magnús Hákonarson in 1271.

Jónsbók: Law code given to Iceland by Norway in 1281 to replace the unpopular *Járnsíða* code.

Konungasögur: Kings' sagas. Old Norse narrative histories of the kings of Norway (or, in *Knýtlinga saga*, the kings of Denmark).

Landnámabok: "The Book of Settlements." An account of the early settlers of Iceland, with much genealogical information and some brief narrative anecdotes. Originally compiled in the thirteenth century but surviving in later versions.

Möðruvallabók: MS AM 132 fol. The most important surviving manuscript collection of sagas of Icelanders. Dating from the mid-fourteenth century, it contains texts of eleven sagas, some of them found in full in no other medieval manuscript.

Riddarasögur: "Sagas of Knights." Old Norse romances, translated from French or original compositions following the same conventions.

Saga Age: The period circa 930–circa 1030 during which most events in the sagas of Icelanders took place (not the period in which the sagas were written).

Samtíðarsögur: "Contemporary sagas" about events in Iceland in the twelfth and thirteenth centuries.

Skáldasögur: Sagas of poets, a subgroup of sagas of Icelanders.

Skaldic (scaldic) verse: Poetry in a variety of complex metrical forms and generally attributed to named poets. Skaldic verse (from Old Norse *skáld*, "poet") is incorporated in many of the sagas of Icelanders.

Sturlung Age: The period of Icelandic history from circa 1220 to circa 1262 that was marked by the increasing concentration of power in the hands of a small number of chieftainly families (including the Sturlung family) in conflict with one another. The conflict ended when Iceland submitted to the Norwegian monarchy in 1262–64.

Þáttr (pl. þættir): Literally, "a thread." Term used for saga-like short stories, mostly preserved in the context of kings' sagas.

The Sagas of Icelanders: Editions, Translations, Possible Dates

The following table enables readers to locate each saga of Icelanders in the standard Íslenzk fornrit edition and in the five-volume *Complete Sagas of Icelanders* translation. It also indicates which CS translations have been reprinted in *Sagas of Icelanders: A Selection*, labeled +SI, and/or separately in the Penguin Classics series, labeled +PC. The fourth column lists other selected translations including, but not limited to, those discussed in chapter 5 above.

The possible dates of composition given in the second column below are necessarily approximate. In many cases, scholars have proposed a variety of other dates for a saga's composition (see also the discussion of dating the sagas in ch. 2 above). I give here first the date proposed in the Íslenzk fornrit edition (preceded by ÍF), then the date given in the CS translation (preceded by CS). The information on Íslenzk fornrit dates is drawn from a valuable table by Vésteinn Ólason (2005: 114–15), which also lists some significantly different dates proposed by individual scholars and the date of the earliest surviving manuscript or fragment for each saga (not included below).

Title	Possible date	Íslenzk fornrit volume:pages	English title in CS, volume and pages, translator's name[a]	Selected other English translations
Bandamanna saga	ÍF ca. 1250 CS Late thirteenth century	VII:291–363	*The Saga of the Confederates,* V:283–312, Ruth C. Ellison +SI +PC (Viðar Hreinsson 2013: 119–54)	Morris and Eiríkr Magnússon 1891– 1905, I:73–121
Bárðar saga Snæfellsáss	ÍF 1350–1380 CS Late fourteenth century	XIII:99–172	*Bard's Saga,* II:237–66, Sarah M. Anderson	
Bjarnar saga Hítdœlakappa	ÍF 1215–1230 CS Late thirteenth century	III:109–211	*The Saga of Bjorn, Champion of the Hitardal People,* I:255–304, Alison Finlay +PC (Whaley 2002: 153– 221)	
Droplaugarsona saga	ÍF 1200–1240 CS Mid-thirteenth century	XI:135–80	*The Saga of Droplaug's Sons,* IV:355–78, Rory McTurk	Haworth and Young 1990: 75–105
Egils saga Skallagrímssonar	ÍF 1220–1230 CS Early thirteenth century	II	*Egil's Saga,* I:33–177, Bernard Scudder +SI +PC (Svanhildur Óskarsdóttir 2004)	Eddison 1932; Fell 1975; Hermann Pálsson and Edwards 1976
Eiríks saga rauða	ÍF 1200–1230 CS Early thirteenth century	IV:193–237	*Eirik the Red's Saga,* I:1– 18, Keneva Kunz +SI +PC (Gísli Sigurðsson 2008: 25–50)	Jones 1961: 126–57; Magnus Magnusson and Hermann Pálsson 1965: 73–105
Eyrbyggja saga	ÍF ca. 1220 CS Mid-thirteenth century	IV:1–184	*The Saga of the People of Eyri,* V:131–218, Judy Quinn	Morris and Eiríkr Magnússon 1891– 1905, II:1–186; Hermann Pálsson and Edwards 1989
Finnboga saga ramma	ÍF 1300–1350 CS Early fourteenth century	XIV:251–340	*The Saga of Finnbogi the Mighty,* III:221–70, John Kennedy	
Fljótsdœla saga	ÍF 1500–1550 CS Fourteenth or fifteenth century	XI:213–96	*The Saga of the People of Fljotsdal,* IV:379–433, John Porter	Haworth and Young 1990: 1–74
Flóamanna saga	ÍF 1290–1330 CS Early fourteenth century	XIII:229–327	*The Saga of the People of Floi,* III:271–304, Paul Acker	

Title	Possible date	Íslenzk fornrit volume:pages	English title in CS, volume and pages, translator's name[a]	Selected other English translations
Fóstbrœðra saga	ÍF ca. 1200 CS Late thirteenth century	VI:119–276	*The Saga of the Sworn Brothers*, II:329–402, Martin S. Regal +PC (Viðar Hreinsson 2013: 3–108)	
Gísla saga Súrssonar	ÍF ca. 1250 CS Mid- or Late thirteenth century	VI:1–118	*Gísli Sursson's Saga*, II:1–48, Martin S. Regal +SI	Johnston 1963 (reprinted in Faulkes 2001: 3–68)
Grettis saga Ásmundarsonar	ÍF 1310–1320 CS ca. 1400	VII:1–290	*The Saga of Grettir the Strong*, II:49–191, Bernard Scudder +PC (Örnólfur Thorsson 2005)	Hight 1913; Fox and Hermann Pálsson 1974; Faulkes 2001: 71–263; Byock 2009
Grœnlendinga saga	ÍF ca. 1300 CS Early thirteenth century (1200–1230)	IV:239–69	*The Saga of the Greenlanders*, I:19–32, Keneva Kunz +SI +PC (Gísli Sigurðsson 2008: 3–21)	Magnus Magnusson and Hermann Pálsson 1965: 49–72
Gunnars saga Keldugnúpsfífls	ÍF 1400–1500 CS Fourteenth or fifteenth century	XIV:341–79	*The Saga of Gunnarr, the Fool of Keldugnup*, III:421–36, Sarah M. Anderson	
Gunnlaugs saga ormstungu	ÍF 1270–1280 CS Late thirteenth century	III:49–107	*The Saga of Gunnlaug Serpent-Tongue*, I:305–33, Katrina C. Attwood +SI +PC (Whaley 2002: 111–49)	Morris and Eiríkr Magnússon 1875: 7–47; Foote and Quirk 1957, Durrenberger and Durrenberger 1992
Hallfreðar saga vandrǽðaskálds	ÍF ca. 1220 CS Early thirteenth century	VIII:133–200	*The Saga of Hallfred the Troublesome Poet*, I:225–53, Diana Whaley +PC (Whaley 2002: 71–108)	
Harðar saga Grímkelssonar [also known as *Harðar saga ok Holmverja*]	ÍF 1235–1245 or fourteenth century CS Late fourteenth century	XIII:1–97	*The Saga of Hord and the People of Holm*, II:193–236, Robert Kellogg	Faulkes 2001: 267–327

(continued)

(Continued)

Title	Possible date	Íslenzk fornrit volume:pages	English title in CS, volume and pages, translator's name[a]	Selected other English translations
Hávarðar saga Ísfirðings	ÍF 1300–1350 CS Fifteenth century	VI:289–358	*The Saga of Havard of Isafjord,* V:313–47, Frederik J. Heinemann +PC (Viðar Hreinsson 2013: 155–204)	Morris and Eiríkr Magnússon 1891– 1905, I:1–69; Durrenberger and Durrenberger 1996
Heiðarvíga saga	ÍF ca. 1200 CS Mid-thirteenth century	III:213–326	*The Saga of the Slayings on the Heath,* IV:67–129, Keneva Kunz	Morris and Eiríkr Magnússon 1891– 1905, II:191–259
Hrafnkels saga Freysgoða	ÍF By 1300 CS Late thirteenth or early fourteenth century	XI:95–133	*The Saga of Hrafnkel Frey's Godi,* V:261–81, Terry Gunnell +SI	Jones 1961: 89– 129; Hermann Pálsson 1971: 35– 71; O'Donoghue 2004: 202–23; Miller 2017: 217–34
Hœnsa-Þóris saga	ÍF 1250–1270 CS Late thirteenth century	III:1–47	*Hen-Thorir's Saga,* V:239–59, Peter A. Jorgensen	Morris and Eiríkr Magnússon 1891– 1905, I:125–63; Jones 1961: 3–38
Kjalnesinga saga	ÍF 1310–1320 CS Mid fourteenth century	XIV:1–44	*The Saga of the People of Kjalarnes,* III:305–28, Robert Cook and John Porter	
Kormáks saga	ÍF By 1220 CS Early thirteenth century	VIII:201–302	*Kormak's Saga,* I:179– 224; Rory McTurk +PC (Whaley 2002: 5–67)	Collingwood 1902
Króka-Refs saga	ÍF 1325–1375 CS Late fourteenth century	XIV:117–60	*The Saga of Ref the Sly,* III:397–420, George Clark +SI +PC (Viðar Hreinsson 2013: 205–38)	
Laxdœla saga	ÍF 1230–1260 CS Mid-thirteenth century	V	*The Saga of the People of Laxardal,* V:1–120, Kuneva Kunz +SI +PC (Bergljót S. Kristjánsdóttir 2008)	Press 1899; Magnús Magnússon and Hermann Pálsson 1969
Ljósvetninga saga	ÍF 1230?–1250 CS Late thirteenth century	X:1–139	*The Saga of the People of Ljosavatn,* IV:193–255, Theodore M. Andersson and William Ian Miller	

Title	Possible date	Íslenzk fornrit volume:pages	English title in CS, volume and pages, translator's name[a]	Selected other English translations
Njáls saga [Brennu-Njáls saga]	ÍF 1275–1285 CS Late thirteenth century	XII	Njal's Saga, III:1–220, Robert Cook	Dasent 1861; Bayerschmidt and Hollander [1955] 1998; Magnús Magnússon and Hermann Pálsson 1960
Reykdœla saga	ÍF ca. 1250 CS Late thirteenth century	X:149–243	The Saga of the People of Reykjadal and of Killer-Skuta, IV:257–302, George Clark	
Svarfdœla saga	ÍF 1350–1400 CS Late fourteenth century	IX:127–211	The Saga of the People of Svarfadardal, IV:149–91, Frederik J. Heinemann	
Valla-Ljóts saga	ÍF 1220–1240 CS Thirteenth or fourteenth century	IX:231–60	Valla-Ljot's Saga, IV:131–47, Paul Acker	
Vápnfirðinga saga	ÍF 1225–1250 CS Late thirteenth century	XI:21–65	The Saga of the People of Vopnafjord, IV:313–34, John Tucker	
Vatnsdœla saga	ÍF 1270–1280 CS Late thirteenth or early fourteenth century	VIII:1–131	The Saga of the People of Vatnsdal, IV:1–66, Andrew Wawn +SI	Jones 1961: 39–77
Víga-Glúms saga	ÍF 1220–1250 CS Early or mid-thirteenth century	IX:1–98	Killer-Glum's Saga, II:267–314, John McKinnell	Head 1866
Víglundar saga	ÍF ca. 1400 CS ca. 1400	XIV:61–116	Viglund's Saga, II:411–41, Marianne Kalinke +PC (Whaley 2002: 225–67)	Morris and Eiríkr Magnússon 1875: 81–126
Þórðar saga hreðu	ÍF ca. 1350 CS Late fourteenth century	XIV:161–226	The Saga of Thord Menace, III:362–96, Katrina C. Attwood	
Þorskfirðinga saga eða Gull-Þóris saga	ÍF 1300–1350 CS Fourteenth century	XIII:173–227	Gold-Thorir's Saga, III:335–59, Anthony Maxwell	
Þorsteins saga hvíta	ÍF 1275–1300 CS ca. 1300	XI:1–19	The Saga of Thorstein the White, IV:303–13, Anthony Maxwell	

(continued)

(Continued)

Title	Possible date	Íslenzk fornrit volume:pages	English title in CS, volume and pages, translator's name[a]	Selected other English translations
Þorsteins saga Síðu-Hallssonar	ÍF ca. 1250 CS Early fourteenth century	XI:297–320	*Thorstein Sidu-Hallsson's Saga*, IV:447–59, Katrina C. Attwood	
Ǫlkofra saga	ÍF ca. 1250 CS Late thirteenth century	XI:81–94	*Olkofri's Saga*, V:231–37, John Tucker +PC (Viðar Hreinsson 2013: 109–18)	

Note: a. +SI indicates the translation is also in *Sagas of Icelanders: A Selection*; +PC indicates reprinting of the translation in Penguin Classics.

NOTES

Preface

1. Last accessed August 28, 2019: https://www.washingtonpost.com/posteverything/wp/2017/05/31/white-supremacists-love-vikings-but-theyve-got-history-all-wrong/?utm_term=.e912de499dbb.

2. A more recent complete edition of the sagas and tales of Icelanders in Bragi Halldórsson et al. 1987 uses modernized spelling but has useful editorial material (in Icelandic).

A Note on Names and Pronunciation

1. I add the English -'s ending to the Icelandic nominative form to indicate possession, producing forms that must look rather barbaric to an Icelander, though this is now normal practice in English-language scholarship (thus, e.g., Egill's, rather than Icelandic Egils or Anglicized Egil's).

Chapter 1. Encountering the Sagas

1. Those wishing to learn to read Old Norse/Old Icelandic might try Byock 2013 and 2015. A full and detailed but accessible recent grammar is available in Barnes 2008, with a companion *Reader* of short texts from across Norse literature in Faulkes 2011 and a glossary in Faulkes 2007 (these three volumes are also available online as PDFs at http://vsnrweb-publications.org.uk/, last accessed August 28, 2019). The standard Old Icelandic-English dictionary remains Cleasby-Vigfusson 1963; a handy abridged version is Zoëga 1910. The text of these dictionaries may also easily be found online.

2. Excellent recent introductions to Norse-Icelandic literature include: O'Donoghue 2004, which surveys verse and prose, including mythological texts as well as sagas, and pays particular attention to the Anglophone reception of Norse literature, and Clunies Ross 2010a, which succinctly and authoritatively covers all saga genres. A slightly older book, Sørensen 1993 is particularly good at relating the literature to the society that produced it. Other recommended accounts of Old Norse–Icelandic literature include: Jónas Kristjáns-

son 1988, Clunies Ross 2000, McTurk 2005, Ármann and Sverrir Jakobsson 2017. For general reference consult Pulsiano 1993 and Simek and Herman Pálsson 1987 (in German).

3. Previous book-length studies of the saga of Icelanders genre include: Hallberg 1962, Andersson 1967, Tucker 1989 (a collection of essays), Bredsdorff 2001, and Vésteinn Ólason 1998. For a survey of scholarship on the genre to the mid-1980s, see Clover 1985.

4. On genre and the sagas, the best starting point is now Bampi 2017; see also Cardew 2004 and Clunies Ross 2010a: 27–36 (where she refers to what I have called genres as "sub-genres"). I discuss the issue in relation primarily to the kings' sagas, rather than the sagas of Icelanders, in Phelpstead 2007a, chapter 2.

5. The best all-around account of Norse paganism and mythology remains Turville-Petre 1964; for a fresh recent take on Norse myth, see Abram 2011.

Chapter 2. Traditions in Time

1. Among the many books on the Vikings, some that can be recommended for their scholarship and readability are: Foote and Wilson 1970, Jones 1984, Roesdahl 1991, Sawyer 1997, Helle 2003 (covering Scandinavian history from prehistory to 1520), and Brink and Price 2008. An engaging account of Norse discovery and colonization in the North Atlantic is Jones 1986 (with translations of primary texts). On medieval Icelandic history see: Jón Johannesson 1974, Jones 1986, Byock 1993, Byock 2001. Short 2010 documents everyday life in saga Iceland. For the medieval and later history of Iceland, see Gunnar Karlsson 2000.

2. Centuries earlier, the Roman Pliny quotes from the lost account of a voyage to the northern seas by Pytheas of Massalia in circa 330 BCE in which Pytheas mentions an island called Thule, six days' sailing north of Britain: this indicates knowledge of Iceland.

3. Sturlubók (ca. 1275–1280) by Sturla Þórðarson (1214–1284); Hauksbók (ca. 1306–1308) by Haukr Erlendsson (d. 1334); two vellum leaves from Melabók (ca. 1300–1310); and two seventeenth-century redactions, Skarðsárbók and Þórðarbók. Landnámabók is edited in ÍF I.2: 3–397 and translated in Edwards and Hermann Pálsson 1972.

4. Listed by Guðrún Nordal (2013: 204): Bárðar saga Snæfellsáss, Egils saga, Eyrbyggja saga, Flóamanna saga, Gísla saga Súrssonar, Grettis saga, Harðar saga, Hrafnkels saga, Kjalnesinga saga, Kormáks saga, Laxdæla saga, Reykdæla saga, Svarfdæla saga, Vatnsdæla saga, Víga-Glúms saga, Þórðar saga hreðu, and Þorskfirðinga saga. Of these, only Grettis saga includes skaldic verse referring to the settlement (Guðrún Nordal 2013: 206).

5. Bandamanna saga, exceptionally, is entirely set after the so-called Saga Age, circa 1050.

6. On the Conversion and Christianization, see further Strömbäck 1975, Orri Vésteinsson 2000.

7. His father Gizurr the White led the attack on Gunnarr of Hlíðarendi in Njáls saga but was subsequently baptized by Þangbrandr. One of Ísleifr's sons was Teitr, Ari's informant and teacher.

8. The classic account of thirteenth-century Icelandic history is Einar Ólafur Sveinsson 1953.

9. Jón Viðar Sigurðsson notes, "It was usual for chieftains to be [Christian] priests in the eleventh and twelfth centuries" (1999: 190). At the end of the twelfth century, the archbishop in Trondheim, to whose province Iceland belonged, forbade chieftains to become priests.

10. For the history of scholarly debate on saga origins, including a detailed account of the free prose/book prose debate, see Andersson 1964. For an up-to-date account of more recent scholarship on the origins of saga writing, see Callow 2017.

11. Articles in Mundal and Wellendorf 2008 provide a comparative perspective on the transition from oral to written in Old Norse and other medieval and later European literatures.

12. The saga is dated to after 1237 in Ursula Brown 1952: xxix. For commentary see, for example, Foote 1984; Sørensen 1993: 42–50, 68–69. While most scholars assume these stories existed only in oral form at that date, Hermann Pálsson 1999: 77–78 suggests that they were read aloud from manuscript texts, noting that *setja saman* is usually used of written rather than oral narratives.

13. On skaldic verse, see especially Turville-Petre 1976, Frank 1978, and Clunies Ross 2005; on its use in sagas, see initially Bjarni Einarsson 1974, Harris 1997, and O'Donoghue 2005. Specifically on the relationship between verse and prose in poets' sagas, see O'Donoghue 1991, Marold 2001, Poole 2001, and Sørensen 2001.

14. Bjarni Einarsson 1974 has been a particularly influential account of this distinction; Clunies Ross (2005, ch. 4, especially pp. 70–71, 78–82) provides a useful account of the matter.

15. Gade 2001 is an exemplary detailed analysis of the authenticity of verse in four poets' sagas (see further ch. 4 below).

16. Hreinn Benediktsson 1972: 246–47. By the time that *Hungrvaka*, a brief account of the earliest Icelandic bishops, was composed in the first decade of the thirteenth century, a similar list includes "sagas" (ÍF 16: p. 2).

17. See also Wellendorf 2017 for an up-to-date account of scholarship on the relationship between saga-writing and Latin learned literature.

18. *Flóamanna saga* is particularly rich in examples of influence from hagiographic and other learned Latin literature: see Perkins 1974–1977 and 1978.

19. For a useful account of recent work on saga style, see Sävborg 2017. Hallberg 1962, ch. 9, examines humor and irony in the sagas. Some particularly valuable studies of specific aspects of saga style include: Lönnroth 1969a on rhetoric and apparent narratorial objectivity; Hume 1973 on beginnings and endings of sagas; and Sävborg 2018 on formulaic language in the sagas.

20. Driscoll and Svanhildur Óskarsdóttir 2015 is a beautiful guide to manuscripts in the Arnamagnæan collection, with a concise account of book production in the Middle Ages (pp. 211–25); Jónas Kristjánsson 1993 includes many illustrations. For an accessible brief introduction to saga manuscripts, their survival, and their preservation in libraries, see Clunies Ross 2010a, ch. 8; Svanhildur Óskarsdóttir 2012 surveys recent developments in Icelandic manuscript studies. The Indices volume of the *Dictionary of Old Norse Prose* (*Ordbog* 1989) lists and dates surviving manuscripts by saga.

21. This continuous tradition was facilitated by the stability over time of the Icelandic language (cf. Driscoll 2010: 87).

22. The debate is neatly summarized in Schach 1993: 216 and 219.

23. Quinn and Lethbridge 2010 is an important collection of articles on saga textuality, variant versions, and editorial method.

Chapter 3. Icelandic Identities

1. Note, however, that Patricia Pires Boulhosa (2005) argues that Icelanders had a closer relationship with and stronger sense of loyalty to the Norwegian crown than most previous scholarship has recognized.

2. Turville-Petre 1996 and Hastings 1997, for example, argue that nations, even nation-states, existed in the Middle Ages, in opposition to recent scholarly orthodoxy that nationalism, as it developed from the eighteenth century onward, created nations.

3. Of course, it shared its language, allowing for some dialectal differences, with other West Norse–speaking communities. It is the combination of language, geography, laws, and memories that adds up to an identity, and some sharing of one or other of these with other communities no more undermines this than the common use of English means that the United Kingdom, the United States, Canada, and Ireland are not separate nations.

4. The nature of the subject matter means that this is more often the case in genres such as the *fornaldarsögur* and *riddarasögur* than in the sagas of Icelanders.

5. Unlike other sources, *Njáls saga* (ch. 97) claims that the Fifth Court was established before the conversion when Njáll engineered a legal impasse in a quarter court so as to necessitate the creation of a superior court and more chieftaincies, including one for his foster-son, Hǫskuldr.

6. Besides the version by Terry Gunnell in CS, translations of *Hrafnkels saga* include Jones 1963: 89–125, Hermann Pálsson 1971: 35–71, O'Donoghue 2004: 202–23, and Miller 2017: 217–34.

7. On the relationship of *Hrafnkels saga* to history, see Gordon 1939, Nordal 1958, and Danielsson 2002 (in Swedish). On this saga, see also Óskar Halldórsson 1989, Fulk 1986–1989, and Sayers 2007. Miller 2017 offers a fresh perspective in an extended and thought-provoking analysis of the saga.

8. Stimulating recent book-length studies of gender in Old Norse–Icelandic literature include Clark 2012 and Jóhanna Katrín Friðriksdóttir 2013. Both discuss, but also range beyond, the sagas of Icelanders. For a fine account of recent research in the area, see Jóhanna Katrín Friðriksdóttir 2017. The first book-length study of men and masculinity in the sagas of Icelanders has appeared even more recently in Evans 2019, a book that matches insightful close reading with impressive theoretical sophistication.

9. Jochens 2002: 137 reports that the names listed in *Landnámabók* suggest that there were six times as many men as women among the first generation of settlers, but the imbalance is unlikely to have been this severe. Jochens also points out that three-quarters of the men listed fathered children, and many female settlers, including slaves and concubines as well as wives thought too unimportant to name or remember, must be unrecorded.

10. Fundamental studies on this topic are Ström 1974 and Sørensen 1983.

11. Bjørn Bandlien, however, argues that *ergi* for women is desire for a man of lower social status rather than nymphomania as such (2005: 30n28).

12. Though usually used in relation to male-male intercourse, in the poorly preserved obscene poem *Grettisfærsla*, the verb is used to describe Grettir Ásmundarson's vigorous relations with a wide range of both male and female "partners": see Heslop 2006.

13. Ecocriticism is only just beginning to have an impact on saga studies: see Phelpstead 2014. Abram 2019, the splendid first book-length ecocritical study of Norse myth and literature, is essential reading. On landscape and the sagas, see, for example, Barraclough 2010 and 2012, Falk 2007, and Overing and Osborn 1994. Hastrup 1985, ch. 6 correlates climate and environmental changes with population and social changes in medieval Iceland. The fullest published account of human-animal relations in the sagas is Rohrbach 2009 (in German).

14. This theme in the saga may be a response to the requirement of the *Jónsbók* laws of 1281 that those with a surplus of hay must sell it when it was in short supply.

15. Though "foster-child" is the more common meaning, *fóstri* can also mean "foster-brother," and predictions concerning the difference in time between foster-brothers' deaths are a saga topos.

16. The following discussion draws on Phelpstead 2012, but I now have reservations regarding the ease with which I there equated Todorov's "unlikely" with that which is "improbable" (27–28). For an example of the use of Todorov's ideas in relation to the sagas, see Clunies Ross 2002, but note that she has developed a more historically appropriate approach in Clunies Ross 2010a, ch. 6.

17. But what a thirteenth- or fourteenth-century Icelander may have regarded as plausibly having happened in the period of settlement may have seemed to him or her less likely to occur in the present. Magic or witchcraft, for example, is notably less prevalent in the contemporary sagas than in the sagas of Icelanders.

18. On this episode, see further Phelpstead 2014: 14–15.

19. On dreams and destiny in the sagas of Icelanders, see Hallberg 1962, ch. 7. A foundational study of dreams in the sagas is Kelchner 1935.

20. Key studies include Dillmann 2006 and Mitchell 2011.

21. The þáttr is translated in CS II: 459–62. It is memorably titled "Thidrandi Whom the Goddesses Slew" in Gwyn Jones's translation (1961: 158–62).

22. Norse quoted from the edition in *Óláfs saga Tryggvasonar en mesta*, ed. Ólafur Halldórsson, II, 149.

Chapter 4. Reading Selected Sagas

1. On *þættir* in general, see Harris 1972, 1976; Rowe and Harris 2005; and Rowe 2017.

2. *Auðunar þáttr* is edited (from Morkinskinna) in ÍF VI (1943), 361–68. The new standard edition of Morkinskinna is Ármann Jakobsson and Þórður Ingi Guðjónsson 2011. The Flateyjarbók text of *Auðunar þáttr* is in Vigfússon and Unger 1860–1868: III, 411–15. Many introductory textbooks of Old Norse include an edition of the story (e.g., Faulkes

2011: 207–15). A translation of the þáttr by Anthony Maxwell appears in CS I: 369–74 and is reprinted in SI pp. 717–22. Among other translations, Gwyn Jones 1961: 163–70 follows the Morkinskinna text, whereas Hermann Pálsson 1971: 121–28 follows that of Flateyjarbók. Miller's elegant book-length study of *Auðunar þáttr* (2008) is essential reading.

3. See Clunies Ross 2001 for the definition and membership of this group of texts. She distinguishes between a "core" (the sagas of Kormákr, Hallfreðr, Bjǫrn, and Gunnlaugr) and "outliers," which include *Egils saga* and *Fóstbrœðra saga*. See the table of sagas at the end of this book for details of the Íslenzk fornrit editions of the Norse texts of the skáldasögur. The CS translations of poets' sagas (not including *Fóstbrœðra saga*, but with *Víglundar saga*) have been handily reprinted as *Sagas of Warrior Poets* in Penguin Classics with useful editorial material (Whaley 2002). Poole 2001 is an excellent and indispensable collection of articles on the poets' sagas.

4. For classic descriptions of heroic society and poetry, see Chadwick 1912, Bowra 1952, and De Vries 1963. Benedict 1946 and Peristiany 1966 are influential accounts of guilt and shame cultures (in Japan and the Mediterranean, respectively).

5. *Kormáks saga* has received book-length attention in O'Donoghue 1991.

6. Useful studies of *Gunnlaugs saga* include Foote and Quirk 1957; Poole 1989 and 2001. Durrenberger and Durrenberger 1992 takes an unusual approach to translating *Gunnlaugs saga* and has a thought-provoking introduction.

7. The CS translation of *Egils saga* by Bernard Scudder has been reprinted with helpful editorial material in Svanhildur Óskarsdóttir 2004. Two useful collections gather essays on a range of topics relating to the saga and provide further bibliographical guidance: Hines and Slay 1992 and De Looze et al. 2015. On the possibility that Snorri Sturluson wrote the saga, see Vésteinn Ólason 1998: 252n38.

8. The two main manuscripts besides Möðruvallabók are a fourteenth-century text in Wolfenbüttel and the seventeenth-century Ketilsbók copies of a lost fourteenth-century manuscript (AM 453 and 462 4to).

9. Turville-Petre 1976: 15–41 is perhaps the best place to begin exploring Egill's poetry. On the relation of verse to prose in the saga, see Clunies Ross 2010b.

10. For a recent study with references to earlier scholarship on this issue, see Haukur Þorgeirsson 2014.

11. The sagas are edited in ÍF IV *Eyrbyggja saga* and its supplement. They are the most frequently translated sagas of Icelanders and have most recently been published together in Kunz and Gísli Sigurðsson 2008, which includes useful editorial material. For a fascinating and richly documented account of the sagas and of their multifaceted reception in the nineteenth and twentieth centuries, see Barnes 2001.

12. Helluland may correspond to the southern part of Baffin Island, Markland to the south coast of Labrador or west coast of Newfoundland, and Vínland to the Canadian Maritime Provinces or north New England (Barnes 2001: xvi), but there has been much disagreement about the locations. See the recent discussion in Kunz and Gísli Sigurðsson 2008: xxx–xxxvi and the convenient table of scholarly views on pp. 66–67 of that book or in Gísli Sigurðsson 2004: 277.

13. It has, nevertheless, recently been used on the cover of Kunz and Gísli Sigurðsson 2008, with a caption stating that the map is "probably 15th century."

14. The final chapter of *Grœnlendinga saga* tells how, after Karlsefni's death, Guðríðr went "south" (i.e., to Rome) on pilgrimage and on her return to Iceland became an anchoress and nun.

15. Translations of the three sagas are presented together in Faulkes 2001. The use of verse in *Gísla saga* and *Grettis saga* is discussed in detail in O'Donoghue 2005 chapters 3 and 4.

16. On the textual transmission of *Gísla saga*, see Þórður Ingi Guðjónsson 2010 and Lethbridge 2010.

17. See Clark 2012 ch. 4 more generally on sexual themes and the heroic in *Gísla saga*.

18. On the "noble heathen" figure in the sagas, see Lönnroth 1969b (repr. in Lönnroth 2011: 45–74).

19. For representative expressions of opposing views on this issue, see Orchard 1995: 140–68 and Fjalldal 1998.

20. The classic case for female authorship is Kress 1980, but the idea goes back much further. H. M. Chadwick (1870–1947), for example, thought the saga was written by a woman (see Scott 2002: 238). On the saga's focus on female experience, see also Jesch 1991: 193–202, Auerbach 1998–2001, and Bandlien 2005: 87–90.

21. Ch. 19 similarly mentions the marriage and divorce between Hrútr and Unnr, daughter of Mǫrðr gígja, which features in the opening chapters of *Njáls saga*, without mentioning the sexual problems that are described so graphically in *Njála*.

22. The CS translation has Kjartan eat "dry food" throughout Lent; the Norse *fastaði þurrt* (literally "fasted drily") means avoiding meat and eating only fish and plant foods.

23. *Bolla þáttr* is included in the ÍF edition of *Laxdæla saga* with the chapters numbered as part of the saga; in CS and its reprints, it is a separate text printed immediately after the saga.

24. The saga inspired several book-length studies in the 1970s (Allen 1971, Einar Ólafur Sveinsson 1971, and Lönnroth 1976) and one more recent one, Miller 2014. Hines and Slay 1992 is a handy collection of articles aimed at students.

25. On this topic, see especially Dronke 1981, O'Donoghue 1992, and Ármann Jakobsson 2007.

26. This remarkable poem, which survives only in *Njáls saga*, is discussed in detail and with reference to Norse and Irish historical traditions in Poole 1991: 116–56.

Chapter 5. The Sagas in English

1. This involved anachronistically identifying the Catholic medieval Norse-speakers with modern Protestant Scandinavians. On the links between identity politics and the reception of the Vínland sagas and "Viking America," see Barnes 2001 and Steel 2018.

2. Eiríkr describes their meeting and collaboration in Morris and Eiríkr Magnússon 1891–1905: VI, vii–xvi. See also Wawn 2001. Eiríkr spelled his name thus in his publications, though the normal modern Icelandic spelling is Eiríkur. A recent book-length

study of William Morris and the sagas examines the translations he produced with Eiríkr alongside creative writings in which Morris was influenced by his reading of the sagas: see Felce 2018.

3. On Eiríkr Magnússon's involvement, see Wawn 2000: 304; Kennedy 2007: 81.

4. On Eddison's *Egils saga* translation, see further Townend 2018.

5. Kennedy provides an interesting account of different critical reactions to Hermann Pálsson's work (2007: 161–64).

BIBLIOGRAPHY

Icelandic authors are listed by first name rather than patronymic (unless they have a hereditary surname). Following Icelandic practice, the letters Ö and Þ appear at the end of the alphabet. Where more than one publication is listed for an author, they appear in order of date of publication.

1. Primary Texts (Original Language)

1.1. Íslenzk fornrit edition of the sagas of Icelanders

ÍF II: *Egils saga Skalla-Grímssonar*. Ed. Sigurður Nordal. Reykjavík, Iceland: Hið íslenzka fornritafélag, 1933.

ÍF III: *Borgfirðinga sögur*. Ed. Sigurður Nordal and Guðni Jónsson. Reykjavík, Iceland: Hið íslenzka fornritafélag, 1938.

ÍF IV: *Eyrbyggja saga*. Ed. Einar Ól. Sveinsson and Matthías Þórðarson. Supplement to second edition, ed. Ólafur Halldórsson. Reykjavík, Iceland: Hið íslenzka fornritafélag, [1935] 1985.

ÍF V: *Laxdœla saga*. Ed. Einar Ól. Sveinsson. Reykjavík: Hið íslenzka fornritafélag, 1934.

ÍF VI: *Vestfirðinga sögur*. Ed. Björn K. Þórólfsson and Guðni Jónsson. Reykjavík, Iceland: Hið íslenzka fornritafélag, 1943.

ÍF VII: *Grettis saga Ásmundarsonar*. Ed. Guðni Jónsson. Reykjavík, Iceland: Hið íslenzka fornritafélag, 1936.

ÍF VIII: *Vatnsdœla saga*. Ed. Einar Ól. Sveinsson. Reykjavík, Iceland: Hið íslenzka fornritafélag, 1939.

ÍF IX: *Eyfirðinga sögur*. Ed. Jónas Kristjánsson. Reykjavík, Iceland: Hið íslenzka fornritafélag, 1956.

ÍF X: *Ljósvetninga saga*. Ed. Björn Sigfússon. Reykjavík, Iceland: Hið íslenzka fornritafélag, 1940.

ÍF XI: *Austfirðinga sögur*. Ed. Jón Jóhannesson. Reykjavík, Iceland: Hið íslenzka fornritafélag, 1950.

ÍF XII: *Brennu-Njáls saga*. Ed. Einar Ól. Sveinsson. Reykjavík, Iceland: Hið íslenzka fornritafélag, 1954.

ÍF XIII: *Harðar saga*. Ed. Þórhallur Vilmundarson and Bjarni Vilhjálmsson. Reykjavík,
Iceland: Hið íslenzka fornritafélag, 1991.

ÍF XIV: *Kjalnesinga saga*. Ed. Jóhannes Halldórsson. Reykjavík, Iceland: Hið íslenzka
fornritafélag, 1959.

1.2. Other Primary Texts

Parallel text editions with both the original and an English translation are listed here and
not in the list of translations below.

Adam of Bremen. *Gesta Hammaburgensis ecclesiae pontificum*. In *Quellen des 9. und 11. Jahr-
hunderts zur Geschichte der hamburgischen Kirche und des Reiches*. Ed. W. Trillmich and
R. Buchner. 7th ed. Darmstadt, Germany: Wissenschaftliche Buchgesellschaft, 2000.
160–499.

Ari Þorgilsson. Íslendingabók. Ed. Jakob Benediktsson. In *Íslendingabók. Landnámabók*.
ÍF I.1. Reykjavík, Iceland: Hið íslenzka fornritafélag, 1968. 3–28.

Ármann Jakobsson and Þórður Ingi Guðjónsson, eds. *Morkinskinna*. 2 vols. ÍF XXIII–
XXIV. Reykjavík, Iceland: Hið íslenzka fornritafélag, 2011.

Bergljót S. Kristjánsdóttir, ed., and Keneva Kunz, trans. *The Saga of the People of Laxardal
and Bolli Bollason's Tale*. London: Penguin Classics, 2008.

Bjarni Aðalbjarnarson, ed. Snorri Sturluson: *Heimskringla*. 3 vols. ÍF XXVI–XXVIII.
Reykjavík, Iceland: Hið íslenzka fornritafélag, 1941–1951.

Bragi Halldórsson, Jón Torfason, Sverrir Tómasson, and Örnólfur Thorsson, eds. *Íslendinga sögur og þættir*. 3 vols. Reykjavík, Iceland: Svart á Hvitu, 1987.

Brown, Ursula, ed. *Þorgils saga ok Hafliða*. London: Oxford University Press, 1952.

Dicuili Liber de mensura orbis terrae. Ed. J. J. Tierney with contributions by L. Bieler. Dublin: Dublin Institute for Advanced Studies, 1967.

Foote, P. G., ed., and R. Quirk, trans. *Gunnlaugs saga ormstungu/The Story of Gunnlaug
Serpent-Tongue*. London: Nelson, 1957.

Guðbrandur Vigfússon, and C. R. Unger, eds. *Flateyjarbók: En samling af norske konge-
sagaer med indskudte mindre fortællinger om begivenheder i og udenfor Norge samt an-
naler*. 3 vols. Christiania, Oslo: Malling, 1860–1868.

Hreinn Benediktsson, ed. and trans. *The First Grammatical Treatise*. Reykjavík, Iceland:
Institute of Nordic Linguistics, 1972.

Hungrvaka in *Biskupa sögur* 2. Ed. Ásdís Egilsdóttir. ÍF XVI, 3–43. Reykjavík, Iceland: Hið
íslenzka fornritafélag, 2002.

Kålund, Kr., ed. *Alfræði íslenzk: Islandsk encyklopædisk litteratur. I. Cod. mbr. AM. 194, 8vo*.
Copenhagen, Denmark: Samfund til udgivelse af gammel nordisk litteratur, 1908.

Landnámabók. Ed. Jakob Benediktsson. In *Íslendingabók. Landnámabók*. ÍF I.2, 3–28.
Reykjavík, Iceland: Hið íslenzka fornritafélag, 1968.

Óláfs saga Tryggvasonar en mesta. Ed. Ólafur Halldórsson. Editiones Arnamagnæanæ,
Series A, 1–3. Copenhagen, Denmark: Munksgaard, 1958–2000.

Saxo Grammaticus. *Gesta Danorum: The History of the Danes.* Ed. Karsten Friis-Jensen and trans. Peter Fisher. 2 vols. Oxford: Clarendon, 2015.

2. English Translations of Primary Texts

Bayerschmidt, Carl F., and Lee M. Hollander, trans. *Njál's Saga* [1955]. Reprinted with an introduction by Þorsteinn Gylfason. Ware, U.K.: Wordsworth, 1998.

Byock, Jesse, trans. *Grettir's Saga.* Oxford: Oxford University Press, 2009.

Clunies Ross, Margaret, ed. *The Old Norse Poetic Translations of Thomas Percy: A New Edition and Commentary.* Turnhout, Belgium: Brepols, 2002.

Coles, John. *Summer Travelling in Iceland.* London: Murray, 1882.

Collingwood, W. G., trans. *The Life and Death of Cormac the Skald.* London: Viking Club, 1902.

Dasent, George Webbe, trans. *The Story of Burnt Njal; or Life in Iceland at the End of the Tenth Century.* Edinburgh: Edmonston and Douglas, 1861.

Durrenberger, E. Paul, and Dorothy Durrenberger, trans. *The Saga of Gunnlaugur Snake's Tongue.* Madison, N.J.: Fairleigh Dickinson University Press, 1992.

———, trans. *The Saga of Hávarður of Ísafjörður.* Enfield Lock, U.K.: Hisarlik, 1996.

Eddison, E. R., trans. *Egil's Saga.* Cambridge: Cambridge University Press, 1930.

Faulkes, Anthony, ed. and trans. *Three Icelandic Outlaw Sagas.* London: Viking Society for Northern Research, 2001.

Faulkes, Anthony, and Alison Finlay, trans. Snorri Sturluson: *Heimskringla.* 3 vols. London: Viking Society for Northern Research: 2011–2015.

Fell, Christine, trans. *Egils Saga.* London: Dent, 1975.

Fox, Denton, and Hermann Pálsson, trans. *Grettir's Saga.* Toronto: University of Toronto Press, 1974.

Gísli Sigurðsson, ed., and Keneva Kunz, trans. *The Vinland Sagas.* London: Penguin Classics, 2008.

Grágás. Laws of Early Iceland: Grágás. Trans. Andrew Dennis, Peter Foote, and Richard Perkins. 2 vols. Winnipeg: University of Manitoba Press, 1980–2000.

Grønlie, Siân, trans. *Íslendingabók, Kristni saga: The Book of the Icelanders, The Story of the Conversion.* London: Viking Society for Northern Research, 2006.

Gudbrand Vigfusson [Guðbrandur Vigfússon], and Sir G. W. Dasent, eds. and trans. *Corpvs Poeticvm Boreale: The Poetry of the Old Northern Tongue from the Earliest Times to the Thirteenth Century.* 2 vols. Oxford: Clarendon, 1883.

———, eds. and trans. *Icelandic Sagas and Other Historical Documents Relating to the Settlements and Descents of the Northmen on the British Isles.* Rolls Series, 4 vols. London: HMSO, 1887–94.

———, eds. and trans. *Origines Islandicae.* 2 vols. Oxford: Clarendon, 1905.

Haworth, Eleanor, and Jean Young, trans. *The Fljotsdale Saga and The Droplaugarsons.* London: Dent, 1990.

Head, Sir Edmund, trans. *Viga Glum's Saga.* London: Williams and Norgate, 1866.

Hermann Pálsson, trans. *Hrafnkel's Saga and Other Icelandic Stories.* Harmondsworth, U.K.: Penguin, 1971.

Hermann Pálsson, and Paul Edwards, trans. *The Book of Settlements: Landnámabók.* Winnipeg: University of Manitoba Press, 1972.

Hermann Pálsson, and Paul Edwards, trans. *Egil's Saga.* Harmondsworth, U.K.: Penguin Classics, 1976.

Hermann Pálsson, and Paul Edwards, trans. *Eyrbyggja Saga* [1972]. London: Penguin Classics, 1989.

Johnston, George, trans. *The Saga of Gisli.* With an essay on the *Saga of Gisli* by Peter Foote. London: Dent, 1963.

Jones, Gwyn. *Eirik the Red and Other Icelandic Sagas.* Oxford: Oxford University Press, 1961.

Kunin, Devra, trans., and Carl Phelpstead, ed. *A History of Norway and the Passion and Miracles of the Blessed Óláfr.* London: Viking Society for Northern Research, 2001.

Magnus Magnusson, and Hermann Pálsson, trans. *Njál's Saga.* Harmondsworth, U.K.: Penguin, 1960.

———, trans. *The Vinland Sagas: The Norse Discovery of America. Grænlendinga saga and Eirik's saga.* Harmondsworth, U.K.: Penguin, 1965.

McDougall, David, and Ian McDougall, trans. *Theodoricus monachus: The Ancient History of the Norwegian Kings.* London: Viking Society for Northern Research, 1998.

Morris, William, and Eiríkr Magnússon, trans. *Grettis Saga: The Story of Grettir the Strong.* London: Ellis, 1869.

———, trans. *Three Northern Love Stories and Other Tales.* London: Ellis and White, 1875.

———, trans. *The Saga Library.* 6 vols. London: Quaritch, 1891–1905.

———, trans. *The Story of Egil the Son of Scaldgrim.* In *William Morris: Artist, Writer, Socialist,* ed. May Morris, 564–636. Oxford: Blackwell, 1936.

———, trans. *The Story of Kormak the Son of Ogmund.* London: William Morris Society, 1970.

Press, Muriel A. C., trans. *Laxdœla Saga.* London: Dent, 1899.

Scott, Sir Walter. "Abstract of the Eyrbyggja-Saga." In *Illustrations of Northern Antiquities,* ed. Robert Jamieson and Henry Weber, 517–49. Edinburgh: Ballantyne, 1814; reprinted in Percy 1847: 517–40.

Stephens, George, trans. *Frithiof's Saga: A Legend of Norway.* London: Black and Armstrong, 1839.

Svanhildur Óskarsdóttir, ed., and Bernard Scudder, trans. *Egils saga.* London: Penguin Classics, 2004.

The Sagas of Icelanders: A Selection. With an Introduction by Robert Kellogg. London: Viking Penguin, 2000.

Viðar Hreinsson, ed. *The Complete Sagas of Icelanders, Including 49 Tales.* 5 vols. Reykjavík, Iceland: Leifur Eiríksson, 1997.

———, ed. *Comic Sagas and Tales from Iceland.* London: Penguin Classics, 2015.

Whaley, Diana, ed. *Sagas of Warrior-Poets.* London: Penguin Classics, 2002.

Örnólfur Thorsson, ed., and Bernard Scudder, trans. *The Saga of Grettir the Strong.* London: Penguin Classics, 2005.

3. Secondary Literature

Abram, Christopher. *Myths of the Pagan North: The Gods of the Norsemen.* London: Continuum, 2011.

———. *Evergreen Ash: Ecology and Catastrophe in Old Norse Myth and Literature.* Charlottesville: University of Virginia Press, 2019.

Allen, Richard. *Fire and Ice: Critical Approaches to Njáls saga.* Pittsburgh: Pittsburgh University Press, 1971.

Anderson, Benedict. *Imagined Communities: Reflections on the Origin and Spread of Nationalism.* London: Verso, 1983; rev. ed. 2016.

Anderson, Sarah M., with Karen Swenson, eds. *Cold Counsel: Women in Old Norse Literature and Mythology.* New York: Routledge, 2002.

Andersson, Theodore M. *The Problem of Saga Origins.* New Haven: Yale University Press, 1964.

———. *The Icelandic Family Saga: An Analytic Reading.* Cambridge, Mass.: Harvard University Press, 1967.

———. "The Long Prose Form in Medieval Iceland." *Journal of English and Germanic Philology* 101 (2002): 380–411.

———. *The Growth of the Medieval Icelandic Sagas (1180–1280).* Ithaca: Cornell University Press, 2006.

Ármann Jakobsson. "Masculinity and Politics in *Njáls saga.*" *Viator* 38 (2007): 191–215.

———. "The Taxonomy of the Non-Existent: Some Medieval Icelandic Concepts of the Paranormal." *Fabula* 54 (2013): 199–213.

Ármann Jakobsson, and Sverrir Jakobsson, eds. *The Routledge Research Companion to the Medieval Icelandic Saga.* London: Routledge, 2017.

Auerbach, Loren. "Female Experience and Authorial Intention in *Laxdœla saga.*" *Saga-Book* 25 (1998–2001): 30–52.

Bampi, Massimiliano. "Genre." In Ármann Jakobsson and Sverrir Jakobsson 2017: 4–14.

Bandlien, Bjørn. *Strategies of Passion: Love and Marriage in Old Norse Society.* Turnhout, Belgium: Brepols, 2005.

Baring-Gould, Sabine. *Iceland: Its Scenes and Sagas.* London: Smith, Elder, 1863; repr. Oxford: Signal, 2007.

Barnes, Geraldine. *Viking America: The First Millennium.* Cambridge: Brewer, 2001.

Barnes, Michael. *A New Introduction to Old Norse: Part 1 Grammar.* 3rd ed. London: Viking Society for Northern Research, 2008.

Barraclough, Eleanor. "Inside Outlawry in *Grettis saga Ásmundarsonar* and *Gísla saga Súrssonar*: Landscape in the Outlaw Sagas." *Scandinavian Studies* 82 (2010): 365–88.

———. "Land-naming in the Migration Myth of Medieval Iceland: Constructing the Past in the Present and the Present in the Past." *Saga-Book* 36 (2012): 79–101.

Bartlett, Robert. *The Natural and the Supernatural in the Middle Ages.* Cambridge: Cambridge University Press, 2008.

Beamish, North Ludlow. *The Discovery of America by the Northmen in the Tenth Century.* London: Boone, 1841.

Benedict, Ruth. *The Chrysanthemum and the Sword: Patterns of Japanese Culture*. London: Oxford University Press, 1946.

Bjarni Einarsson. *Skáldasögur: Um uppruna og eðli ástaskáldasagnanna fornu*. Reykjavík, Iceland: Bókaútgáfa Menningarsjóðs, 1961.

———. "On the Rôle of Verse in Saga-Literature." *Mediaeval Scandinavia* 7 (1974): 118–25.

Boulhosa, Patricia Pires. *Icelanders and the Kings of Norway: Mediaeval Sagas and Legal Texts*. Leiden, Netherlands: Brill, 2005.

Bowra, C. M. *Heroic Poetry*. London: Macmillan, 1952.

Bredsdorff, Thomas. *Chaos and Love: The Philosophy of the Icelandic Family Sagas*. Trans. John Tucker. Copenhagen, Denmark: Museum Tusculanum, 2001.

Brink, Stefan, and Neil Price, eds. *The Viking World*. London: Routledge, 2008.

Butler, Judith. *Gender Trouble: Feminism and the Subversion of Identity*. 10th anniversary edition. London: Routledge, [1990] 1999.

Byock, Jesse. *Feud in the Icelandic Saga*. Berkeley: University of California Press, 1982.

———. *Medieval Iceland: Society, Sagas, and Power*. Enfield Lock, London: Hisarlik, 1993.

———. *Viking Age Iceland*. London: Penguin, 2001.

———. *Viking Language 1: Learn Old Norse, Runes, and Icelandic Sagas*. Pacific Palisades, Calif.: Jules Williams, 2013.

———. *Viking Language 2: The Old Norse Reader*. Pacific Palisades, Calif.: Jules Williams, 2015.

Callow, Chris. "Dating and Origins." Ármann Jakobsson and Sverrir Jakobsson 2017: 15–33.

Cannadine, David. *The Undivided Past: History Beyond Our Differences*. London: Allen Lane, 2013.

Cardew, Phil. "The Question of Genre in the Late *Íslendinga sögur*: A Case Study of Þorskfirðinga saga." In *Sagas, Saints and Settlements*, ed. Gareth Williams and Paul Bibire, 13–27. Leiden, Netherlands: Brill, 2004.

Carlé, Birte. "Some Observations Regarding Narrative Patterns in the Medieval Sagas of Holy Maids." In *Les Sagas de chevaliers (riddarasögur): Actes de la Ve conférence internationale sur les sagas (Toulon, Juillet 1982)*, ed. Régis Boyer, 393–404. Paris: Presses de l'Université de Paris-Sorbonne, 1985.

Cerquiglini, Bernard. *In Praise of the Variant: A Critical History of Philology*. Trans. Betsy Wing. Baltimore: Johns Hopkins University Press, 1993.

Chadwick, H. M. *The Heroic Age*. Cambridge: Cambridge University Press, 1912.

Clark, David. *Gender, Violence, and the Past in Edda and Saga*. Oxford: Oxford University Press, 2012.

Clark, David, and Carl Phelpstead, eds. *Old Norse Made New: Essays on the Post-Medieval Reception of Old Norse Literature and Culture*. London: Viking Society, 2007.

Cleasby, Richard, and Gudbrand Vigfusson. *An Icelandic-English Dictionary*. 2nd ed. with a supplement by Sir William Craigie. Oxford: Clarendon, 1963.

Clover, Carol J. "Icelandic Family Sagas (*Íslendingasögur*)." In *Old Norse–Icelandic Literature: A Critical Guide*, ed. Carol J. Clover and John Lindow, 239–315. Ithaca: Cornell University Press, 1985.

———. "The Long Prose Form." *Arkiv för nordisk filologi* 101 (1986): 10–39.

———. "The Politics of Scarcity: Notes on the Sex Ratio in Early Scandinavia." In *New Readings on Women in Old English Literature*, ed. Helen Damico and Alexandra Henessey Olsen, 100–134. Bloomington: Indiana University Press, 1990.

———. "Regardless of Sex: Men, Women and Power in Early Northern Europe." *Speculum* 68, no. 2 (1993): 363–87.

———. "Hildigunnr's Lament." In Anderson and Swenson 2002: 15–54.

Clover, Carol J., and John Lindow, eds. *Old Norse–Icelandic Literature: A Critical Guide.* Ithaca: Cornell University Press, 1985.

Clunies Ross, Margaret. "The Art of Poetry and the Figure of the Poet in *Egils saga*." In Tucker 1989: 126–49.

———. *The Norse Muse in Britain, 1750–1820.* Trieste, Italy: Edizione Parnaso, 1998.

———. *Prolonged Echoes: Old Norse Myths in Medieval Northern Society.* Odense, Denmark: Odense University Press, 1994–98.

———, ed. *Old Icelandic Literature and Society.* Cambridge: Cambridge University Press, 2000.

———. "The Skald Sagas as a Genre: Definitions and Typical Features." In Poole 2001: 25–49.

———. "Realism and the Fantastic in the Old Icelandic Sagas." *Scandinavian Studies* 74 (2002): 443–54.

———. *A History of Old Norse Poetry and Poetics.* Cambridge: Brewer, 2005.

———. *The Cambridge Introduction to the Old Norse–Icelandic Saga.* Cambridge: Cambridge University Press, 2010a.

———. "Verse and Prose in *Egils saga Skallagrímssonar*." In Quinn and Lethbridge 2010b: 191–211.

Cole, Richard. "Racial Thinking in Old Norse Literature: The Case of the *Blámaðr*." *Saga-Book* 39 (2015): 21–40.

Colley, Linda. *Britons: Forging the Nation, 1707–1837.* New Haven, Conn.: Yale University Press, 1992.

Danielsson, Tommy. *Hrafnkels saga eller Fallet med den undflyende traditionen.* Hedemora, Sweden: Gidlunds forlag, 2002.

D'Arcy, Julian, and Kirsten Wolf. "Sir Walter Scott and *Eyrbyggja Saga*." *Studies in Scottish Literature* 22 (1987): 30–43.

De Looze, Laurence, Jón Karl Helgason, Russell Poole, and Torfi Tulinius, eds. *Egil the Viking Poet: New Approaches to Egil's Saga.* Toronto: Toronto University Press, 2015.

De Vries, Jan. *Heroic Song and Heroic Legend.* Trans. B. J. Timmer. London: Oxford University Press, 1963.

Dillmann, François-Xavier. *Les magiciens dans l'Islande ancienne: Études sur la représentation de la magic islandaise et de ses agents dans les sources littéraires norroises.* Uppsala: Kungl. Gustav Adolfs Akademien för svensk folkkultur, 2006.

Driscoll, Matthew J. "The Words on the Page: Thoughts on Philology, Old and New." In Quinn and Lethbridge 2010: 87–104.

Driscoll, M. J., and Svanhildur Óskarsdóttir, eds. *66 Manuscripts from the Arnamagnæan Collection.* Copenhagen, Denmark: Museum Tusculanum, 2015.

————, eds. "Love Poetry 2: West Norse." In Pulsiano 1993: 396–98.

Dronke, Peter. *Medieval Latin and the Rise of European Love-Lyric*, 2 vols. Oxford: Clarendon, 1965–1966.

Dronke, Ursula. *The Role of Sexual Themes in Njáls Saga*. London: Viking Society for Northern Research, 1981.

Dufferin, Lord. *Letters from High Latitudes*. [1857] London: Merlin, 1989.

Einar Ólafur Sveinsson. *The Age of the Sturlungs: Icelandic Civilization in the Thirteenth Century*. Trans. Jóhann S. Hannesson. Islandica 36. Ithaca: Cornell University Press, 1953.

————. *Dating the Icelandic Sagas: An Essay in Method*. London: Viking Society for Northern Research, 1958.

————. *Njáls Saga: A Literary Masterpiece*. Trans. Paul Schach. Lincoln: University of Nebraska Press, 1971.

Evans, Gareth Lloyd. *Men and Masculinities in the Sagas of Icelanders*. Oxford: Oxford University Press, 2019.

Falk, Oren. "The Vanishing Volcanoes: Fragments of Fourteenth-century Icelandic Folklore [1]." *Folklore* 118, no. 1 (2007): 1–22.

Faulkes, Anthony, ed. *A New Introduction to Old Norse: Part II. Reader*. 5th ed. London: Viking Society for Northern Research, 2011.

————, ed. *A New Introduction to Old Norse: Part III. Glossary and Index of Names*. 4th ed. London: Viking Society for Northern Research, 2007.

Felce, Ian. "The Old Norse Sagas and William Morris's Ideal of Literal Translation." *Review of English Studies* New Series 67, no. 279 (2016): 220–36.

————. *William Morris and the Icelandic Sagas*. Cambridge: D. S. Brewer, 2018.

Fichtner, Edward G. "Gift Exchange and Initiation in the *Auðunar þáttr vestfirzka*." *Scandinavian Studies* 51 (1979): 249–72.

Finlay, Alison. "Skalds, Troubadours and Sagas." *Saga-Book* 24 (1995): 105–53.

————. "Skald Sagas in their Literary Context 2. Possible European Contexts." In Poole 2001: 232–71.

Fjalldal, Magnús. *The Long Arm of Coincidence: The Frustrated Connection between "Beowulf" and "Grettis saga."* Toronto: Toronto University Press, 1998.

Foote, P. G. "An Essay on the *Saga of Gísli* and Its Icelandic Background." In *The Saga of Gísli*, trans. George Johnston, 93–134. London: Dent, 1963.

————. "Sagnaskemtan: Reykjahólar, 1119." *Saga-Book* 14 (1955): 226–39. Repr. in *Aurvandilstá: Norse Studies*. Odense, Denmark: Odense University Press, 1984.

————. "Saints' Lives and Sagas." In *Saints and Sagas: A Symposium*, ed. Hans Bekker-Nielsen and Birte Carlé, 73–88. Odense, Denmark: Odense University Press, 1994.

Foote, P. G., and David M. Wilson. *The Viking Achievement: The Society and Culture of Early Medieval Scandinavia*. London: Sidgwick and Jackson, 1970.

Foucault, Michel. *The Will to Knowledge: History of Sexuality 1*. Trans. Robert Hurley. London: Penguin, 1979.

Frank, Roberta. "Marriage in Twelfth- and Thirteenth-Century Iceland." *Viator* 4 (1973): 473–84.

————. *Old Norse Court Poetry: The Dróttkvætt Stanza.* Ithaca: Cornell University Press, 1978.

Fulk, R. D. "The Moral System of *Hrafnkels saga Freysgoða.*" *Saga-Book* 22 (1986–1989): 1–32.

Gade, Kari Ellen. "The Dating and Attributions of Verses in the Skald Sagas." In Poole 2001: 50–74.

Gísli Sigurðsson. *Gaelic Influence in Iceland: Historical and Literary Contacts: A Survey of Research,* 2nd ed. Reykjavík: University of Iceland Press, 2000.

————. *The Medieval Icelandic Saga and Oral Tradition: A Discourse on Method.* Trans. Nicholas Jones. Cambridge, Mass.: Harvard University Press, 2004.

Gordon, E. V. "On Hrafnkels saga Freysgoða." *Medium Ævum* 8 (1939): 1–32.

Grønlie, Siân. *The Saint and the Saga Hero: Hagiography and Early Icelandic Literature.* Woodbridge, U.K.: Boydell and Brewer, 2017.

Gudbrand Vigfusson [Guðbrandur Vigfússon]. "Prolegomena." In *Sturlunga Saga Including the Islendinga Saga of Lawman Sturla Thordsson,* I: xvii–ccxiv. 2 vols. Oxford: Clarendon, 1878.

Gunnar Karlsson. *Iceland's 1100 Years: History of a Marginal Society.* London: Hurst, 2000.

Hallberg, Peter. *The Icelandic Saga.* Trans. Paul Schach. Lincoln: University of Nebraska Press, 1962.

Harris, Joseph. "Genre and Narrative Structure in Some *Íslendinga þættir.*" *Scandinavian Studies* 44 (1972): 1–27.

————. "Theme and Genre in Some *Íslendinga þættir.*" *Scandinavian Studies* 48 (1976): 1–28.

————. "The Prosimetrum of Icelandic Saga and Some Relatives." In *Prosimetrum: Cross-Cultural Perspectives on Narrative in Prose and Verse,* ed. Joseph Harris and Karl Reichl, 131–63. Cambridge: Brewer, 1997.

Harris, Richard L. *Concordance of Proverbs and Proverbial Matters in the Old Icelandic Sagas.* http://www.usask.ca/english/icelanders/index.html.

Hastings, Adrian. *The Construction of Nationhood: Ethnicity, Religion and Nationalism.* Cambridge: Cambridge University Press, 1997.

Hastrup, Kirsten. *Culture and History in Medieval Iceland: An Anthropological Analysis of Structure and Change.* Oxford: Clarendon, 1985.

————. *Island of Anthropology: Studies in Past and Present Iceland.* Odense, Denmark: Odense University Press, 1990.

Haukur Þorgeirsson. "Snorri Versus the Copyists: An Investigation of a Stylistic Trait in the Manuscript Traditions of *Egils saga, Heimskringla* and the *Prose Edda.*" *Saga-Book* 38 (2014): 61–74.

Helgi Þorláksson. "Historical Background: Iceland 870–1400." In *A Companion to Old Norse–Icelandic Literature and Culture,* ed. Rory McTurk, 136–54. Oxford: Blackwell, 2005.

Helle, Knut, ed. *The Cambridge History of Scandinavia. Volume I: Prehistory to 1520.* Cambridge: Cambridge University Press, 2003.

Heller, Rolf. *Die literarische Darstellung der Frau in den Isländersagas*. Halle, Germany: Max Niemeyer Verlag, 1958.

Hermann Pálsson. *Oral Tradition and Saga Writing*. Vienna: Fassbaender, 1999.

Heslop, Kate. "Grettisfærsla: The Handing on of Grettir." *Saga-Book* 30 (2006): 65–94.

Hickes, George. *Linguarum vett: Septentrionalium thesaurus grammatico-criticus et archæologicus*. 2 vols. Oxford: Sheldonian Theatre, 1703–1705.

Hines, John, and Desmond Slay, eds. *Introductory Essays on Egils saga and Njáls saga*. London: Viking Society for Northern Research, 1992.

Hoare, Dorothy M. *The Works of Morris and of Yeats in Relation to Early Saga Literature*. Cambridge: Cambridge University Press, 1937.

Hume, Kathryn. "Beginnings and Endings in the Icelandic Family Sagas." *Modern Language Review* 68 (1973): 593–606.

———. *Fantasy and Mimesis: Responses to Reality in Western Literature*. London: Methuen, 1984.

Jesch, Judith. *Viking Women*. Woodbridge: Boydell, 1991.

Jochens, Jenny. "Consent in Marriage: Old Norse Law, Life, and Literature." *Scandinavian Studies* 58 (1986a): 142–76.

———. "The Medieval Icelandic Heroine: Fact or Fiction?" *Viator* 17 (1986b): 35–50.

———. "Before the Male Gaze: The Absence of the Female Body in Old Norse." In *Sex in the Middle Ages: A Book of Essays*, ed. Joyce E. Salisbury, 3–29. New York: Garland, 1991.

———. *Old Norse Images of Women*. Philadelphia: University of Pennsylvania Press, 1996.

———. *Women in Old Norse Society*. Ithaca: Cornell University Press, 1995, repr. 1998.

———. "Race and Ethnicity in the Old Norse World." *Viator* 30 (1999a): 79–103.

———. "Triangularity in the Pagan North: The Case of Bjǫrn Arngeirsson and Þórðr Kolbeinsson." In *Conflicted Identities and Multiple Masculinities: Men in the Medieval West*, ed. Jacqueline Murray, 111–34. New York: Garland, 1999b.

———. "Representations of Skalds in the Sagas 2: Gender Relations." In Poole 2001: 309–32.

———. "Vikings Westward to Vínland: The Problem of Women." In Anderson and Swenson 2002: 129–58.

Jóhanna Katrín Friðriksdóttir. *Women in Old Norse Literature: Bodies, Words, and Power*. New York: Palgrave Macmillan, 2013.

———. "Gender." In Ármann Jakobsson and Sverrir Jakobsson 2017: 226–39.

Jón Johannesson. *A History of the Old Icelandic Commonwealth: Íslendinga Saga*. Trans. Haraldur Bessason. Winnipeg: University of Manitoba Press, 1974.

Jón Viðar Sigurðsson. *Chieftains and Power in the Icelandic Commonwealth*. Trans. Jean Lundskær-Nielsen. Odense, Denmark: Odense University Press, 1999.

Jónas Kristjánsson. *Eddas and Sagas: Iceland's Medieval Literature*. Trans. P. Foote. Reykjavík, Iceland: Hið íslenska bokmenntafélag, 1988.

———. *Icelandic Manuscripts: Sagas, History and Art*. Trans. Jeffrey Crosser. Reykjavík: Icelandic Literary Society, 1993.

Jones, Gwyn. *A History of the Vikings*. 2nd ed. Oxford: Oxford University Press, 1984.

———. *The Norse Atlantic Saga: Being the Norse Voyages of Discovery and Settlement to Iceland, Greenland, and North America.* 2nd ed. Oxford: Oxford University Press, 1986.

Kelchner, Georgia Dunham. *Dreams in Old Norse Literature and Their Affinities in Folklore: With an Appendix Containing the Icelandic Texts and Translations.* Cambridge: Cambridge University Press, 1935.

Kennedy, John. *Translating the Sagas: Two Hundred Years of Challenge and Response.* Turnhout, Belgium: Brepols, 2007.

Ker, W. P. *Epic and Romance: Essays on Medieval Literature.* London: Macmillan, 1896.

Kress, Helga. "'Mjǫk mun þér samstaft þykkja': Um sagnahefð ok kvenlega reynslu í *Laxdœla sögu*." In *Konur Skrifa*, ed. Valborg Bentsdóttir, Guðrún Gísladóttir and Svanlaug Baldursdóttir, 97–109. Reykjavík, Iceland: Sögufélag, 1980.

Lethbridge, Emily. "*Gísla saga Súrssonar*: Textual Variation, Editorial Constructions and Critical Interpretations." In Quinn and Lethbridge 2010: 123–52.

Lincoln, Bruce. *Between History and Myth: Stories of Harald Fairhair and the Founding of the State.* Chicago: University of Chicago Press, 2014.

Lindow, John. "Skald Sagas in their Literary Context: 1. Other Icelandic Genres." In Poole 2001: 218–231.

Lönnroth, Lars. *Njáls saga: A Critical Introduction.* Berkeley: University of California Press, 1976.

———. "Rhetorical Persuasion in the Sagas." *Scandinavian Studies* 41 (1969a): 157–89; repr. in Lönnroth 2011: 77–109.

———. "The Noble Heathen: A Theme in the Sagas." *Scandinavian Studies* 41 (1969b): 1–29; repr. in Lönnroth 2011: 45–74.

———. *The Academy of Odin: Selected Papers on Old Norse Literature.* Odense: University Press of Southern Denmark, 2011.

Marold, Edith. "The Relation Between Verses and Prose in *Bjarnar saga Hítdœlakappa*." In Poole 2001: 75–124.

———. "*Mansǫngr*—A Phantom Genre?" In Quinn, Heslop, and Wills 2007: 240–62.

Martin, John D. "Law and the (Un)dead: Medieval Models for Understanding the Hauntings in *Eyrbyggja saga*." *Saga-Book* 29 (2005): 67–82.

Mayburd, Miriam. "The Paranormal." In Ármann Jakobsson and Sverrir Jakobsson 2017: 265–78.

McTurk, Rory, ed. *A Companion to Old Norse-Icelandic Literature and Culture.* Oxford: Blackwell, 2005.

Miller, William Ian. *Bloodtaking and Peacemaking: Feud, Law, and Society in Saga Iceland.* Chicago: University of Chicago Press, 1990.

———. *Audun and the Polar Bear: Luck, Law, and Largesse in a Medieval Tale of Risky Business.* Leiden, Netherlands: Brill, 2008.

———. *Why Is Your Axe Bloody? A Reading of Njáls saga.* Oxford: Oxford University Press, 2014.

———. *Hrafnkel or the Ambiguities: Hard Cases, Hard Choices.* Oxford: Oxford University Press, 2017.

Mitchell, Stephen A. *Witchcraft and Magic in the Nordic Middle Ages*. Philadelphia: University of Pennsylvania Press, 2011.

Mundal, Else, ed. *Dating the Sagas: Reviews and Revisions*. Copenhagen, Denmark: Museum Tusculanum, 2013.

Mundal, Else, and Jonas Wellendorf, eds. *Oral Art Forms and Their Passage into Writing*. Copenhagen, Denmark: Museum Tusculanum, 2008.

Nordal, Guðrún. "The Art of Poetry and the Sagas of Icelanders." In Quinn, Heslop, and Wills 2007: 219–38.

———. "Skaldic Citations and Settlement Stories as Parameters for Saga Dating." In *Dating the Sagas: Reviews and Revisions*, ed. Else Mundal, 195–212. Copenhagen, Denmark: Museum Tusculanum, 2013.

Nordal, Sigurður. *Hrafnkels Saga Freysgoða*. Trans. R. G. Thomas. Cardiff: University of Wales Press, 1958.

O'Donoghue, Heather. *The Genesis of a Saga Narrative: Verse and Prose in Kormaks saga*. Oxford: Oxford University Press, 1991.

———. "Women in *Njáls saga*." In Hines and Slay 1992: 83–92.

———. *Old Norse–Icelandic Literature: A Short Introduction*. Oxford: Blackwell, 2004.

———. *Skaldic Verse and the Poetics of Saga Narrative*. Oxford: Oxford University Press, 2005.

Ong, Walter, S. J. *Orality and Literacy: The Technologizing of the Word*. London: Methuen, 1982.

Orchard, Andy. *Pride and Prodigies in the Monsters of the Beowulf Manuscript*. Revised ed. Toronto: Toronto University Press, 1995.

Ordbog over det norrøne prosasprog: Registre/A Dictionary of Old Norse Prose: Indices. Copenhagen, Denmark: Den arnamagnæanske commission, 1989.

Orri Vésteinsson. *The Christianization of Iceland: Priests, Power, and Social Change, 1000–1300*. Oxford: Oxford University Press, 2000.

Óskar Halldórsson. "The Origin and Theme of *Hrafnkels saga*." In Tucker 1989: 257–71.

Overing, Gillian R., and Marijane Osborn. *Landscapes of Desire: Partial Stories of the Medieval Scandinavian World*. Minneapolis: University of Minnesota Press, 1994.

Percy, Thomas, trans. *Northern Antiquities: Or, a Description of the Manners, Customs, Religion and Laws of the Ancient Danes, and Other Northern nations; Including Those of Our Own Saxon Ancestors*. London: Carnan, 1770; new edition revised by I. A. Blackwell. London: Bohn, 1847.

Peristiany, J. G., ed. *Honour and Shame: The Values of Mediterranean Society*. Chicago: University of Chicago Press, 1966.

Perkins, Richard. "The Dreams of *Flóamanna saga*." *Saga-Book* 19 (1974–1977): 191–238.

———. *Flóamanna saga, Gaulverjabær and Haukr Erlendsson*. Studia Islandica 36. Reykjavík, Iceland: Menningarsjóður, 1978.

Phelpstead, Carl. *Holy Vikings: Saints' Lives in the Old Icelandic Kings' Sagas*. Tempe: Arizona Center for Medieval and Renaissance Studies, 2007a.

———. "Size Matters: Penile Problems in Sagas of Icelanders." *Exemplaria* 19, no. 3 (2007b): 420–37.

———. "Adventure-time in *Yngvars saga víðförla*." In *Fornaldarsagaerne: Myter og virkelighed*, ed. Agneta Ney, Ármann Jakobsson, and Annette Lassen, 331–46. Copenhagen, Denmark: Museum Tusculanum, 2009.

———. "Fantasy and History: The Limits of Plausibility in Oddr Snorrason's *Óláfs saga Tryggvasonar*." *Saga-Book* 36 (2012): 27–42.

———. "Hair Today, Gone Tomorrow: Hair Loss, the Tonsure, and Masculinity in Medieval Iceland." *Scandinavian Studies* 85, no. 1 (2013): 1–19.

———. "Ecocriticism and *Eyrbyggja saga*." *Leeds Studies in English* 45 (2014): 1–18.

Poole, Russell. "Verse and Prose in *Gunnlaugs saga Ormstungu*." In Tucker 1989: 160–84.

———. *Viking Poems on War and Peace: A Study in Skaldic Narrative*. Toronto: University of Toronto Press, 1991.

———, ed. *Skaldsagas: Text, Vocation, and Desire in the Icelandic Sagas of Poets*. Berlin: de Gruyter, 2001.

———. "The Relations Between Verses and Prose in Hallfreðar saga and Gunnlaugs saga." In Poole 2001: 125–71.

Propp, Vladimir. *Morphology of the Folktale*. 2nd ed. Austin: University of Texas Press, 1968.

Pulsiano, Phillip, and Kirsten Wolf, eds. *Medieval Scandinavia: An Encyclopedia*. London: Garland, 1993.

Quinn, Judy. "Introduction." In Quinn and Lethbridge 2010: 13–37.

Quinn, Judy, Kate Heslop, and Tarrin Wills, eds. *Learning and Understanding in the Old Norse World: Essays in Honour of Margaret Clunies Ross*. Turnhout, Belgium: Brepols, 2007.

Quinn, Judy, and Emily Lethbridge, eds. *Creating the Medieval Saga: Versions, Variability and Editorial Interpretations of Old Norse Saga Literature*. Odense: University Press of Southern Denmark, 2010.

Roesdahl, Else. *The Vikings*. Trans. Susan M. Margesen and Kirsten Williams. London: Penguin, 1991.

Rohrbach, Lena. *Der tierische Blick: Mensch-Tier Relationen in der Sagaliteratur*. Tübingen, Germany: Francke, 2009.

Rowe, Elizabeth Ashman. "The Long and the Short of It." In Ármann Jakobsson and Sverrir Jakobsson 2017: 151–63.

Rowe, Elizabeth Ashman, and Joseph Harris. "Short Prose Narrative (þáttr)." In McTurk 2005: 462–78.

Sävborg, Daniel. "Style." In Ármann Jakobsson and Sverrir Jakobsson 2017: 111–26.

———. "The Formula in Icelandic Saga Prose." *Saga-Book* 42 (2018): 51–86.

Sawyer, Peter, ed. *The Oxford Illustrated History of the Vikings*. Oxford: Oxford University Press, 1997.

Sayers, William. "The Alien and Alienated as Unquiet Dead in the Sagas of Icelanders." In *Monster Theory: Reading Culture*, ed. Jeffrey Jerome Cohen, 242–63. Minneapolis: University of Minnesota Press, 1996.

———. "Ethics or Pragmatics; Fate or Chance; Heathen, Christian, or Godless World? (*Hrafnkels saga*)." *Scandinavian Studies* 79, no. 4 (2007): 385–404.

Schach, Paul. "*Fóstbrœðra saga*." In Pulsiano 1993: 216–19.

Scott, Forrest S. "The Woman Who Knows: Female Characters in *Eyrbyggja saga*." In Anderson and Swenson 2002: 225–43.

Sedgwick, Eve Kosofsky. *Between Men: English Literature and Male Homosocial Desire*. New York: Columbia University Press, 1985.

Short, William R. *Icelanders in the Viking Age: The People of the Sagas*. Jefferson, N.C.: McFarland, 2010.

Simek, Rudolph, and Hermann Pálsson. *Lexikon der altnordischen Literatur*. Stuttgart, Germany: Kröner, 1987.

Smith, Joshua Toulmin. *The Discovery of America by the Northmen in the Tenth Century*. London: Tilt, 1839.

Steel, Karl. "Bad Heritage: The American Viking Fantasy, from the Nineteenth Century to Now." In *Nature, Culture, Ecologies: Nature in Transcultural Contexts*, ed. Gesa Mackenthun and Stephanie Wodianka, 75–94. Münster, Germany: Waxmann, 2018.

Ström, Folke. *Níð, Ergi and Old Norse Moral Attitudes*. Dorothea Coke Memorial Lecture. London: Viking Society for Northern Research, 1974.

Strömbäck, Dag. *The Conversion of Iceland: A Survey*. Trans. Peter Foote. London: Viking Society for Northern Research, 1975.

Svanhildur Óskarsdóttir. "Expanding Horizons: Recent Trends in Old Norse–Icelandic Manuscript Studies." *New Medieval Literatures* 14 (2012): 203–23.

Swannell, J. N. "William Morris as an Interpreter of Old Norse." *Saga-Book* 15 (1961): 365–82.

Sørensen, Preben Meulengracht. *The Unmanly Man: Concepts of Sexual Defamation in Early Northern Society*. Trans. Joan Turville-Petre. Odense, Denmark: Odense University Press, 1983.

———. *Saga and Society: An Introduction to Old Norse Literature*. Trans. John Tucker. Odense, Denmark: Odense University Press, 1993.

———. "The Prosimetrum Form: 1. Verses as the Voice of the Past." In Poole 2001: 172–90.

Todorov, Tzvetan. *The Fantastic: A Structural Approach to a Literary Genre*. Trans. Richard Howard. Ithaca: Cornell University Press, 1975.

Townend, Matthew. *Language and History in Viking Age England: Linguistic Relations between Speakers of Old Norse and Old English*. Turnhout, Belgium: Brepols, 2002.

———. *The Vikings and Victorian Lakeland: The Norse Medievalism of W. G. Collingwood and His Contemporaries*. Kendal, U.K.: Cumberland and Westmorland Antiquarian and Archaeological Society, 2009.

———. "E. R. Eddison's *Egil's Saga*: Translation and Scholarship in Inter-War Old Northernism." *Saga-Book* 42 (2018): 87–124.

Tranter, Stephen N. *Clavis Metrica: Háttatal, Háttalykill and the Irish Metrical Tracts*. Basel: Helbing & Lichtenhahn, 1997.

Tucker, John, ed. *Sagas of Icelanders: A Book of Essays*. New York: Garland, 1989.

Turville-Petre, E. O. Gabriel. *Origins of Icelandic Literature*. Oxford: Clarendon, 1953.

———. "Introduction." In *The Story of Burnt Njal*, trans. G. W. Dasent, v–ix. London: Dent, 1957.

———. *Myth and Religion of the North: The Religion of Ancient Scandinavia*. London: Weidenfield and Nicolson, 1964.

———. "*Dróttkvætt* and Irish Syllabic Measures." In *Nine Norse Studies*, 154–78. London: Viking Society for Northern Research, 1972.

———. *Scaldic Poetry*. Oxford: Oxford University Press, 1976.

Turville-Petre, Thorlac. *England the Nation: Language, Literature, and National Identity, 1290–1340*. Oxford: Clarendon, 1996.

Vésteinn Ólason. *Dialogues with the Viking Age: Narration and Representation in the Sagas of the Icelanders*. Trans. Andrew Wawn. Reykjavík, Iceland: Heimskringla, 1998.

———. "Family Sagas." In McTurk 2005: 101–18.

Wawn, Andrew. *The Vikings and the Victorians: Inventing the Old North in Nineteenth-Century Britain*. Cambridge: D. S. Brewer, 2000.

———. "*Fast er drukkið og fátt lært": Eiríkur Magnússon, Old Northern Philology, and Victorian Cambridge*. H. M. Chadwick Memorial Lectures 11. Cambridge: Department of Anglo-Saxon, Norse, and Celtic, University of Cambridge, 2001.

———. "The Post-Medieval Reception of Old Norse and Old Icelandic Literature." In McTurk 2005: 320–37.

———. "The Grimms, the Kirk-grims, and Sabine Baring-Gould." In *Constructing Nations, Reconstructing Myth: Essays in Honour of T. A. Shippey*, ed. Andrew Wawn with Graham Johnson and John Walter, 215–42. Turnhout, Belgium: Brepols, 2007a.

———. "*Vatnsdæla saga*: Visions and Versions." In Quinn, Heslop, and Wills 2007b: 399–446.

Wellendorf, Jonas. "Ecclesiastical Literature and Hagiography." Ármann Jakobsson and Sverrir Jakobsson 2017: 48–58.

Whaley, Diana. "Skalds and Situational Verses in *Heimskringla*." In *Snorri Sturluson: Kolloquium anläßlich der 750. Wiederkehr seines Todestages*, ed. Alois Wolf, 245–66. Tübingen, Germany: Gunter Narr, 1993.

———. "Representations of Skalds in the Sagas 1. Social and Professional Relations." In Poole 2001: 285–308.

———. "The 'Conversion Verses' in *Hallfreðar saga*: Authentic Voice of a Reluctant Christian?" In *Old Norse Myths, Literature and Society*, ed. Margaret Clunies Ross, 234–57. Odense: University Press of Southern Denmark, 2003.

Wolf, Kirsten. "Amazons in Vínland." *Journal of English and Germanic Philology* 95 (1996): 469–85.

Zoëga, Geir T. *A Concise Dictionary of Old Icelandic*. Oxford: Clarendon, 1910.

Þórður Ingi Guðjónsson. "Editing the Three Versions of *Gísla saga Súrssonar*." In Quinn and Lethbridge 2010: 105–21.

INDEX

Note: The letter æ is treated as ae and œ as oe; ð appears after d. Þ and ǫ appear at the end of the alphabet in that order. Accents on vowels are ignored in the alphabetization. For saga characters other than the few major characters indexed here, see the saga in which they appear.

CARL PHELPSTEAD is professor of English literature at Cardiff University, Wales. His previous books include *Holy Vikings: Saints' Lives in the Old Icelandic Kings' Sagas* and *Tolkien and Wales: Language, Literature and Identity*.

New Perspectives on Medieval Literature: Authors and Traditions

EDITED BY R. BARTON PALMER AND TISON PUGH